SEX SELLS!

RODGER STREITMATTER

SEX SELLS!

*The Media's Journey from
Repression to Obsession*

A Member of the
Perseus Books Group

Copyright © 2004 by Westview Press, A Member of the Perseus Books Group

Published in 2004 in the United States of America by Westview Press.

Find us on the world wide web at www.westviewpress.com

Westview Press books are available at special discounts for bulk purchases in the United States by corporations, institutions, and other organizations. For more information, please contact the Special Markets Department at the Perseus Books Group, 11 Cambridge Center, Cambridge, MA 02142, or call (800) 255-1514 or (617) 252-5298, or e-mail special.markets@ perseusbooks.com.

Library of Congress Cataloging-in-Publication data

Streitmatter, Rodger.
  Sex sells! / The Media's Journey from Repression to Obsession / Rodger Streitmatter.
    p. cm.
  ISBN 0-8133-4248-1 (hardcover : alk. paper)
  1. Sex in mass media. I. Title.
P96.S45S77 2004
306.7—dc22

                                                        2004017383

Text design by Jeff Williams

10   9   8   7   6   5   4   3   2   1

To Tom, again and always

Contents

Contents

Illustrations
Images related to the content of the various chapters in this
book have been placed on the author's Web site at American University.
Readers may view these illustrations at http://nw08.american.edu/~rstreit/.

Introduction

IN 1953 WHEN LUCILLE BALL HAD THE AUDACITY TO BECOME PREGNANT, THE CHAR-acters on *I Love Lucy* had to limit themselves to facial expressions, hand ges-tures, and coded phrases when making reference to the wacky redhead's swollen stomach. Executives at CBS absolutely refused to allow anyone on the nation's number one TV program to say "pregnant" on the air, fearing that the word would conjure up, in the minds of viewers, images of a man and woman having sexual intercourse.

By 2003, *Sex and the City* had not only built one plotline around repeated use of the word—without shame or apology—that many people consider the most offensive in the English language, but the Emmy-winning HBO hit had also shown TV viewers a close-up of that female body part. (Yes, we're talking "cunt.")

Who was responsible for this seismic shift?

What cultural and economic forces contributed to it?

When were the various sexual thresholds crossed?

Where have media "gone too far" regarding sexual content?

Why has such remarkable change occurred in a mere fifty years?

This book answers these questions.

To do so, each of the following chapters illuminates a specific media product that has, during the past five decades, contributed to this intriguing journey from sexual repression to sexual obsession.

The topics of some of the chapters will be familiar to anyone with a basic knowledge of popular culture. *Playboy* and *Cosmo*. James Bond and Madonna. *Fatal Attraction* and *Will & Grace*. And how could the story be complete without looking at how the media covered Bill and Monica?

Other of the sexual provocateurs who play starring roles in the chapters may be less familiar—or more debatable. Suzanne Somers and Underwear Man. Queen Latifah and 2 Live Crew. *Head Over Heels* and www.tits-paradise.com.

They all come to life in the following pages because each one has served as a foot soldier in the Sexual Revolution that has transformed this nation.

That last sentence is a significant one, as it summarizes the driving thesis underpinning this book: The media have not merely reflected the remarkable changes in sexual attitudes and sexual practices that have taken place in this country, but they have helped propel those changes.

As the following chapters—both individually and in the aggregate—document, the media have repeatedly been in the vanguard of shaping the American public's collective sexual self. From magazine editor Hugh Hefner to Internet porn star Vince Voyeur, this gallery of randy trailblazers has slain taboos and inhibitions at a breathtaking rate—and often while breathing quite heavily.

The number of chapters totals only eighteen. Since the beginning of my process of researching and writing this book, I have been determined to keep the list short because I did not want to create an encyclopedic list of names, dates, and titles that would make the reader's eyes glaze over. Instead, my goal has been to focus on a limited number of topics that would allow me to treat them in the engaging narrative style—including highly textured descriptions—that each of these often larger-than-life players clearly deserves. This approach also keeps this book to a manageable length, which also means an affordable price.

The decision to restrict the number of topics means that not every media product and every individual provocateur has been included. So, for example, even though I readily acknowledge that some scenes from

Midnight Cowboy contained strong sexual content, the 1969 film did not make the cut. Readers will, instead, learn about the sexual messages that Hollywood was sending during the 1960s by looking at the James Bond films—including such analytical tidbits as what the most successful film franchise in history had to say about marriage, redheads, and casual sex.

I have placed each media product in the specific time period in which it was most influential. The chapter on *Playboy* looks at the magazine during its halcyon days in the 1960s when it brought pornography into the mainstream of American life; the chapter on Madonna focuses on the Queen of Pop during the 1980s when she pioneered an entirely new art form called the music video. Readers who want more information about any of the media products or individuals before or after the years that I concentrate on can look to my endnotes for other sources.

Another parameter of this book is its single-minded devotion to sex. Because of this focus, the chapter on a particular musician or television show is not a comprehensive study of that topic but only of the subject's sexual dynamics. With Jim Morrison, I make only passing reference to the quality of the music that The Doors produced and the social issues that the group's lyrics tackled; with *All in the Family,* I mention that the program had a great deal to say about racial bigotry and generational conflict, but I do not go into detail. Again, readers who thirst for the non-sexual elements for any of these topics can look to the endnotes for guidance.

The genres of the media that I write about in the following pages include magazines, motion pictures, music, advertising, print and broadcast journalism, and the Internet, but the one that receives the most attention is television. This is not merely because this particular medium has the most apropos nickname for a book such as this one—the "boob tube"—but also because I consider it to be the most powerful medium in the history of communication. Programs such as *Three's Company, Friends,* and *The Real World* may appear to be nothing more than light entertainment, but I believe they have profound impact not only on our attitudes about sex but on our sexual behavior—and this book will articulate why I have come to this conclusion.

The final essay describes an entirely new concept. Specifically, in these pages I diverge from much of the conventional wisdom by arguing that the

pervasiveness of sexual content in the media is not in itself "bad." Indeed, much of the material is beneficial, I contend, because it exposes media consumers—especially young people—to sexual topics that they desperately need to be familiar with.

During this era of AIDS, of rampant STDs, and of increasingly reckless sexual behavior, the well-being of Americans is threatened every bit as much by sexual activity as by tobacco or alcohol and other drugs. And so, in order to survive and to thrive in this libidinous world, individuals need to learn how to navigate the sexual terrain.

They need to become "sexually literate."

In that final essay, therefore, I highlight examples both from the previous chapters and from contemporary media products such as *Maxim* magazine and the music of Christina Aguilera and Lil' Kim to show how the media continually send out sexual messages—some good, some bad, all important. I also show how media consumers can learn from those messages and, in so doing, arm themselves to live in a world that has been shaped so profoundly during the last half century by the symbiotic relationship between sex and the media and by the principle that is at the heart of this book: *Sex Sells!*

The 1950s

No Sex, Please, We're American

THE HALFWAY POINT IN TWENTIETH-CENTURY AMERICA WAS DEFINED BY A SEXUAL paradox. On the one hand, a landmark study found that men and women were much friskier in the bedroom than most people had previously believed, a finding that was reinforced by the fact that a massive baby boom pushed the birthrate to the highest level in the nation's history. On the other hand, the public attitude toward sex was decidedly repressive, with the leaders of society doing everything within their considerable power to discourage discussion of the topic.[1]

The year 1948 is a good point to begin examining the country's sexual self at mid-century. That was the year that *Sexual Behavior in the Human Male*, better known as the Kinsey Report, provided the first comprehensive look at sexual practices in the United States. How the book was received reveals a great deal about the communal mindset vis-à-vis all things carnal.[2]

To conduct the study, Alfred C. Kinsey of Indiana University interviewed 12,000 American men. His major finding was that his subjects, when the bedroom doors were tightly closed, behaved very differently from what society had traditionally prescribed. Indeed, he found that men who violated prevailing sexual dictates were in the majority; so men who "misbehaved" sexually, in fact, were defining what was "normal."[3]

For example, during an era when the U.S. Naval Academy insisted that a candidate for admission "shall be rejected by the examining surgeon for evidence of masturbation," the Kinsey Report found that fully 92 percent of American males masturbated.[4]

Among the other specifics:

- 85 percent of married men had engaged in premarital sex,
- 50 percent of married men had engaged in extramarital sex, and
- 37 percent of men had, at least once, reached orgasm through homo-sexual contact.[5]

After hearing the statistics, the leaders of American society—first appalled, then outraged—attacked both the findings and the finder.[6]

Some of the criticism came from the church. The president of Catholic University denounced Kinsey for publishing "the most anti-religious book of our times," the editor of a religious publication accused him of being "against purity, against morality, against the family," and Norman Vincent Peale, the pastor of a large New York City church and soon-to-be author of the best-selling *The Power of Positive Thinking,* challenged Kinsey's definition of the word "normal," saying, "No matter how many murderers there are, murder will never be normal."[7]

The non-clergy struck out at Kinsey as well. An internationally respected psychologist from Stanford University called him "reckless," one of the nation's most prominent psychoanalysts dubbed him "inaccurate," and renowned anthropologist Margaret Mead chastised him for threatening the well-being of the nation's young people. Even the director of the FBI, J. Edgar Hoover, took it upon himself to lambaste Kinsey for endangering the democratic form of government. "Man's sense of decency declares what is normal and what is not," Hoover insisted. "Whenever the American people, young or old, come to believe there is no such thing as right or wrong, normal or abnormal, those who would destroy our civilization will applaud a major victory over our way of life."[8]

Kinsey suffered another vociferous public thrashing five years later when he published *Sexual Behavior in the Human Female,* based on interviews with 6,000 women. Among the specifics:

- 62 percent of women masturbated,
- 50 percent of married women had engaged in premarital sex,
- 26 percent of married women had engaged in extramarital sex, and

• 13 percent of women had, at least once, reached orgasm through homosexual contact.[9]

The most controversial aspect of the findings involved virginity. Kinsey reported that women who did not have intercourse until their wedding night subsequently had a difficult time developing a satisfying sex life after marriage. Virgin brides were, in fact, only one-third as likely to achieve orgasm during their marriage as women who had engaged in intercourse while they were still single. "When there are long years of abstinence and restraint, and an avoidance of physical contacts before marriage," the Kinsey Report warned, "acquired inhibitions may do such damage that it may take some years to get rid of them after marriage, if indeed they are ever dissipated." The research said, in short, that if a single woman wanted to have a fulfilling marriage, she should become sexually active before her wedding night.[10]

The onslaught of criticism began as soon as the book was published. A widely respected minister from Union Theological Seminary in New York City condemned Kinsey's "absurd hedonism" and "moral anarchism," and one of the nation's leading psychiatrists denounced Kinsey as not only saying that every human being should have as much sex as possible every single day but also as declaring that romantic love was "to put it simply, unimportant." The most stinging of all the comments came from the Rev. Billy Graham, a young minister fast becoming the most powerful evangelist in the country, who concluded, "It is impossible to estimate the damage this book will do to the already deteriorating morals of America."[11]

With the publication of Kinsey's second volume, the attacks moved into the world of politics—and became more than mere words. First, a New York congressman demanded that the U.S. Post Office stop distributing the book on the grounds that the author was "contributing to the depravity of a whole generation, to the loss of faith in human dignity and human decency." Other members of Congress soon adopted an even more aggressive strategy by threatening to investigate the organization that paid for Kinsey's research. With the political pressure mounting, the Rockefeller Foundation consequently cut off the professor's funding. That action ended Kinsey's ability to publish and threw him into a professional, emo-

tional, and physical tailspin. Three years after publishing his second book, the sixty-two-year-old Kinsey died—an exhausted and broken man.[12]

America's closed-door policy regarding carnal topics was also reflected elsewhere in the national culture. The classic how-to book for teenagers made the point by prescribing the way a proper first date should end: "Once back at Mary's home, Mary gets out her key, unlocks the door, and then turns to John with a smile. She says, 'It's been a lovely evening. Thank you, John,' or something similar that lets John know she has enjoyed the date. John replies, 'I have enjoyed it too. I'll be seeing you.' Then she opens the door and goes in without further hesitation. Since this is the first date, neither John nor Mary expects a goodnight kiss. So Mary is careful not to linger at the door, which might make John wonder what she expects him to do." Consistent with the conventions of the time, *Facts of Life and Love for Teenagers* placed the burden of establishing amorous limits squarely on Mary's chaste shoulders—one heading in the book read "How to Stop: The Girl's Responsibility."[13]

Neither the girls nor the boys living in the 1950s could expect much dating guidance from the country's newest form of entertainment. Although critics liked to call television the "boob tube," that nickname was as close as the medium came to discussing or showing images of the human anatomy. In the world created by *Father Knows Best*, *Leave It to Beaver*, and *The Adventures of Ozzie and Harriet*, stay-at-home moms vacuumed while wearing pearls and starched dresses, and no member of these idealized families ever, ever, *ever* talked about sex. The only couple in all of TV land who was allowed to be shown in the bedroom together was Lucille Ball and Desi Arnaz on *I Love Lucy*, because the audience knew that the two stars were married to each other in real life. Yet censors drew the line on that show, too, when the world's most famous redhead became pregnant. Even though Ball giving birth was a major news story—mother and son graced the cover of the first issue of *TV Guide* in 1953—and the pregnancy was a continuing story line in seven episodes of the show, none of the actors was allowed to utter the word "pregnant" on air.[14]

Another legendary example of the restraints imposed on American television during the era involved Elvis Presley. Much of the young singer's popularity clearly was driven by the on-stage eroticism created by his

gyrating hips and the suggestive nature of his lyrics—"Hold me close, hold me tight, make me thrill with delight," "When I feel like this, baby, don't say no." But when Ed Sullivan invited the sexy star to appear on his venerable Sunday night variety show in 1957, the vaunted impresario set strict limits on the young man he considered "the devil incarnate." Sullivan not only dictated which songs Presley would sing but also refused to expose his audience—which numbered 60 million that night, the largest in TV history up to that point—to the vulgarity of a grinding pelvis. Sullivan directed CBS cameramen to shoot the King of Rock 'n' Roll only from the waist up, threatening to fire anyone who violated his order.[15]

Restrictions on the movie screen were even more stringent. The Motion Picture Production Code—written by a Catholic priest and enforced by a rigid Catholic layman—prohibited Hollywood from creating any film that might "lower the moral standards of those who see it." That phrase translated into no "excessive kissing," no "lustful embraces," no "suggestive postures or gestures," and most certainly no "exposed navels, thighs, or breasts." All those no's turned Doris Day and Rock Hudson into America's motion picture sweethearts. The archetype of their series of sugarcoated romantic comedies, 1959's *Pillow Talk*, featured the blonde as a die-hard virgin who steadfastly resisted the advances of the hunk—never mind that Hudson would be exposed, after his AIDS-related death thirty years later, as having been gay.[16]

How homosexuals were treated during the 1950s was one of the era's darkest chapters. The witch-hunt was set on its course when the head of the vice squad in the nation's capital estimated that the federal government was employing some 3,500 "sex perverts." That bombshell launched a Senate investigation that produced a parade of law enforcement officials and psychologists who, during Capitol Hill hearings, characterized all homosexuals as "lacking emotional stability and moral fiber." J. Edgar Hoover then announced that the FBI had identified 406 "sex deviates" in government service. (Hoover did not mention his own intimate relationship with another man nor his proclivity for wearing black cocktail dresses in the privacy of the home they shared.) The senators promptly gave Hoover the money to launch an initiative to expose the sexual orientation—and destroy the careers and personal lives—of hundreds of gay

men and lesbians. Typical of the comments made during the investigation, which helped create stereotypes that still exist today, was one by an assistant attorney general for the State of California. "The homosexual is an inveterate seducer of the young," the lawyer said, "and he represents a social problem because he is not content with being degenerate himself: He is ever seeking younger victims."[17]

America's fear for its children's safety, coupled with the repressive attitude toward sex, extended to the comic books that young people were reading. Calling the publications "immoral" and "detrimental to the youth of the nation," critics expressed particular concern about Batman and Robin. "They live in sumptuous quarters, with beautiful flowers in large vases, and have a butler, Alfred," wrote the *Saturday Review of Literature*. "Batman is sometimes shown in a dressing gown. It is like a wish dream of two homosexuals living together." Robin's detractors had lots to say as well. "He is buoyant with energy and devoted to nothing on earth or in interplanetary space as much as Bruce Wayne," wrote the author of a book titled *Seduction of the Innocent*. "He often stands with his legs spread, the genital region discreetly evident."[18]

Rather than responding to such ludicrous claims with laughter and derision, the Powers That Be cracked down. Civic leaders across the country enlisted the help of local Cub Scouts to confiscate every comic book they could find and then threw them into raging bonfires built on public squares in a long list of cities such as Rumson, New Jersey, and Cape Girardeau, Missouri. Publishers became so fearful that their titles would be banned from newsstands that they established the Code of the Comics Magazine Association of America. Prepared with the spiritual guidance of church leaders, the rules banned all nudity, suggestive poses, and "exaggeration of any physical qualities," while stipulating that "romance stories shall emphasize the sanctity of marriage and never be treated in such a way as to stimulate the lower and baser emotions."[19]

The "no sex, please, we're American" philosophy was expressed in any number of other aspects of the culture as well. When car buyers around the country heard that the grill on Ford Motor Company's latest model—highlighted by a large hole at its center—was, in fact, an automotive engineer's facsimile of a vagina, it was considered a sin to buy one; the Edsel

quickly became the biggest disaster in automotive history. In the fashion world, by contrast, Christian Dior struck gold by replacing the curvaceous hourglass shape with that of the straight-lined H, which inspired the sack dress; his designs struck the consumer's fancy by creating "chastity garments" that hid and hobbled the female form, rendering it virtually sexless. Schools established strict dress codes for teenage students; many a principal would force a golf ball down a boy's trouser leg to make sure his pants were not inappropriately tight.[20]

Although a reader fifty years later might find some of these practices amusing, others were deadly serious. Widespread opposition to interracial sex, for instance, sometimes resulted in tragedy. In August 1955, a fourteen-year-old African-American boy from Chicago named Emmett Till was visiting relatives in Mississippi. The young man, who was unfamiliar with the racial rules of the stridently segregated South, bought some bubble gum at the local grocery store and, as he walked out the front door, showed his admiration for an attractive white woman by whistling at her. Three days later, the woman's husband, Ray Bryant, and his half brother, J. W. Milam, dragged the boy out of bed, stripped him naked, beat him, and fired a .45 bullet into his head. They then used barbed wire to tie a propeller from a cotton gin around the young man's neck and dumped his body into the Tallahatchie River. Although law enforcement officials arrested the two killers—they hadn't even hidden their faces when they kidnapped the boy from his relatives' home—and brought them to trial, the all-white, all-male jury acquitted the men after only an hour of deliberation. Milam later bragged, "When a nigger even gets close to mention sex with a white woman, he's tired of livin'." Milam wanted to make an example of the boy, he said, "just so everybody can know how me and my folks stand."[21]

The Pill and the Media

Spawning a Revolution

THE DEVELOPMENT OF A SINGLE MEDICAL PRODUCT STANDS ALONE AS—
far and away—the most influential factor in moving American society full
tilt into the Sexual Revolution that erupted during the 1960s: the birth
control pill.

The fact that a ten-milligram dose of synthetic hormones, popped into
a woman's mouth once a day, was virtually 100 percent effective in preventing pregnancy led to changes that were sweeping in scope, profound
in impact, and, in every sense of the word, *revolutionary*.[1]

In 1990, the *Ladies' Home Journal* celebrated the thirtieth anniversary of
the pill being approved as an oral contraceptive, describing it as having
transformed American women's lives as no single event before or since:
"Nothing else in this century—perhaps not even winning the right to
vote—made such an immediate difference in women's lives."[2]

- The pill gave women an unprecedented sense of freedom. For the
  first time in human history, women were in control of their reproductive systems—and, therefore, their bodies. Biology no longer determined their destiny.

- The pill changed the sex lives of men as well as women. Without the
  fear of unwanted pregnancy hovering over them, both partners could
  enjoy the full dimensions of lovemaking. Sexual intercourse and sexual experimentation skyrocketed.

- The pill had even greater impact outside the bedroom. By 1960, relatively few women had been able to break into the professions. But with the ability both to postpone and to limit childbirth, huge numbers of women could, for the first time, stop restricting themselves to short-term jobs and begin thinking in terms of lifelong careers.

Although the genesis for all of these changes in American society can rightly be traced back to the birth control pill, a second force also was essential for this tiny tablet to alter the cultural landscape in these myriad ways: the media.

That the oral contraceptive is now so widely used obscures the fact that initially, in the late 1950s, it was a little-known medication that gynecologists prescribed only to the small number of their patients who suffered from certain rare menstrual disorders—*not* to prevent pregnancy. Indeed, the era's physicians considered the fact that the drug suppressed a patient's ovulation to be a minor side effect.[3]

Then the media heard about it. When the nation's leading magazines and newspapers began promoting the tablet as a form of contraception, women started requesting that their doctors, in a phrase they picked up from the media, "put me on the pill." Initially, the vast majority of those physicians consented only for their married patients. Urged on by the abundance of news articles they were reading, single women began slipping wedding rings on their fingers before they went to the doctor's office—and then they began *demanding* the pill, bare-fingered.[4]

Also obscured by the passage of time is the fact that reporting on a new medication that made it possible for a woman to prevent pregnancy was, during this period in American history, an act of courage. The 1950s had been a manifestly conservative era in which a sizable portion of the population insisted, at least publicly, that contraception was immoral—an affront both to God and to nature. According to those adamant voices, woman's role in life was first to procreate and then to devote herself to raising the children she had dutifully borne. These functions were seen as even more important in the wake of World War II, as a critical mass of young GIs had been killed in battle. To suggest that a woman's childbearing responsibility could or should be disrupted was considered by many

to be both sinful and unpatriotic. President Dwight Eisenhower reflected the strength of this position by steadfastly refusing, from the time he entered the White House in 1953 until he left in 1961, to allow a single federal dollar to be used to research contraception or to provide birth control medication of any kind.[5]

The initial articles about the pill in such widely respected news magazines as *Time, Fortune,* and *Newsweek* played a leading role in impelling the American public to embrace this revolutionary capsule. Popular magazines soon jumped on the bandwagon, with both those targeted directly at women—*Good Housekeeping, Ladies' Home Journal, Mademoiselle*—and those aimed at both sexes—*Esquire, Reader's Digest, Ebony*—using their pages to promote the birth control pill. Although the specific themes contained in the editorial content of the publications spanned a wide spectrum, they shared the common goal of casting their subject in a positive light. Spawning the Sexual Revolution, encouraging female autonomy, overcoming opposition from the Catholic Church—these were among the momentous achievements that the media had consistently credited, by the mid-1960s, to the birth control pill.

Celebrating the "Scientific Dream-Come-True"

The earliest news articles about the pill began appearing more than three years *before* the Food and Drug Administration licensed it as a contraceptive in May 1960. And those stories reflected the controversial nature, during the era, of a medical treatment to prevent pregnancy.[6]

Time magazine placed a question mark at the end of the headline above its first article, which appeared in early 1957—"Contraceptive Pill?" The tone of uncertainty continued in the first sentences of the piece. "Hush-hush medical research has been pursued in dozens of laboratories in the effort to find a contraceptive pill. Last week, after months of rumors, President John Searle of Chicago drug manufacturers G.D. Searle & Co. guardedly told stockholders that the company 'hopes to introduce an item for a variety of menstrual disorders. There has been speculation that the drug may have a use in the field of physiological birth control.'"[7]

And yet the tone of those early articles was, at the same time, decidedly supportive and optimistic. "The continued testing should throw more light on a technique that is full of promise," *Fortune* magazine told its readers in the lead paragraph of a 1958 article, before going on, later in the piece, to proclaim that "The promise is an inspiring one." The business magazine also reported that initial research had brought "encouragement to the scientists" and then, to make sure that readers did not dismiss the researchers as immoral radicals, went out of its way to describe them as "brilliant" and to devote the time and space necessary to create flattering character sketches of the two men who were credited with developing the pill. *Fortune* labeled Dr. John Rock a "distinguished" Harvard professor and described him as "tall, white-haired, and immaculately groomed," while describing Dr. Gregory Pincus as "a middle-aged Einstein" whose breakthroughs regarding the treatment of reproductive disorders was "outstanding."[8]

Other members of the media were soon singing the pill's praises as well. In the headline above one item, *Newsweek* dubbed the oral contraceptive "The Remarkable Pill"—a phrase that ignited a battle royal to see which publication could find the most exuberant way to laud the tiny tablet. *Reader's Digest* labeled it "one of the outstanding research accomplishments of our day," and a front-page story in the *New York Times*, widely regarded as the country's newspaper of record, crowned the birth control pill "a scientific dream-come-true."[9]

Publications targeted toward narrower audiences soon joined the chorus. *Ebony*, a leading African-American magazine, hailed the pill as "the ideal contraceptive." To support its assertion, the magazine created a list of seven criteria required for a product to receive such a designation and then, one by one, reported how the oral contraceptive met them all—from safety ("completely harmless") to low cost ("a month's supply is $3.50") to convenience ("can be taken at a time completely removed from the sexual act so the couple does not have to bother about birth control every time they have intercourse").[10]

Women's magazines were particularly eager to tell their readers about the pill. Like the publications aimed at both sexes, those targeting the actual consumers of the new scientific discovery were enthusiastic about its

possibilities. But more important than giving an endorsement was providing women with details. "The oral contraceptive pill is essentially a hormone drug," *Good Housekeeping* told its readers. "The pill prevents the production of the egg normally liberated from ovaries every month." The final line of the explanation about how the pill worked its magic carried a sense of reassurance, suggesting that the process was not so different from the biological processes routinely taking place inside a woman's body: "The synthetic hormones act very much like the natural hormones that prevent eggs from being produced during pregnancy."[11]

Downplaying the Downside

From the earliest stages of the development of an oral contraceptive, researchers as well as potential users were understandably concerned about the medication's side effects. The various publications dutifully reported this part of the story, but then, generally in the next breath, characterized them as mere inconveniences that were easily dealt with.

"A few patients experience mild nausea and a bloated feeling similar to that which often occurs during the early months of pregnancy," *Ebony* told its readers. But then the magazine quickly continued, "These symptoms usually disappear after one or two months. They may be lessened by antacids such as Gelusil, Tums or Sodamints." In case a reader was still troubled by lingering concerns about the minor side effects, *Ebony* immediately produced a long list of the pill's benefits: "There are three menstrual advantages of the pill. The amount of bleeding is less, there is usually total freedom from pain, and the cycle is very regular. Premenstrual discomfort or tension is also relieved."[12]

Ladies' Home Journal's coverage of the side effects followed the same pattern of naming the most common complaints—and then minimizing them. The *Journal* also inserted quotation marks as a subtle way of suggesting that the complaints amounted to, in the magazine's opinion, little more than whining: "Some women have complained of certain undesired 'reactions' such as occasional headaches, dizziness, nausea and breast tenderness. With continued regular use of the medication, these complaints usually disappear. Since such 'reactions' also occur in women

not taking the pills, their incidence, particularly after the first month or two, is probably not significant. In any event, they are not serious."[13]

The downside of taking the pill also received short shrift in news-oriented publications. "When side effects appear, they are likely to be nausea, breast tenderness and other symptoms of early pregnancy," reported the *New York Times*. The paper then added, "They often disappear as medication is continued." On other occasions, publications with a strong commitment to news responded to complaints by mocking them. When scientists at the University of Oregon released a study showing that the most widely used brand of oral contraceptive, Enovid, accelerated the growth of existing breast cancer in rats, *Newsweek* dispensed with the issue by reporting, "As one New York physician scoffed last week, 'All this proves is that if you're a rat and have breast cancer, you shouldn't take Enovid.'"[14]

Launching a Revolution

The story surrounding the pill had, by mid-1961, grown even larger than that of a major medical phenomenon. For the repercussions of the little tablet had begun to ripple through the culture, propelling a sizable number of Americans to change their bedroom habits, which, in turn, prompted *Esquire* magazine to announce—boldly and bluntly—that the nation had entered a new phase in its evolution: "We appear to be living through a sexual revolution."[15]

Esquire reinforced the thesis of the lengthy piece by titling it "Sex: The Quiet Revolution" and then adding the subtitle "Among the Fallen Idols: Virginity, Chastity, and Repression." The pioneering trend story left no doubt that the birth control pill was the catalyst for transforming sex, at least among many young adults, from a means of procreation to a form of recreation. Sources for the story ranged from a theology professor who observed, "A good deal of the old repressiveness is gone—what we generally associate with the word 'puritanism,'" to a plethora of sexually active young women whose quotes included such candid statements as, "In my milieu, I don't know any virgins," and "I used to think it was terrible if people had intercourse before marriage. Now I think each person should find his own values. Why not?"[16]

After *Esquire* attached a name to the radical changes that were taking place in American bedrooms, other publications soon began reporting the new sexual permissiveness as well. In January 1961, *Mademoiselle,* which called itself "the magazine for the smart young woman," carried a story by staff writer Ellen Willis that was built around comments by students at a women's college. Some of the quotes sounded almost identical to those from the *Esquire* piece—"Sex is a matter for each individual to decide according to her own personal values." Other quotes were even more blunt—"The first time I had relations, I thought I was deeply in love with the boy, but eventually we broke up. Since my inhibitions had been conquered once, it was easier the next time, and the next, and the next. Now I find it almost impossible *not* to sleep with any boy I like more than casually, and it means very little to me."[17]

Introducing the "Autonomous Girl"

Coverage of the birth control pill also eroded the concept of women being dependent on men. Some of the early articles discussing the tiny tablet's central role in the Sexual Revolution had hinted at a shift toward women becoming more independent—the *Mademoiselle* piece reported that "the majority of college girls favor contraception for the purposes of planning families wisely." But it took feminist icon Gloria Steinem to articulate the point clearly and directly. She did so in a blockbuster 1962 article in *Esquire* that introduced readers to a new category of American woman.[18]

Steinem first asserted that "the development of the 'autonomous girl' is important," and then proceeded to list this independent woman's unique characteristics. "She has work she wants to do and with which she feels identified," Steinem wrote. "She can marry later than average and have affairs if she wishes, but she can also marry without giving up her work. She can lay aside her job during childbearing years and resume it full or part time afterward."[19]

The pill was an essential element in achieving female autonomy, Steinem continued, because it allowed a woman to delay childbirth until she completed her education and established her career. What's more, the

author pointed out, a career woman now had the ability to limit how many children she had and to space them in a time frame that suited her plans. A woman with this level of autonomy and control "does not feel forced to choose between a career and marriage, and is therefore free to find fulfillment in a combination of the two," Steinem said, before concluding, "Like men, they are free to take sex, education, work and even marriage when and how they like."[20]

After Steinem's breakthrough article identified female autonomy as a clear by-product of the birth control pill, other publications followed suit. The *New York Times* reported that large numbers of young women were choosing "not to rush into marriage" but, at the same time, were seeing "no reason why they should not have a sex life of their own during their early adult years." *Time* magazine, for its part, supported the same idea by running a profile of a woman who was the epitome of the autonomous woman. "When I got married I was still in college, and I wanted to be certain that I finished," the twenty-three-year-old said. "With the pill, I know I can keep earning money and not worry about an accident that would ruin everything."[21]

Combating the Catholic Church

In choosing to promote the birth control pill, the country's magazines and newspapers took a position in direct opposition to the Catholic Church. Clerical officials from the Pope on down the ecclesiastical chain of command to bishops and finally to the nationwide network of parish priests told women that if they prevented or even delayed childbirth, they were violating God's will and, therefore, were committing a sin.

The most comprehensive treatment of the topic came in a *Newsweek* cover story labeled "Birth Control: The Pill and the Church." The lengthy article began by laying out the issue: "The traditional church view is that the 'primary' end of marriage—and therefore of sexual intercourse—is the procreation and rearing of children. Interference with the 'power to generate life' violates natural and divine law."[22]

That *Newsweek* considered the pill to be beneficial to society, despite the Catholic Church's opposition to it, became stunningly apparent as the article continued, as the news magazine abandoned all pretense of objectivity and read like an editorial. Before the end of the first page, the piece already had pointed out that the Church's opposition to birth control had forced many Catholic families to live in poverty and that the Church was out of pace with most of society because "all major Protestant sects sanction birth control." At other points, the article praised the oral contraceptive as "ingenious," called it the "Magic Pill," and credited it with having improved the marriages of many American couples because "sex is more fun with oral contraceptives."[23]

In one direct affront to the world's most powerful religion, the story pointed out that, despite what officials said, "moral theories about contraception are not always observed" by Catholic couples. Indeed not. *Newsweek* reported that "as many as 70 percent of U.S. Catholics use some form of contraception" and bolstered its point by quoting a New Jersey woman who defiantly stated, "I don't confess that I take the pill because I don't believe it is a sin."[24]

The article was so bold in its assault on the Church's anti-contraception stand that on at least one occasion it adopted a tone of blatant mockery. After reporting that the only form of birth control that officials sanctioned was the rhythm method and then explaining that the technique involved a woman avoiding intercourse during ovulation, the article ridiculed the method by dubbing it "Vatican roulette."[25]

The cover story's strongest pro-contraception stance came when it argued that the Catholic Church was wrong to oppose the pill because taking it did not, in fact, fit into the category of *artificial* birth control. The oral contraceptive was altogether different from such "mechanical contrivances" as the diaphragm or intrauterine device, *Newsweek* insisted, because it simply modifies the time sequence in the body's functions by suppressing ovulation—much like the rhythm method. The article concluded this pivotal argument by firmly stating: "The pill should be considered morally acceptable."[26]

A Critical Minority

While the vast majority of media outlets embraced the birth control pill as a medical marvel that offered enormous benefits both for individuals and for humanity writ large, some publications took a different view. These dissident voices, in keeping with the journalistic tradition of skepticism, raised a variety of questions regarding the immediate as well as the long-term effects of the little tablet.

Perhaps the strongest of the critics was *The New Republic* magazine, which published a withering article titled "The Golden Pill: We Can't Yet Be Sure It's Safe." The piece raised concerns about a variety of severe medical repercussions—including strokes, sterility, and depression—that women using the pill were reporting. "The question of utmost importance is whether The Pill causes cancer," the magazine stated. Pharmaceutical companies had been so eager to sell oral contraceptives to the public, it reported, that the first brand went on the market after being tested on a mere 132 women for only three years. The Food and Drug Administration's approval after such limited testing, *The New Republic* continued, directly contradicted the agency's official position that "all known human carcinogens require a latent period of approximately one decade." Therefore, before the birth control pill had become available, the magazine concluded, it should have been tested on at least 20,000 women for a minimum of ten years.[27]

A second skeptic, the *Saturday Evening Post,* focused on whether the pill might contribute to "a widening of the rift between the generations." The *Post,* one of the largest-circulation magazines in the country at the time, reported that many parents and religious leaders in their fifties and older questioned the benefits of the new tablet, while younger people embraced it wholeheartedly. "Many seek in sexual activity the confirmation of their 'identity' as free adults," the weekly magazine stated, "and, whether by legitimate or underground routes, the pill has found its way to the college campuses and even to the high-school hallways." The two separate reactions to the birth control pill, the *Post* argued, threatened to split the country into what an increasing number of cultural observers were referring to as a "generation gap."[28]

Another publication that fit into the disbeliever camp was *U.S. News & World Report,* which raised concerns about how the pill was affecting American morals. "With birth control now so easy and effective, is the last vestige of sexual restraint to go out the window?" the most conservative of the three major news magazines asked, followed by the point-blank question: "Will mating become casual and random—as among animals?" Clearly convinced that the pill was causing the nation's morality to plummet, the magazine quoted an official at one California college as saying, "There is less talk than there used to be about right or wrong." *U.S. News* clearly believed that the pill was changing the morals not only of young singles but also of married couples, as it stated—with no attribution to any source—"Marital infidelity is becoming accepted by many Americans as being of little importance."[29]

The Pill and the Media: A Dynamic Duo

The handful of negative articles was far outweighed by the hundreds of positive ones that portrayed the pill as a medical and social advancement of the highest order. Two books devoted to the history of oral contraception have both documented the seminal role that the media played in promoting the tiny tablet. *On the Pill: A Social History of Oral Contraceptives, 1950–1970,* for example, stated that, "In the early 1960s, the media depicted the pill as holding tremendous promise and potential."[30]

Although it is always difficult to know how events would have unfolded had the media *not* portrayed a particular topic in a positive light, American magazines and newspapers were clearly instrumental in popularizing the birth control pill and, thereby, bringing about social and cultural changes that otherwise would have occurred much more slowly, if at all. In the late 1950s before articles about the oral contraceptive had begun to appear, it was being prescribed only for a small number of women suffering from rare menstrual disorders; by 1966, it was being used on a daily basis by an astonishing six million American women.[31]

What's more, a mere half dozen years after the pill had been approved for contraceptive use, its long-term impact on the culture was already being felt. According to a front-page *New York Times* article by reporter

Jane E. Brody, the birthrate in the United States had dropped, in a mere six years, by an astonishing 24 percent. Perhaps even more dramatic evidence of the pill's effect on American life was that, as the birthrate had plunged, the frequency of sexual intercourse had soared, studies showed, by an even more dramatic 40 percent.[32]

Based both on the number of articles about the birth control pill that were published and on the supportive tone that the vast majority of those articles adopted—such as the *New York Times* labeling it "a scientific dream-come-true," *Newsweek* calling it the "Magic Pill," and *Ebony* weighing in with "the ideal contraceptive"—there is no question that the American media embraced and promoted this new phenomenon.

This reality begs another question that can be summarized in a single word: Why?

To put this another way: During an era when the long-term effectiveness and safety of the pill had not yet been proven and when a large segment of the population was still highly suspicious of this revolutionary medical experiment, what drove such a broad range of media voices to take the risk of unabashedly endorsing it?

Although there is no single reason, one factor clearly was the time period in which the majority of the articles were written. In the fall of 1960, the youngest man in the history of the American presidency was elected to the White House. Forty-three-year-old John F. Kennedy and his even younger wife—Jackie Kennedy was only thirty-one when she became first lady—symbolized a period in which the country celebrated new ideas. It was an era defined by a *zeitgeist* of vigor and vitality that informed virtually every aspect of the culture. And with the Space Race rushing forward at full throttle, scientific breakthroughs were embraced with particular zeal because anything and everything seemed possible—including an end to unwanted pregnancy.[33]

Media promotion of the pill also fit snugly with the suggestion that often has been made, though generally not in a positive tone, that the media tend to reflect a liberal bias. The idea that a little tablet could enhance the sex lives of millions of American men and women most certainly appealed to the progressively minded reporters and editors who peopled the nation's newsrooms. What's more, the fact that such a remark-

able little capsule flew in the face of the stodgy and socially repressive Catholic Church may have resonated with the ill will that many liberal journalists felt toward both organized religion and The Establishment.

Publishing articles that promoted the revolutionary potential of the birth control pill—as well as the benefits for the American public's sex life—also can be seen as reinforcing the widely held notion that the media are driven by the bottom line: *Sex Sells!* While it is impossible to prove that 1960s journalists wrote and gave prominent placement to articles in order to sell more magazines and newspapers, there is little question that millions of potential buyers who were strolling by the corner newsstand stopped for a second look when they saw headlines such as "The Remarkable Pill" (*Newsweek*), "Contraception: Freedom from Fear" (*Time*), and "Sex: The Quiet Revolution"—and the subtitle "Among the Fallen Idols: Virginity, Chastity, and Repression" (*Esquire*).[34]

It also is relevant that the pill's potential for redefining gender roles in American society held a particular appeal for a group of journalists who were, during this same era, edging their way into the newsroom: women. Throughout most of its history, the Fourth Estate had been largely a male domain. World War II had been a watershed event in women's efforts to break down the barriers against their gaining a presence in the field, and by the early 1960s a few talented and tenacious pioneers had succeeded. The birth control pill represented an ideal topic for these stalwart few, as here was a story that could become major news while also being a subject that women were uniquely suited to cover. It may be more than a coincidence that several of the most significant articles on the topic—the *Mademoiselle* piece that documented a new era in sexual behavior on college campuses, the *Esquire* piece that announced the emergence of the "autonomous woman," the front-page *New York Times* piece that dubbed the oral contraceptive "a scientific dream-come-true"—all carried the bylines of female reporters: Ellen Willis, Gloria Steinem, and Jane E. Brody. This triumvirate was only a small part of a legion of women journalists who wrote about the pill.[35]

In the final analysis, though, the most significant factor propelling favorable media coverage was that this medical development was, indeed, an extraordinarily newsworthy story.

When journalists go about the business of determining the importance of an event, they apply a series of time-honored news values. Several of the items on the list clearly were present with this story:

Impact. Does a news story affect a large number of people? Does it affect those people in significant ways?

Timeliness. Does a news story include information that is, in fact, *new*?

Novelty. Does the story include unusual or out-of-the-ordinary elements that people will be interested in reading about?

Conflict. Does the telling of a story include portraying people or institutions that are struggling against each other?[36]

The birth control pill story contained all of these news values—and in large doses. It had potentially major impact on millions of people; the Food and Drug Administration approving the medication as a contraceptive in May 1960 provided timeliness; the idea of a tiny tablet changing the entire world's sexual habits spoke to the novelty factor; and opposition from the Catholic Church added plenty of conflict.

The media and the pill, in short, represented a perfect marriage.

Playboy Magazine

Taking Pornography into the Mainstream

CHRISTINE WILLIAMS IS A YOUNG WOMAN WITH SIMPLE TASTES. HER favorite food is pizza, and her favorite hobby is reading science fiction. She doesn't spend a lot of time shopping for clothes, as she's fully satisfied to wear the straightforward sheath dresses that fill the typical American woman's closet in the 1960s—nothing fancy or out of the ordinary.

At the same time, the eighteen-year-old Williams has faced her share of adversity. Her father was career military, so she was shuttled from one Army base to another while growing up; by the time she finished high school, she'd been forced to leave behind five different sets of friends. Her height didn't make it any easier for the self-conscious young woman. "I was always the tallest and gawkiest girl in my class," Williams said, "and it really embarrassed me."[1]

The details about her life and the words coming out of her mouth paint the subject as, in a phrase: the girl next door.

But as the half dozen photos surrounding the block of magazine copy attest, she also is drop-dead gorgeous. Flowing blond hair tops her six-foot frame that has filled out quite nicely—she measures 37–26–37, to be exact—to create nothing less than an absolutely stunning specimen of nubile womanhood.

Christine Williams being both wholesome in her background and eye-popping in her appearance transformed her into a foot soldier in the Sexual Revolution.

As one of the all-American beauties who graced the pages of the biggest publishing success story of the decade, the Playmate of the Month for October 1963 was living proof that the sky did not fall and mothers did not march in protest when a magazine dared to build its identity around the image of lovely young women exposing lots of bare skin.

Playboy illustrated better than any other single media product of the era that the time had come for old sexual taboos to be relegated to the history books as society reached the point that the empress, so to speak, no longer needed to wear clothes. The Chicago-based monthly replaced the smutty "girly" magazines of earlier times by removing the plain brown wrapper to reveal a glossy cover and a bevy of fresh-faced, luscious-bodied beauties such as Christine Williams to fashion a surefire formula for presenting erotica to a mass audience that no publication before it had dared to contemplate but that many after it would be eager to imitate:

Playboy moved pornography into the mainstream.[2]

The magazine's founder, Hugh Hefner, became an international sexual icon and a major figure in—some say the catalyst for—the Sexual Revolution. Hefner had introduced *Playboy* in 1953, but it was during the 1960s that the magazine captured the public imagination and its circulation soared to a remarkable seven million. By the middle of the decade, no one questioned that the publication had become the revolution's signature printed voice.[3]

Playboy achieved that stature by spearheading an effort to alter the national consciousness on sexual topics. Thanks to this bible of the young urban male, a critical mass of the population now found it perfectly acceptable to ogle naked women—the magazine became a fixture on the coffee table of every red-blooded American bachelor—and to talk publicly about sex in ways that previous generations had never dared. Indeed, the legions of libidinous readers who eagerly awaited the arrival of the new issue each month embraced not only the concept of having intercourse before marriage but also of having sex with multiple partners at the same time—the more the merrier.

These messages stood in particularly dramatic contrast to the limitations that were in place regarding sex on American television during the

1960s. Only a man and woman who were married to each other could be depicted in bed together, and to avoid any suggestion of under-the-covers nudity, it was a firm requirement that the viewer had to be able to see at least one shoulder strap on the wife's nightgown peeking over the top of the blanket.[4]

Reinventing the "Men's Magazine"

Before *Playboy* debuted, the phrase "men's magazine" conjured up images of sleazy publications filled with grainy black-and-white photos of women who looked like they'd just spent the night on the street—the bags under their eyes surpassed only by their balloon-sized bosoms. The lone words that were printed between the low-quality images were the fabricated names of the world-weary models such as "Virginia Hams" and "Beatrice Beaver."[5]

When *Playboy* arrived, it offered readers a very different experience— full-color images that ultimately would come to be classified as "soft-core," rather than "hard-core," pornography. The main attraction in that premier issue was a glorious image of Marilyn Monroe, one of the country's most glamorous stars, posing seductively against a lush background of crimson velvet and with, as she later would say, "nothing on but the radio." Hugh Hefner had purchased the nude image, taken four years earlier when Monroe was still unknown, for a mere $200.[6]

After readers had feasted on the delicious blond bombshell, they moved on to nourishment for their minds. During the late 1950s, the magazine reprinted literary classics by such notable authors as Somerset Maugham, John Steinbeck, and Ernest Hemingway. And in the 1960s, the content included important new fiction by James Baldwin, Ray Bradbury, and Truman Capote, as well as in-depth interviews with top newsmakers ranging from Frank Sinatra and the Beatles to Fidel Castro, the Rev. Martin Luther King Jr., and Malcolm X.[7]

Feature-length articles by *Playboy* staff writers leaned toward sexual topics such as "Uncovering a Nudist Wedding," "A Stripper Goes to College," and "The Pros of Paris"—the last story complete with names, prices, and photos of French prostitutes. But even the pieces that were

pornographic because of their subject matter were treated with journalistic integrity, forcing even the magazine's critics to acknowledge that the
content was not "smutty or dirty."[8]

Advertising reflected the same sense of class and sophistication as the
writing. Items that might remind a young man-about-town that his youth
and vitality could fade—toupees and hair-restoring lotions—were banned
from the pages; products deemed essential for the *bon vivant*—stereo systems and fine clothing—were welcomed. Indeed, *Playboy*'s advertising
content broke new ground at a pace similar to the magazine itself. "Ten
years ago, none of our clients would have dared to place an ad in *Playboy*,"
an official with the world's largest advertising agency told a *Business Week*
reporter in 1969. "Today it's a routine buy."[9]

During the 1960s, the country's leading publications reported that
Hugh Hefner's pioneering magazine had dramatically influenced the nation's sexual self. *Look* stated that *Playboy*'s success marked the "triumph
of sexuality" and the "end of Puritanism," and *Time* announced that, because of Hefner's publishing venture, "Nudity is now accepted in this
country as a legitimate expression of sex appeal."[10]

Propelled partly by the publicity but mostly by its own content, *Playboy*
became a phenomenon of legendary proportions. By the mid-1960s, one
out of every four male college students in the country was buying a
copy—and then passing it around to the other three. Many campuses held
monthly parties to celebrate the arrival of the latest issue, and professors
at some of the nation's most prestigious institutions, including Harvard,
incorporated the magazine into their courses. A popular comedian of the
era quipped that an entire generation of men was growing up convinced
that a woman folded in three places and had staples in her navel.[11]

Showcasing the Girl Next Door

The most salient pages of *Playboy*—as well as those that bore the most
fingerprints—were the three that unfolded at the center of the magazine.
Each issue showcased a single young woman whose physical attributes
were made readily apparent by the expansive nude image of her. The
Playmate photo was innovative not only because the magazine invented

the foldout concept but also because of the style in which the photo was taken; the image was shot with a soft-focus filter and airbrushed to perfection—pubic hair was strictly *verboten*.[12]

Also revolutionary were the few paragraphs of copy next to the image. This thumbnail sketch of the particular month's beauty painstakingly portrayed the Playmate not as the kind of brazen trollop who previously had bared her body for public view, but as an all-American young woman who possessed three characteristics to be admired as much as her voluptuous form: She was of high moral character. She was wholesome. She was eager to meet men.

The centerfold's morality came through in a variety of ways—some blunt, others subtle. Miss September 1963 was described as having "distinctively Victorian views" rather than the radical ones of many young people of the era, and Miss January 1967 was labeled humanitarian Albert Schweitzer's "fairest disciple," having been so inspired by the famous doctor's good works with African natives that she had enrolled in nursing school. One of the less direct means of communicating a woman's moral center was by discussing the central role that her parents played in her life. Miss May 1966 was quoted as saying she was flattered when offered the opportunity to appear in the magazine but "like any well-bred girl, I had to clear it with my parents first." One sketch reported that a centerfold's mother had accompanied her to the photo shoot and another said that the girl's father had provided some of the nude photos of his daughter that appeared in the magazine.[13]

To illustrate that Playmates were wholesome, the magazine showed that they had simple tastes—with absolutely no suggestion, despite their good looks, of being conceited. Miss October 1962 was described as "a girl who is endowed with refreshingly unpretentious tastes including Alfred Hitchcock's thrillers and heaping helpings of all foods Italian." Another called herself a "home girl" because her greatest loves were "people, pretty shoes, spaghetti, chocolate ice cream, and fried chicken." The down-to-earth nature of a large number of the women was subtly communicated by showing their affection for animals. One was described as being so attached to her dog that she brought him with her to her photo session and another as saying that she liked dogs because "They have no affectations."

Some of the descriptions related to a Playmate's love for animals did double duty by also conveying her fondness for men; the copy for Miss March 1969 included the statement, "Of her three pets, Cinder gets most of Kathy's attention—it's no coincidence that he's the only male."[14]

Playboy most frequently told its readers about a centerfold's eagerness to meet men by portraying her as uncommonly friendly toward the opposite sex. "All it really takes to make me happy," Christine Williams was quoted as saying, "is male friends who are indulgent about my two major vices—talking and eating large amounts of chocolate." Miss March 1963 was characterized as "making friends easily with men, who are invariably taken with the fact that she so obviously enjoys masculine company." The joint concepts of availability and friendliness were repeated month after month. One Playmate was described as "refreshingly friendly and happy-go-lucky," another as "charming and cooperative," a third as "loving animals, and the male animal most of all."[15]

Personifying the American Playboy

Second only to the centerfolds as *Playboy*'s human symbol was a subject most often pictured not in the nude but in a tuxedo: Hugh Hefner.

During his youth and early adulthood, this skinny son of a Chicago accountant spent his free time drawing cartoons. He created several comic strips and humor publications, first in high school and then while earning a psychology degree from the University of Illinois. Along the way, Hefner married his high school sweetheart, fathered two children, and worked in a variety of positions in the publishing world.

It was a pair of those jobs, juxtaposed back to back, that gave Hefner the inspiration that changed his life—and, ultimately, the sexual habits of millions of Americans. The first was as a writer in the promotions department of the upscale literary magazine *Esquire,* the second as circulation manager for a "men's magazine" titled *Modern Man.* In early 1953, a light bulb went off in the twenty-six-year-old's head: Why not combine literary content and naked women in a single publication?

The first issue of *Playboy* sold 50,000 copies, and the circulation climbed steadily throughout the late 1950s. But the big breakthrough came early

in the new decade when Hefner expanded his enterprise beyond the printed page. Again, the inspiration came by happenstance. When Hefner published an article about a Chicago nightclub known for its scantily clad waitresses, the piece prompted a flood of 3,000 letters. Another light bulb begot another question: Why not adapt the concept and create a string of nightclubs tailored specifically for *Playboy* readers?

As the trademark of the first Playboy Club that opened in 1960, Hefner created "the bunny." This was the woman, an animated version of the centerfold, who greeted a club member at the door, checked his hat, served him a drink, and chatted with him until he bought a few more drinks. To add to the fun, Hefner dressed each bunny in a super-tight and bright-colored satin corset, perky bunny ears, three-inch heels, and a fluffy tail positioned squarely on the woman's curvaceous backside.

As the bunnies multiplied to staff the string of Playboy Clubs that arose across the United States and Europe, so did the magazine profiles portraying Hefner as a sexual icon. Having divorced his wife and moved into a forty-room mansion that also served as home to two dozen dazzling centerfolds and bunnies, the visionary entrepreneur had created a fantasy world for himself that other men were living only in their dreams. Various publications dubbed Hefner, though he was neither handsome nor well built, "The Playboy of the Western World," and *Newsweek* called him "the guru of a nirvana for the Urban Guy."[16]

Nirvana indeed.

By the late 1960s, Hefner was sitting atop a $1 billion empire that had expanded to include three dozen Playboy Clubs, half a dozen luxury hotels, a publishing house, a Hollywood film company, a syndicated television program with him in the starring role, and a marketing operation that was hawking some ninety products, from key chains to leisure wear, encrusted with the ubiquitous bunny logo.[17]

Talking About Sex

Though Hugh Hefner developed Playboy Enterprises into a multifaceted corporation, the jewel in the crown continued to be the magazine. Likewise, even though *Playboy*'s editorial content provided information

and amusement on a broad spectrum of topics such as what the "hip" modern man was wearing and where he was traveling, the single subject that gave the publication its unique identity, as well as the one that attracted most of its readers, boiled down to S-E-X.

Some articles echoed the media's consistent pattern of promoting the birth control pill, such as a piece assuring Americans that while the number of women using the pill was soaring, so was the number of men using condoms to prevent passing venereal diseases to their partners. But most of the stories published in *Playboy* chronicled aspects of the Sexual Revolution that other publications wouldn't touch, expanding American journalism far beyond its previous parameters. Typical of this huge category of items was one announcing that, by 1969, fewer than half of female college seniors were virgins and another—headlined "Use It or Lose It"—cautioning readers that a Tulane University research study found that "Males not allowed to copulate suffer atrophy of the penis."[18]

Sex was also the topic of choice in the Playboy Forum, a section devoted to articles from readers. Again, some items reinforced the media's love affair with the pill, such as one from an attorney demanding that the government provide all Americans with free birth control. But most readers who took advantage of *Playboy*'s open-forum concept opted to discuss aspects of sexuality that other publications banned from their pages. An Australian reader, for example, made a case for legalizing prostitution while also condemning his local police for entrapment: "One man was stopped by police after a disguised policewoman offered herself to him for ten dollars and he accepted," the Aussie wrote. "He pleaded not guilty but was convicted."[19]

Such serious items were in the minority, as *Playboy*'s general tone was light and entertaining. An abundance of full-page cartoons added to the amusement quotient. One showed a young woman with large, well-formed breasts posing in front of her dressing table and saying, "Mirror, Mirror, on the wall, *Whose* are the fairest of them all . . . ?" Another pictured a young woman sitting at one end of a sofa while a man sitting at the other end said, "Boy, for the Now Generation, you're sure full of a lot of 'Not nows.'" Still another was set in a bar with a "No One Under 21 Allowed" sign hovering overhead as a buxom young woman sat on one

of the stools, pulling back her trench coat to expose a pair of extraordinarily perky breasts; the smiling bartender clearly appreciated the show but, nevertheless, said, "I'm afraid I'll still have to see your driver's license."[20]

Although the magazine was the first containing nude images to be sent through the mail, it faced obscenity charges only once. The 1963 nude photos of actress Jayne Mansfield were no more revealing than those of other women who had appeared in the magazine. What upped the risqué factor this time was the presence of a man—fully clothed and with a book in his hands, but still a man—sitting on the edge of the bed as the luscious blonde, in the terms used in the copy next to the photos, "writhed" and "gyrated" in an effort to distract her bedfellow from his reading. Post Office authorities took the magazine to court, but, when the jury failed to reach a verdict, the charges were dropped.[21]

Promoting Casual Sex

Threaded throughout the magazine's articles as well as its photos and cartoons was the message that sex is too pleasurable to confine it to marriage.

Indeed, even Americans who only read *about* the publication recognized this as its signature concept. The first paragraph of one magazine article about *Playboy* labeled it "the oracle for communicating that unmarried sex is fine and good and clean," and another piece quoted Hugh Hefner as citing the fact that the national divorce rate had climbed to 25 percent as support for his assertion that "We're not a monogamous society." The numerous articles published about Hefner reinforced the point by reporting his propensity for designating one particular Playmate his "special girl," at least for a few weeks or months, while simultaneously having sex with other women, too.[22]

Much of the country appeared to agree with the hedonistic publisher's attitude toward promiscuity. An article titled "The Campus Mood" included a quote from a University of Colorado junior. "At least twenty percent of this campus is shacking up," she bluntly stated. "There's no question about 'Are you getting married?' You're living together, it's fine,

it's nice. That's all. The end." Other pieces moved beyond reporting to the point of blatantly promoting the benefits of casual sex. Typical was one celebrating premarital sex as an essential step toward a successful marriage. "We throw married people into bed together with absolutely no experience whatsoever, if we follow society's rules," the story began. "If couples had a variety and a frequency of experience with intercourse beforehand, many of the basic problems that afflict most new marriages could be avoided." Another article suggested that students who engaged in intercourse on a regular basis were more likely to earn high grades. "With sex a matter of course in the lives of college students, they become less preoccupied with it," the article argued, therefore giving them more time to devote to their studies.[23]

Playboy Forum items also encouraged no-strings-attached sex. A piece from an Ohio reader who identified herself as "an other woman" listed the advantages of her situation compared to that of a wife. "I don't have to wash his clothes or pick up his socks," she wrote. "I don't have to prepare three meals a day. I don't have to look after his children when they are ill or cranky." Another reader's argument in favor of sex outside of marriage was made particularly compelling by the fact that it was written by a former chairman of the Temple University Medical School. "There are certain people," the Philadelphia psychiatrist insisted, "who for their mental and emotional welfare have a very significant need to seek a certain type of person with whom they can give sexual relations more significance than they can possibly obtain in marriage."[24]

The editor whose job it was to respond to letters from readers also took the opportunity to encourage men to move their romantic relationships into the bedroom whenever they had the chance. A Massachusetts man sent in a question about a quandary he faced. "I've been making it with a very hip Scandinavian chick. She's everything one could ask for, but there's one problem. Although she has fine manners and does very well in company, she can't resist trying to caress me in very intimate and obvious ways when we're in public. What should I do?" The editor's answer was brief and to the point: "Stay home, avoid crowds, and get plenty of bed rest."[25]

Celebrating Group Sex

Second only to casual sex as a pervasive theme in *Playboy* was the concept that the pleasures of carnal activities were heightened considerably when more than two people participated. Although no official statistics document the percentage of Americans who incorporated group sex into their lives during the 1960s, the magazine's editorial content suggested that the figure was substantial.

"Swinging, once a carefully guarded pastime indigenous to upper-income groups," one article reported, "has lately been embraced by schoolteachers, mutual-fund salesmen, aerospace engineers and other members of the predominant middle class." The piece went on to provide specifics about the social trend at hand, first taking readers to an "annual New Year's Eve orgy" in a home in the Hollywood Hills and then introducing them to a "cell of 2,500 Chicago-area mate swappers" and to "antique-hunting couples [who] journey through the New England countryside, pausing to browse in quaint roadside shops—and to swap mates at small inns." The article also gave readers a sense of the social forces behind the new popularity that group sex was enjoying: "Its swift surfacing from the clandestine to the commonplace has coincided with general acceptance of the birth control pill."[26]

As with casual sex, *Playboy* went beyond reporting to the point that it unabashedly promoted group sexual encounters. In some instances, the support came in the form of the magazine using specific details and erudite words to paint orgies as chic events. "Uniformed waiters were pouring 12-year-old Scotch and jeroboams of Dom Perignon in the sunken 40-foot living room of the penthouse apartment situated high above Sunset Strip," one article read. "A major television personality warmly welcomed 100 guests. Relaxed by the free-flowing liquor and the oleaginous Mantovani strings purring over a stereo intercom, secure in the comfort of a large kindred group, they repaired at regular intervals to the five mirrored bedrooms."[27]

The magazine further encouraged modern-day Bacchanalias by reporting that the divorce rate among married swingers was low, that the inci-

dence of sexually transmitted disease was minimal because most people involved in orgies were "hip on hygiene," and that the possibility of getting arrested was slight because police officers who observed group sex invariably joined in to become "enthusiastic participants." The magazine even argued that orgies were in concert with the increasing value that 1960s young people placed on equality. "Disparities in income and social status are characteristically forgotten, as sex in these circles is the great equalizer," one piece stated, going on to quote a man as saying, "It's hard to be a snob when you're bare-assed."[28]

Playboy's identity with group sex was solidified by the abundant coverage of the magazine's founder that appeared in other publications. It became *de rigueur* for layouts to include an image of Hugh Hefner with several young women—always beautiful, always well built, always showing lots of skin—either draped over him or standing so close the reader could almost feel the body heat. Some images were sufficiently erotic, in fact, that they could have qualified as *Playboy* centerfold shots; one accompanying the *Time* cover story pictured Hefner surrounded by a bevy of bunnies sunbathing in the nude—the bare breasts of a woman in the foreground were fully visible. Another *Time* article was illustrated by a provocative photo of Hefner and four shapely young women lying on a bed, and another layout included a shot of Hefner sitting beside a swimming pool, two bikini-clad women snuggling close to him and two more kneeling at his feet, their mouths only inches from his crotch. Similarly suggestive photos appeared in *Look* and *Newsweek, Forbes* and *Business Week*.[29]

Facing Challenges on Two Fronts

By the late 1960s, *Playboy* was being attacked by two dramatically different forces. First, feminists lambasted the magazine as sexist because it did not portray women as multidimensional human beings with minds and hearts, but only as sex objects with breasts and thighs. Second, other publishers imitated Hugh Hefner's successful formula and created other men's magazines that competed with the original. On both fronts, the battle focused on the *Playboy* centerfold.

Typical of the feminist-oriented articles was one in the *Saturday Evening Post* that accused the publication of "reducing women to the status of a commodity." Each month's Playmate was selected strictly on the basis of her physical attributes, the piece said, while no consideration whatsoever was given to any other aspect of her person: "She exists only to give pleasure, and the sex she proffers is, quite literally, skin deep." Other stories in other publications made equally critical assessments. A *Life* magazine attack titled "In Hefnerland, Women Are Status Symbols" argued that *Playboy* readers considered their girlfriends or wives to be "no more or less important than the sleekest sports car or most expensive bottle of Scotch. A woman becomes de-personalized, an object for man's pleasure."[30]

With regard to its publishing imitators, *Playboy* faced the first of a long line of formidable competitors in 1969 with the appearance of *Penthouse.* Founder and editor Bob Guccione followed his predecessor's model of mixing substantive editorial content with nude photos but offered readers more explicit images than those that Hefner printed—including pubic hair. *Time* magazine also noted that the women in *Penthouse* were "more lifelike" than those in *Playboy:* "They have moles and appendicitis scars, and sometimes their breasts even sag a little."[31]

Fueling the Revolution

Feminist criticism and competition notwithstanding, *Playboy* clearly played an epic role in propelling the American media on the arc that ultimately moved from sexual repression to sexual obsession. One historian credited the publication with single-handedly "inciting a sexual revolution," a second praised the magazine for "giving American popular culture a sex life," and a third pronounced that "Society and the world have been changed forever because of *Playboy.*"[32]

The most important specific contribution that should be credited to the magazine is its success at moving pornography into the cultural mainstream. Before *Playboy,* most people considered images of naked women to be disgusting smut. But thanks to the magazine's depiction of beautiful young women such as Christine Williams, both in its images

and in its prose, as the epitome of the girl next door, many more readers—the seven million who read the magazine combined with the millions more who read *about* it in other publications—came to view nudity as a much more acceptable phenomenon. Likewise, the magazine played a pivotal role in popularizing the practice of intercourse outside of marriage and, presumably to a lesser degree, of sex with multiple partners. Although these activities would remain controversial, the editorial content and cartoons in the pages of *Playboy* compelled some people to incorporate these activities into their lives, while causing many more to daydream about doing so.

In 1999, seventy-three-year-old Hugh Hefner wrote the foreword for a book about the Sexual Revolution: "I believe that sex is the primary motivating factor in the course of human history, and in this twentieth century it has emerged from the taboos and controversy that have surrounded it throughout the ages to claim its rightful place in society."[33]

Playboy was a leading force in bringing about that new mindset.

James Bond

Bringing Sex into the Movies

SHE SEEMS TO APPEAR OUT OF NOWHERE. FIRST HER BLOND HAIR emerges from the white foam, then her lovely tanned shoulders—mere prelude to her magnificently round breasts undulating in their effort, valiant but futile, to struggle free of the white bikini top that constrains them. There is still more to come—the slender waist, the scant bikini bottom just barely covering the V that will become an object of fantasy for generations of male viewers, then a pair of shapely legs as the voyeuristic eye moves slowly from thigh to knee to calf to ankle. Finally, the full figure of womanhood walks sensually out of the surf—water dripping from her voluptuous curves—to stand so tall and statuesque that her beauty and erotic appearance were fully worthy of worship and yet her nubile innocence making her seem so vulnerable.

It had been a challenge for the film's casting director to find an actress who could fill the role, which the script had described as a Venus comparable to the one Florentine painter Sandro Botticelli had created in *The Birth of Venus* around 1480. But when a photo of a twenty-six-year-old Swiss model posing in a wet T-shirt appeared at the United Artists studio, the search abruptly ended.

Ursula Andress rising out of the ocean onto a deserted stretch of sand in Jamaica went on to be heralded as one of the most memorable entrances by a woman in the history of motion pictures—one poll crowned it "the sexiest screen moment" ever committed to film. And those are exactly the kind of superlatives required for the image to be an appropriate

symbol of the sexual content in the James Bond movies created during the 1960s.[1]

Andress appeared in *Dr. No,* which launched the series that would become Hollywood legend. The films were not only highly profitable and extraordinarily popular, but they also appeared with an uncommon regularity—*Dr. No* in 1962, *From Russia With Love* in 1963, *Goldfinger* in 1964, *Thunderball* in 1965, *You Only Live Twice* in 1967, *On Her Majesty's Secret Service* in 1969—that allowed them to achieve a remarkable level of influence on the nation's collective sexual self.

And so, while *Playboy* was fueling the Sexual Revolution on paper, the Bond movies were doing much the same on celluloid. Indeed, the two media products overlapped and reinforced each other in several instances. When Ursula Andress took it all off for a twelve-page spread—the longest in *Playboy* history—in mid-1965, the photos caused such a sensation that she not only returned for two more nude spreads but also paved the way for no fewer than a dozen of Bond's other cinematic sex kittens to grace the pages of the magazine. Ian Fleming, the novelist who created the James Bond character, and Sean Connery, the actor who most often portrayed the secret agent, were also the subjects of lengthy *Playboy* interviews, and, in one film, James Bond is shown unfolding a copy of the magazine to admire the centerfold.[2]

The films sent many of the same provocative sexual messages—*Life* magazine described the movies as "glamorizing amorality"—as their print counterpart. Like the pages of *Playboy,* the world of James Bond featured a parade of gorgeous women, every one of them blessed with perfect facial features and curvaceous bodies. The Hugh Hefner role was, in the first five movies released in the 1960s, filled by Sean Connery and, in the last one, by George Lazenby—both men much more handsome and with much better physiques than the publishing mogul. The celebration of casual sex that was a major element in *Playboy* was easily translated to film, this time not only talked about in words but accompanied by suggestive visuals as well. New themes that emerged on the theater screen included women being portrayed as dangerous femme fatales and voyeurism as a technique to stir the loins of male viewers.[3]

Bringing Sex to the Big Screen

James Bond first came to life in Ian Fleming's string of adventure novels written in the 1950s. The high-living British secret service agent—code name 007—was the prototype of the attractive, debonair, witty, and indestructible playboy/hero whose international missions were packed with action, intrigue, espionage, the latest in Space Age gadgetry, and what one magazine of the era called "an acre or so of dazzling girls" who fell victim to his prodigious powers of seduction.[4]

The sexual escapades were a dramatic departure from what Hollywood had offered filmgoers in the 1950s. The most successful movies of that decade had been musicals such as *South Pacific* and *The King and I*, biblical epics such as *Ben Hur* and *The Ten Commandments*, and sugarcoated romantic comedies featuring Doris Day and Rock Hudson. By contrast, James Bond did not sing or dance, go to church, or suffer rejection by women; instead, the hot-for-action sex symbol spent his free time between the sheets.[5]

And audiences loved him for it.

The Bond motion pictures were an unprecedented triumph, both in the amount of money they made and in the number of viewers they pulled into theaters. By mixing sex, action, and humor through self-parody, they created a cinematic phenomenon that still ranks today as the most successful series of films in box-office history. The films grossed more than $2.5 billion in ticket sales, a record that no other series has come even close to matching. James Bond's popularity soared after moviegoers got a taste of his sexual hedonism in his first two films, to the point that *Goldfinger's* release in 1964 drew "lines of eager ticket buyers forming for blocks on opening day and afterward, this enthusiastic reception being duplicated all over the country." In some cities, people were so eager to get into the theater that they waited all night to buy tickets, with the line ultimately stretching for half a mile. "The success of *Goldfinger* was such that in one cinema in New York City, one showing followed another day and night," by one critic's account, "and the management imposed an interval only to sweep away from the auditorium the remains of popcorn

which had reached a depth of several inches." It was soon taken for granted that every new film in the series would be Hollywood's top moneymaker of the year, and, by the end of the decade, it was estimated that the number of theatergoers worldwide who had seen at least one James Bond movie had reached the unprecedented figure of one billion.[6]

The impact of the films transcended the theater to become such a powerful phenomenon that *Time* magazine coined a new term to describe it; in 1965, the nation's largest-circulation news magazine reported that "Bondomania" was spreading like wildfire and that "James Bond has developed into the biggest mass-cult hero of the decade." The sexual rogue's penetration into the culture was evident at many levels. Toy companies introduced the first generation of action figures in the secret agent's likeness, *Life* magazine featured one of the female stars from *Goldfinger* on its cover, and the sensational popularity of the films prompted new interest in the Ian Fleming novels, sending total sales to an impressive eighteen million copies.[7]

Perhaps the strongest evidence of Bond's influence on the sexual culture evolved not from the response of moviegoers or consumers but from that of a much smaller group of social observers. For the first time in history, Vatican officials in Rome became so concerned with the sexual messages being communicated on motion picture screens that they publicly condemned the Bond films as representing a "dangerous threat" to global morality.[8]

The Girl Next Door Leaves the Neighborhood

The women who starred in the movies were as integral to the productions as the centerfolds were to *Playboy*. The "Bond girls," as they were widely known, were as ravishing and well-built—several of them were international beauty queens—as their magazine equivalents. And yet the two sets of "lookers" also differed in several fundamental ways.[9]

First and foremost, the Playmates showed far more skin than the actresses did. In particular, the exposed breasts that protruded from the magazine's three center pages each month were the women's most memorable feature, but the Hollywood standards of morality were con-

siderably more restrictive than those for print publications. The price of a movie theater ticket would buy a Bond fan plenty of glimpses of large and well-shaped breasts bulging out from bikinis, low-cut dresses, and bath towels that seemed on the verge of falling to the floor at any moment, but at least some of each breast—and most definitely the nipple—remained concealed.[10]

The Playmates and "Bond girls" also differed in character. Simply put, all those girl-next-door types with their wholesome values and simple tastes got lost somewhere on the way to the United Artists studio. They were replaced by a bevy of slightly older and considerably more sophisticated women whose worldview was much broader than a single neighborhood.

Sylvia Trench set the standard. The first beauty to appear in *Dr. No,* the glamorous brunette has her hair elegantly coiffed and is wearing a floor-length, off-the-shoulder evening dress and carrying a mink stole when she meets the tuxedoed master of derring-do at a London casino. Trench is in the middle of a losing streak, but she keeps right on betting and smiling—especially after catching James Bond's wandering eye. The situation prompts the suave secret agent to utter his inaugural line of dialogue with a suggestive question at the end: "I admire your courage, *Miss?*"[11]

A few scenes later, Trench appears in Bond's hotel room, still wearing her spike heels but having replaced her striking red gown with a considerably more comfortable shirt from the secret agent's closet. He insists that they'll have to wait until the next day to get to know each other better because he has to leave "immediately" for the airport to catch a plane. But when the sexy woman persists, Bond changes his tune and insists that he must leave "*almost* immediately." As Trench leads the way to the bedroom, the moviegoer knows that this is no inexperienced girl next door.

Nor are the stunning women who appear in the films consistently the same white-bread Americans as *Playboy* readers were accustomed to ogling. *Newsweek's* review of *You Only Live Twice* made special note of "the awesome collection of Japanese lovelies," while other Bond films included beauties from countries such as France, Germany, Italy, and Russia. Although none of Bond's 1960s bed partners could be accurately de-

scribed as black, no one seeing the entire series had trouble tagging the international spy's taste in women as "exotic."[12]

The Über Playboy

Like Hugh Hefner, James Bond became a symbol of the sexually adventurous "babe magnet" of the 1960s. But the two icons also differed significantly.

For anyone who read the magazine and watched the films, the most dramatic distinction was in physical appearance. Hefner's facial features were too nondescript to qualify as handsome, and his frame was more that of a scarecrow than a matinee idol. Hefner also was consistently photographed wearing a full set of clothes; the American public rarely glimpsed his bare arms or legs, much less his chest.

Not so Bond.

Sean Connery, the leading man most frequently identified with the secret agent *extraordinaire*, was the definition of handsome. His rugged facial features were highlighted by smoldering dark brown eyes and a mischievous smirk, and his well-developed body completed the hunky package—the former lifeguard had represented Scotland in the Mr. Universe contest. "I wanted a ballsy guy," producer Harry Saltzman said after choosing Connery, "instead of all the mincing poofs we had applying for the job." After appearing as Bond in five films in as many years, an exhausted Connery left the role. George Lazenby, who took his place, was every bit as attractive as the original.[13]

The production professionals in charge of the scripts and on-screen action took full advantage of the physical attributes of the two strapping specimens of manliness, making sure the films included plenty of close-ups of their faces and as much of their bare skin as the censors would allow. All six films included several scenes in which the leading man removed his shirt to reveal his impressive chest covered with a full crop of the thick, dark hair that communicated "virility" in the 1960s. (Although Lazenby's chest was not as furry as Connery's, his well-toned pectorals fully compensated for his shortcomings in the hair department.)

The movie-going audience got its first glimpses of James Bond's sexy physique in *Dr. No,* first in swimming trunks on the beach and later in a skintight undershirt that had been torn in all the right places to showcase his powerful chest and upper arms. Other sexy images of 007 followed in later films—nothing but a towel in *From Russia With Love,* bare-chested while getting a massage in *Goldfinger,* lots more swimming and massaging in *Thunderball.*

Bond's well-tanned body got its most screen time in *You Only Live Twice,* with the opening image showing him rolling around in the sheets with one of his many paramours. The action hero's bare torso made several return appearances in the film while its owner was swimming, being massaged by yet another blonde, and being bathed by a gaggle of Japanese lovelies—unaccustomed to men with so much body hair, the Asian women repeatedly stroked and caressed his chest. The creative production crew found still more ways to showcase their star's physique in *On Her Majesty's Secret Service.* The opening sequence showed 007 dressed in a tuxedo but then had him racing toward a beach to rescue a damsel in distress, ripping off his jacket and tie as he ran so that, by the end of the scene, his soaked white shirt made him look like the hands-down winner of a male wet T-shirt contest.

That James Bond's looks were the top priority was reinforced by the choice of George Lazenby to replace Sean Connery for the last film of the decade. Even though the newcomer would face the daunting challenge of being critically compared to an enormously popular star, the Powers That Be opted not to go with a professional actor. Lazenby had never, before being cast in the role, been on a theater stage or in a Hollywood studio, having spent his entire career as a professional model. When it came to portraying the most high-profile superhero in the world, looks clearly were more important than acting ability.[14]

Although Sean Connery and George Lazenby were both far more physically attractive than Hugh Hefner, the secret agent and *Playboy's* founder enjoyed one attribute that added enormously to their public personas as sexy *bon vivants:* Women flocked to them.

Just as articles about Hefner consistently included a provocative shot of him surrounded by buxom bunnies and Playmates, James Bond also was

repeatedly at the center of a harem of ravishing women. In *On Her Majesty's Secret Service,* for instance, the intrepid agent's work took him to an exclusive allergy clinic in the Swiss Alps that could accommodate a maximum of a dozen patients at any one time. As luck would have it, all twelve of the residents happened to be young women—each one gorgeous. Denied male companionship during their treatment, the women literally pawed all over Bond during the dinner where they met him. Before the break of dawn, the midnight marauder had already had sex with two of the eager nymphets.[15]

Bond's virility faced its biggest test in *Goldfinger* when he encountered the most provocatively named of the women who crossed his path—Pussy Galore. His challenge did not involve the lovely blonde's name but the fact that all of her previous sexual experiences had been with other women. "You can turn off the charm," the confirmed lesbian told him soon after they met. "I'm immune." Hardly. By the end of the film, the motion picture industry's most manly man had succeeded in going where no man had gone before—not once, but twice.[16]

Casual Sex Becomes More than Mere Words

As in the pages of *Playboy,* one of the most prominent themes threaded through the Bond films was the attitude that sex was too pleasurable an experience to be confined to marriage. This message was more powerfully communicated on celluloid than in print, in fact, because the magazine only talked about casual sex in its articles, while the movie version provided visual depictions, or at least hinted at them. In the straightforward words of one scholar of sex in the twentieth century, "The James Bond movies promoted sex without commitment."[17]

One memorable encounter unfolds in the early scenes of *Goldfinger.* Soon after arriving at a Miami Beach luxury hotel, 007 comes upon a beautiful woman lying seductively on a chaise lounge—dressed only in black lace bra and panties. When the woman makes eye contact with Bond, she asks, "Who are you?" The question sets up one of the licentious secret agent's most celebrated lines: "Bond. James Bond." Apparently that retort and those sensuous eyes are all the woman needs

for enticement, as she immediately follows him to his suite for a randy session of sex—no more than ten minutes after they'd met.[18]

Thunderball's early scenes provide another example. This time, a comely physical therapist is helping Bond recover from minor injuries. Before the session ends, however, she has expanded her services to include providing her patient with a quickie in the steam room. Bond enjoys this particular session of no-strings-attached sex so much that he returns for seconds. The therapist clearly enjoys the trysts as much as Bond does. After they end their second romp, he gives her a coy smile and says, "Keep in touch." She smiles sweetly, strokes his hand, and responds, "Anytime, James. Anyplace."[19]

The virile secret agent enjoys numerous other impromptu sexual encounters, sometimes without even knowing the woman's name, throughout the half dozen films. Bond's sexual terrain of choice seems to be between the sheets of a bed, but he's willing to be flexible. In From Russia With Love, he has spur-of-the-moment intercourse in a tent, on a train, in the backseat of a convertible, and while riding in a gondola as it floats down the Grand Canal in Venice—in full view of tourist cameras.

The strongest endorsement of casual sex comes in On Her Majesty's Secret Service. Bond falls in love with Contessa Teresa de Vincenzo, who is a dramatic departure from most of the "Bond girls" because she is fully capable of taking care of herself. She dodges bullets while skiing, survives an avalanche, fights off an attacker, and holds her own in a high-speed car chase while Bond sits in the passenger seat. Toward the end of the film, the highly independent woman and the international spy marry. Salient messages regarding gender roles as well as sex emerge from the last scene in the film, as the woman who finally tamed James Bond is shot and killed, while still in her wedding gown. The messages are clear: If a woman wants to live, she'd best remain passive and keep the sex casual.[20]

Beware of Femme Fatales

Except for this ill-fated marriage, the cinematic series consistently suggests that carnal activities—at least when there's no whisper of the word "commitment"—are highly pleasurable pursuits that red-blooded American

males should engage in whenever and wherever they get the chance. But a second and much darker message vis-à-vis certain types of sexual partners lies just below the surface.

More precisely, the movies warn that femme fatales are lurking under many bedsheets and can add a hazardous element to an active male sex life. By no means do the films suggest, though, that this potential hazard is so perilous that men should steer clear of women. In fact, 007's numerous encounters with dangerous sex partners are among his most exciting. More important still, each time a woman's malevolent colors surface, she is the one who ultimately pays a high price—never Bond.

One particularly evil vixen appears in *Thunderball*. A dazzling redhead, Fiona Volpe repeatedly uses her perfect body and voracious sexual appetite to seduce and then murder her male prey. She enters Bond's life when he walks into his Nassau hotel room to find her—nude, of course— relaxing in his bathtub. Within a matter of minutes, they move to the bed and make passionate love. As soon as Volpe is sexually satisfied, her associates rush into the room and capture Bond at gunpoint. When he is later wounded while escaping, the femme fatale follows his trail of blood to a nightclub and asks him to dance. Volpe is again setting Bond up for the kill, as an assassin standing in the shadows plans to shoot him. At the last instant, the nimble *bon vivant* whirls his dance partner around so the bullet kills her, not him.[21]

Moviegoers are exposed to another wicked woman in *You Only Live Twice*, as Helga Brandt, also a redhead, strategizes three different murder plots. When she sends gunmen to kill Bond, they end up drowning; when she traps him inside a disabled airplane that is spiraling to the ground, he escapes; and when she ties him up and threatens to use a scalpel to peel off his skin, she sleeps with him instead. Like the other voluptuous traitors, Brandt eventually receives her just desserts. Hers is a particularly gory death, as a pool of hungry piranhas devour her body.[22]

Consistent with a long-standing stereotype, femme fatales in the cinematic productions tend to have either red or black hair, rather than blond. Among the dark women—in both their motivations and their tresses— are Miss Taro in *Dr. No,* who tries to have Bond killed on a mountainous highway, and Bonita in *Goldfinger,* who lures him to her bedroom where

a thug is poised to strike him with a club. As in the other attempts on the playboy's life, the man escapes and the woman pays; the Asian woman is arrested, the Latina knocked out cold.[23]

A Titillating View

While there is no question that the blond and buxom Ursula Andress who emerges from the surf in *Dr. No* is stunning, adding to the sensual delight is the precise way in which the filmmakers introduce her to male viewers.

The technique hinges on the fact that James Bond gets his first look at the sensual woman long before she is aware that he's watching her. She thinks she's stepping out of the surf and onto a stretch of uninhabited beach, not knowing that the international spy is peering at her from the jungle undergrowth. He stays hidden even after her exquisite body comes into full view, enjoying every inch of her bare skin while at the same time gaining a sense of power over her. In other words, the film introduces its most spectacular beauty in a voyeuristic manner that, in essence, treats her body as an object that brings erotic pleasure to male viewers—first Bond and then the millions of men who watch from their theater seats.[24]

Later films follow *Dr. No*'s example by giving male moviegoers more voyeuristic, and therefore highly stimulating, images. In *From Russia With Love,* Bond's first look at his future sex partner comes by way of ogling her exquisite legs—in that first scene, her head is never visible—through a periscope hidden underneath the Russian Embassy. Likewise, in *Goldfinger,* the woman in black lace bra and panties isn't even aware that a stranger has entered her hotel suite and walked through the living room until Bond reaches the balcony where she's sunbathing. And again in *On Her Majesty's Secret Service,* 007 catches his first glimpse of the damsel in distress through a long-distance telescope as she walks along the beach several hundred yards beneath his perch on an oceanside cliff.[25]

Erotic sequences featuring well-formed women are often tossed into a film solely to provide visual pleasure for—perhaps even to sexually arouse—male ticket-holders, as the scenes are not integrated into the plot. Two such instances occur in *From Russia With Love* when Bond inexplicably finds himself in a camp of gypsies. He learns that two young women

have fallen in love with the same man and therefore, in the "gypsy way," are required to fight it out to see which one gets him. Then follows a memorable scene in which the pair of scantily clad women claw and scratch viciously at each other while Bond and the other men—first in the camp, later in movie theaters—watch with rapt attention. The women later become two more notches on Bond's bedpost. The second sequence showcases a belly dancer who performs for the male audience, shimmying for everyone but saving her lap dance exclusively for Bond. As critics later pointed out, neither the fight nor the dance has any relevance whatsoever to the film's main narrative.[26]

The title sequences at the beginning of several James Bond films are another venue for female images designed to excite male viewers. The most memorable one opens *Goldfinger*, with the first three minutes of the picture devoted to the names of cast and crew members being superimposed alongside the curvaceous body of a woman whose skin is painted gold. Other films use the same method but vary the background—the gyrating body of the belly dancer in *From Russia With Love*, female swimmers in *Thunderball*, silhouettes of nude women in *On Her Majesty's Secret Service*. Regardless of the movie or the specific form of the models, the emphasis is on the women's bodies, as their facial features are never visible.

That the "Bond girls" are valued for their physiques rather than their acting ability is reinforced by the fact that the real voices of many women who are featured in the films are not used. The list of half a dozen actresses whose dialogue is dubbed includes Ursula Andress. Denied the use of their own voices, these women are literally reduced to objects that are included in the film solely because of the pleasure that their voluptuous bodies bring to male viewers.[27]

An Unparalleled Filmmaking Legacy

Many of the writers who commented on the 1960s James Bond films readily acknowledged that they communicated sexual messages that cast women as well as monogamy in a decidedly negative light. Reviewers pointed out, for example, that female characters were consistently por-

trayed as dangerous and diabolical femme fatales that sexually active men had to watch out for, and that the only beauty who succeeded in taming 007 was killed while still wearing her bridal attire. Nevertheless, the series did not draw nearly as many voracious feminist attacks as *Playboy* magazine did during the same period.[28]

Indeed, the critics consistently pooh-poohed the questionable messages as either innocent or innocuous. *New Yorker* magazine stated that Ursula Andress was used solely as a sex object, but, in its next breath, defended the depiction as a good-natured one crafted merely to "remind every adolescent of his ideal." *Time* followed the same pattern, calling Bond "an unspeakable cad in his relations with women" and describing how the voyeuristic camerawork rendered women in the films powerless, but then gushing that "All this is marvelously exciting." *Life* traveled the identical route in its cover story on *Goldfinger*, saying that as soon as the various actresses finished their requisite "torrid love scene" with 007, they were killed *toute suite*, but still praising the film as being so good that it most definitely "deserves to break all records" at the box office.[29]

The decision to celebrate the James Bond movies rather than to malign them for their problematic messages regarding sexual roles and conduct was driven at least partially by the fact that the series quickly emerged as the most successful one in the history of motion pictures. The writers—feminist or otherwise—knew that no amount of condemnation was going to keep viewers from trooping off to the nation's movie theaters in unprecedented numbers.

Why beat up on the most popular film franchise in Hollywood history? As the *New York Times* put it in an article about the Bond films: "Serious criticism of such an esteemed institution would be tantamount to throwing rocks at Buckingham Palace."[30]

Because of the huge audiences that the half dozen films attracted, there is no question that they had enormous impact on the American public. Cultural historians have documented that the prototype of the sexually hedonistic "swinging bachelor" that was firmly established by the end of the 1960s had been propelled into that position of prominence by the series of blockbusters. As the producer of the films put it, "Every man wants to be a superman, to make love to anything that walks. With a James Bond

movie, the guy in the audience buys that dream." The author of one of the two dozen books that have been written about the movies made the same point in slightly different words, saying, "Bond is the perfect hero for the permissive society: hedonistic, sexually active, progressing from one girl to the next and treating them with the same casual indifference."[31]

The world's most libidinous secret agent clearly was an effective provocateur who undeniably helped lead the American public toward a more laissez-faire view of sexual activity.

Jim Morrison of The Doors

Pushing the Limits of Sex in Music

IT WAS THE HOTTEST STORY OF THE YEAR.

Every morning at breakfast, readers across the country devoured the juicy details in the newspaper—from the jury being selected all the way through until the judge announced the sentence—so they were fully prepared to join their coworkers in the heated debates that broke out every day at the water cooler, on coffee breaks, and during lunch.

And there was plenty of juice.

First came the prosecution witnesses, including a woman who testified that the defendant most definitely had "rolled down his tight pants to a point midway between his waist and his knees" and "placed his hand on his exposed genitals" before proceeding to masturbate in full view of 12,000 people. Next came the tape recording of the infamous Miami concert. "I want you to have some fun," the rock star told his fans. "I want you to love your neighbor until it hurts. I want love, love, love, love, love, love, love, love," ending with the final quote, as sanitized for newspaper readers, "Grab your f— friend and love him."[1]

Then came the parade of contradictions. Some observers thought the strongest testimony came from a photographer—he'd been within three feet of the stage—who swore that the singer had "not exposed his private parts," but others insisted that the undercover narcotics agent was more persuasive when he, a member of The Establishment, vehemently denied that the singer and his guitarist had "simulated oral copulation" on stage.[2]

As the story unfolded during the summer and fall of 1970, everyone in America seemed to have an opinion—but the judge's carried the most weight. He ruled, after the jury delivered its guilty verdict, that the accused should spend six months in jail. The judge also took the liberty of speaking for all "right-thinking people" when, along with handing down the sentence, he lectured the defendant, "To admit that this nation accepts as a community standard your 'indecent exposure' would be to admit that a small minority who display utter contempt for our institutions and heritage determine the community standards for us all."[3]

The judge's scolding aside, the hedonistic rock star had, indeed, pushed the limits of sexual content in American music.

The Miami incident prompted the press to dub Jim Morrison "the King of Orgasmic Rock." But, in fact, by the late 1960s the lead singer of The Doors had already become the most hypnotic sex symbol the music world had ever known. One of his biographers wrote that "Morrison oozed sex," while another said "Jim Morrison was a kind of cultural superman, larger than life, moving little girls to sexual delight." And with three out of every four singles and half of all albums at the time being purchased by girls between the ages of twelve and seventeen, Morrison's brand of unrepressed eros was a highly marketable commodity.[4]

His superstar persona began with his sultry good looks and palpable sex appeal, which were further enhanced by how he dressed—and sometimes undressed—while on stage. His bawdy performance style and off-stage escapades added to the mystique, as did the erotic lyrics that he wrote, speaking not only to his own youthful generation but to the millions of fans who still see him today, more than thirty years after his untimely death, as the epitome of the sexual rebel.

Jim Morrison's Early Life: Wild Child

James Douglas Morrison was born in 1943 to George Morrison, an officer in the U.S. Navy who would rise to the rank of admiral, and his stay-at-home wife, Clara. Strict discipline was practiced in the household, with the father routinely "dressing down" Jim in military style by berating him,

over and over again, about something he'd done wrong until the boy was reduced to tears.[5]

College offered Jim Morrison his first opportunity to rebel against his strict upbringing, and so he joined many young people of the 1960s in consuming large quantities of alcohol, in experimenting with various drugs, and in growing his hair down to his shoulders. In keeping with the spirit of free love that defined the era, his rebellion had its sexual dimensions as well. When he enrolled at Florida State University as a theater major, Morrison immediately decorated the walls of his dormitory room with *Playboy* centerfolds; later when he moved to California to study film at UCLA, he gained a reputation as the most promiscuous man on campus, often sleeping with several different women during the same week.[6]

Morrison earned his degree in 1965 but had no particular career path in mind. It was fellow student Ray Manzarek, a keyboard player, who suggested that they create a rock band and who found drummer John Densmore and guitarist Robby Krieger to complete the group. But it soon became clear that Morrison, even though he had no previous experience with music, was the one who would set the group apart from all others.

The lead singer took his first step in that direction by naming the band The Doors, inspired by English poet William Blake's passage, "There are things that are known and things that are unknown; in between are doors." Then Morrison produced a notebook bulging with poetry that he'd written and that he soon transformed into compelling lyrics, many of them with strong sexual themes.[7]

Morrison also landed The Doors their first major job. After initially playing at parties and small clubs, they attracted the attention of a woman who was scouting talent for the hottest nightclub in Los Angeles. Ronnie Haran later admitted that she booked the band at the Whiskey a Go-Go not because of its music but because of the lead singer, calling Morrison "the sexiest rock 'n' roll star" she'd ever seen. Specifically, Haran raved about the handsome twenty-two-year-old's ability to caress the microphone in a way that made every woman in the audience feel like he was making love to her—and her alone.[8]

It was also while The Doors were appearing at the Whiskey a Go-Go that Elektra Records offered them a contract. When their debut album, released in 1967, sold a million copies and then their first single, "Light My Fire," shot to number one in the country, the group secured its spot as one of America's premier rock bands. When those triumphs were followed, early the next year, with a second album that also struck gold, proving that this foursome was not just another one-hit wonder, The Doors became the most popular musicians in the country.[9]

While the band possessed plenty of musical talent and also was on the cutting edge of social movements such as opposition to the Vietnam War, the single element that made them distinctive was the sexual heat that radiated from Jim Morrison. A columnist from the *Village Voice* lamented that America had been lacking a male sex symbol for many years: "Now along comes Jim Morrison of The Doors. If my antenna are right, he could be the biggest thing to grab the mass libido in a long time."[10]

Dozens of other reviews and feature stories communicated similar messages. *Rolling Stone* credited Morrison's skintight leather pants and frequently bared chest with making The Doors "the hottest group in America," while another music magazine, *Crawdaddy!*, said listening to him sing was "as good as having sex." The counterculture *Los Angeles Free Press* joined the chorus, calling Morrison's singing the perfect aphrodisiac because it "doesn't touch the heart, it tickles the prostate." Readers of the mainstream press were also soon hearing about Morrison's libidinous ways. *Time* raved about the singer's ability to "preach passion" like no singer before him, and *Newsweek* dubbed him, because of his impact on the Sexual Revolution, the country's first "erotic politician."[11]

Morrison was also thrust into the media spotlight because he refused to play by the rules. When the director of *The Ed Sullivan Show*, the most popular variety program on television, said the lyrics to "Light My Fire" were unacceptable, Morrison agreed to change the line "Girl, you couldn't get much *higher*" to "Girl, you couldn't get much *better*." But during the CBS live broadcast, the singer broke his word and defiantly sang "*higher*"—prompting Sullivan to ban him from ever appearing on the show again.[12]

Sexual Icon: Looks Count

The first major element contributing to Jim Morrison's sex appeal was his appearance. His physical features were highly attractive in their own right, and he emphasized them by choosing a provocative wardrobe unlike anything the music world had ever seen before.

"His blue-gray eyes were penetrating, his cheeks hollow and slightly sunken, like a fashion model's," wrote one Morrison biographer. "There was a softness to him, a gentleness, an almost seductive quality. His face was more than handsome, it was pretty; and the way he cocked his head slightly, exposing his alabaster white neck, displayed a vulnerability that most men would be afraid to reveal. But he was not feminine. In his eyes something definitely masculine burned. More than masculine even. Something dangerous."[13]

Morrison used his looks to full advantage. After his star began to rise and The Doors became one of the highest-paid bands in the country, he hired Hollywood's top hair stylists to fashion his thick brown mane so it looked constantly uncombed, saying he wanted to look like Alexander the Great. Morrison wanted to emulate the military hero partly because he liked the idea of being a conqueror—not of foreign empires but of outdated sexual mores.[14]

With regard to his physique, America's hottest rocker was lean and lanky, standing five feet eleven inches tall and weighing a mere 145 pounds. Trim and agile, Morrison moved with a grace and sleekness that earned him one of his two widely known nicknames: the Young Lion.[15]

Female fans who flocked to see The Doors had other words to describe Morrison. One seventeen-year-old girl was quoted as saying, "The word was out on the street that everyone had to see this lead singer because there had never been anything like him," and a woman in her twenties, who ultimately would see the group perform more than 100 times, said, "He looked like a Greek god, with masses of dark brown curls and a face that sweaty dreams are made of."[16]

Morrison's clothing choices added to those nighttime visions. His trademark leather pants were always black and always clinging tight to his slen-

der hips and legs. What he wore above the waist varied—sometimes a black leather shirt, other times either a black or a white cotton shirt. And often, by midway through a concert, he had removed his shirt to reveal a chest dripping with perspiration. For publicity photos, he often posed in a snakeskin jacket that earned him his second nickname: the Lizard King.

The look worked. On some occasions, a female reviewer sounded as enraptured as the most adoring Morrison groupie. "There isn't another face like that in the world," gushed a woman writing for *Crawdaddy!* "It's so beautiful and not even handsome in the ordinary way. I think it's because you can tell by looking at him that he *IS* God."[17]

On-Stage Eroticism

A typical Doors performance began with three musicians walking quietly onto the stage and taking their positions behind their respective instruments. But everyone knew the show didn't really begin until the shadow of a fourth figure appeared in the wings—a lean phantom in signature leather.

As soon as the crowd spotted Morrison, a massive communal scream erupted. He then walked to the center of the stage and, as if not noticing that anyone else was present, cradled the microphone seductively in his hands. Appearing to enter a trance-like state, the superstar looked upward so the spotlight illuminated his strikingly handsome face and then, often after remaining silent for as long as a minute, slowly and softly emitted his first words.

Although the typical two-hour set started with Morrison singing gently, the decibel level gradually escalated and the singer became far more animated. *Life* magazine tried to catalogue his movements as ranging from gyrating and writhing, to grinding and undulating, to jerking and crouching and swaggering and jumping and twisting—the magazine finally gave up and grouped them all together in the term "elements of carnality." Another observer described the Young Lion's unique approach with this passage: "Morrison started singing. The music wove and screamed into one climax after another. Before long, Jim was *raping* the microphone stand between his thighs, advancing toward the hungry girls who were

pressing harder now toward the stage. He grabbed the mike stand and threw it down hard on the stage—and the girls looked like they were having an orgasm."[18]

It is difficult for many in the twenty-first century to appreciate how innovative Morrison's performance style was. But just as he pioneered the leather trousers that soon became ubiquitous among rock musicians, he also broke new ground in on-stage sexual theatrics.[19]

The media marveled at the Lizard King's eroticism. *New York* magazine said he achieved "total sensual contact with an audience." One writer for the *Village Voice* reported, "I have never seen such an animalistic response from so many different kinds of women," while another from the same publication wrote, "All he has to do is strike a pose, bathed in crimson lights, and it's all over." *Jazz & Pop* magazine was so intrigued by the over-the-top reaction from female fans that it devoted an entire article to the phenomenon, reporting, "By the time an evening is over, the fans are thronging the stage area, arms upstretched, 'Touch Me! Touch Me!' as though Morrison were a piece of the True Cross." The magazine went on to describe members of his audience showering the star with "tokens of affection" in the form of a barrage of bras and panties.[20]

Morrison's antics sometimes caught the attention of the police. One widely reported incident began before a 1967 concert in New Haven, Connecticut. When a police officer saw Morrison kissing and fondling an eighteen-year-old girl in a hallway, he told the singer to stop. Morrison obeyed the order but then, when he went on stage, criticized the lieutenant for intruding into his personal life. Six officers promptly walked onto the stage, halted the concert, and arrested Morrison for giving an "indecent and immoral exhibition." The event escalated in significance because a *Life* magazine writer in the audience made it the centerpiece of an eight-page article, complete with photos of uniformed police officers confronting the singer on stage, titled "Wicked Go The Doors."[21]

The New Haven incident had historic significance as well, marking the first time that a rock artist had been arrested while on stage. It was not, however, the last time Morrison and the police would cross paths. By 1970, the Young Lion had been arrested ten times, with most of the charges revolving around his ribald actions and foul language. Although several of

the arrests resulted in monetary fines, he was never held in jail for more than a few hours.[22]

Off-Stage Escapades

In addition to changing how rock stars dressed and performed on stage, the Lizard King also created a model for a hedonistic tendency that a legion of superstars who have followed in his footsteps have been all too eager to emulate: being promiscuous.

Morrison lived with Pam Courson from 1965 until he died in 1971—his will left everything to her. But even though the beautiful young art student with auburn hair and Snow White complexion was devoted to the charismatic singer, one woman was not enough to satisfy his voracious sexual appetite. And so, throughout their relationship, he slept with other women—sometimes in long-term affairs, more often for one-night stands. Courson was fully aware that Morrison was unfaithful to her and yet she remained with him in their common-law marriage.[23]

In some instances, Morrison's sex partners served to advance his career. Patricia Kennealy, the editor of *Jazz & Pop* magazine, published numerous flattering stories about him. He then invited her not only into his bedroom but also joined her in an ancient pagan rite that some people considered comparable to a wedding, with the ceremony including the couple exchanging each other's blood. The relationship also resulted in a pregnancy. At Morrison's urging, Kennealy agreed to have an abortion, as long as he promised to be with her during the procedure. When the time came, however, he failed to show up.[24]

More disturbing than Morrison's numerous affairs is the fact that he, even at the point when he was the most popular male vocalist in the country, indiscriminately brought complete strangers to the Alta Cienega, a cheap motel he used for impromptu sexual liaisons. "Jim liked to walk the streets of West Hollywood," according to one biographer. "And frequently when he met a young woman, no matter how overweight or unattractive, he took her back to the tiny room."[25]

Although only Morrison's close friends were aware of his sexual promiscuity at the time, his addiction to alcohol was widely known. By

1968, he was appearing drunk for performances so frequently that reviewers began reporting it in their stories. His level of inebriation was relevant to the articles, as it influenced the quality of his singing.[26]

Writing Lyrics for the Generations

Like many successful writers, Jim Morrison focused on topics that were familiar to him and in keeping with his own values. At the same time, the words in his songs had a universal appeal and still resonate with many listeners today.

A discussion of Morrison's lyrics must begin with The Doors's first huge hit and signature song, "Light My Fire." The words most definitely revolve around sex. The chorus—perhaps the best-remembered lines the group ever sang—states, "Come on, baby, light my fire / Come on, baby, light my fire / Try to set the night on fire." The phrase "light my fire" refers to the singer asking his lover to arouse him sexually. Morrison is telling the woman to turn him on, and the line "Try to set the night on fire" is saying that he wants to experience levels of erotic ecstasy so powerful that the bed partners will ignite and—at least metaphorically—burst into flames. Some critics have said that "Light My Fire" ranked as the best song of the 1960s, as it represented "the communal orgasm of that generation and its decade."[27]

The song "Hello, I Love You," another single that soared to the top of the charts, is even more blatant in its sexual messages. Its first, and most memorable, two lines are "Hello, I love you / Won't you tell me your name?" In this instance, the singer is immediately proclaiming his love for the other person, which in Morrison-speak means that he wants to have sex with her—before he even knows her name. In other words, the lyrics are a clear celebration, much like *Playboy* magazine and the James Bond films, of casual sex. Morrison takes his libidinous message a step further when he says, later in the song, "Do you think you'll be the guy / To make the queen of the angels sigh?" Making "the queen of the angels sigh" is a reference to the sound a person utters when reaching the height of physical pleasure and sexual release. Morrison is asking if the person thinks he will be able to make his lover achieve sexual orgasm.[28]

"Love Me Two Times," another of the group's major hits, delivered a timely message when it was released in the late 1960s. The Vietnam War was taking tens of thousands of young men to the jungles of Southeast Asia, forcing them to leave their wives and girlfriends behind. With the words "Love me one time / I could not speak / Love me one time / Yeah, my knees got weak / But love me two times, girl / Last me all through the week," Morrison is again using the word *love* as a synonym for the word *sex*. So the message is that if a woman brings her man to orgasm once during a session of lovemaking, that makes his knees go weak, but doing so twice in the same night has a better chance of keeping him satisfied for the rest of the week—or, at least symbolically, until he returns from the distant battlefield.[29]

Miami: Going Too Far

The singer was already drunk when he arrived at the Dinner Key Auditorium on March 1, 1969. He started out using the word *love,* but everyone knew that, as in his song lyrics, what he was really talking about was *sex.* "Love your brother, hug him," he told the standing-room-only crowd. "Man, I'd like to see a little nakedness around here. Take your clothes off and love each other." Many in the audience dutifully responded, first hundreds of men and women taking off their shirts and blouses, followed by several dozen women loosening their bras and tossing them onto the stage.[30]

But even in this bawdy environment, the crowd seemed stunned when the Young Lion uttered the line that would haunt him for the last two years of his life: "Do you want to see my *cock?*"[31]

The statement was so startling, some witnesses would later say, that the audience went instantly silent. Morrison leered at them, blurry-eyed, and kept talking. "You didn't come here only for *music* did you?" The crowd watched and listened. "You wanna see my *cock,* don't you? That's what you came for isn't it? YEAHHH!"[32]

Precisely what happened next is unclear. Many observers would later claim that Morrison grabbed his shirt—he had been bare-chested since early in the performance—and swung it back and forth in front of his

crotch the way a bullfighter moves his cape. After pulling the shirt to the side for an instant, he taunted the audience, "See it? Did you see it?" Some say he had exposed his genitals to the crowd; others say he had only pretended to.[33]

Most people agree that Morrison continued to strut around the stage, pushing and shoving the other band members and technicians while bellowing at the audience. They also consistently remember that he knelt down on his knees in front of guitarist Robby Krieger and simulated performing oral sex.[34]

After the concert, Morrison was charged with "lewd and lascivious behavior in public by exposing his private parts." And when the infamous trial unfolded in the summer of 1970, the nation turned its eyes toward Miami as the parade of witnesses provided the news media with the kind of testimony—always lively, often titillating—that people love to read and talk about.[35]

More damaging to the Lizard King than the decisions that ultimately were handed down by the jury and the judge, however, was the one made by the nation's arbiters of good taste. As one of his biographers succinctly stated, "The Establishment thought he had gone too far." The Doors had been scheduled to begin a twenty-city tour a week after the Miami performance. But when Morrison was arrested, officials in the various cities began, one after the other, to cancel the concerts. Within a matter of days, sixteen states had banned The Doors from appearing, not only for the tour but ever again. In the colorful words of keyboard player Ray Manzarek, "The shit hit the fan. It was never the same after that."[36]

There were other repercussions as well. Hundreds of radio stations across the country, fearful that being associated with Morrison would cause them to be labeled "indecent," stopped playing his records. Closer to home, the Miami arrests severely damaged the group's internal dynamics. The other three Doors were angry that the lead singer's outrageous behavior now prevented them from performing and earning the hefty salaries that the concerts had provided. The gulf between Morrison and the other band members widened even further when The Doors were invited to join the top rock artists in the country for an open-air concert in the Catskill Mountains in August 1969. Three of the musicians saw the

performance as a chance to redeem the group's reputation, but Morrison didn't like singing outside. His refusal to participate meant that the group failed to appear in the biggest musical event of the era: Woodstock.[37]

The Final Days

The indecent exposure conviction and its aftermath hurled Morrison into a deep depression. He gained weight, stopped paying attention to his hair, and grew a scraggly beard that hid the facial features that had, during happier days, made young girls swoon. He rarely bathed and sometimes wore the same clothes for weeks at a time.[38]

The Doors sporadically returned to the studio and the stage, and many of the records and concerts were successful. The quality of the music was inconsistent, however, and the group suffered intermittent setbacks. During a show in Seattle, for example, one member of the audience threw a paper cup onto the stage, prompting Morrison to pretend to masturbate in the crowd's direction. Many people in the auditorium, no longer amused by the man whose sex appeal was now obscured under the extra pounds and the facial hair, walked out of the concert.[39]

After the trial ended and as the legal appeal of his conviction worked its way through the court system, Morrison moved to Paris with Pam Courson in March 1971, hoping that a change of scenery would bring stability to his life. They rented an apartment on the Right Bank, and he lost some weight and shaved off his beard. They both continued to abuse their bodies, however, with their drugs of choice—alcohol for him, heroin for her. Also problematic was Morrison's frustration when he sat down with his notebook and attempted to write new lyrics, but the pages remained blank.[40]

On July 3, 1971, Jim Morrison died. The circumstances of the death are murky. Courson said he suffered a heart attack in the bathtub in their Paris apartment. Many people who were close to the superstar believe, however, that he died of an overdose of heroin, complicated by the high level of alcohol that was already in his bloodstream. Those who support the second cause-of-death theory say that it explains why Courson was so distraught after her lover's death, positing that she blamed herself for hav-

ing supplied the drug that killed him. If Courson knew the truth, she carried it to her grave, as she died in 1974—of a heroin overdose.[41]

A Sexual Legend

Within a matter of days after Jim Morrison's body had been lowered into the ground at Pere-Lachaise Cemetery in Paris, a steady stream of fans began coming to pay homage to him. For more than three decades, the flow of visitors has continued—they appear every day throughout the year. Indeed, for many Americans, no trip to the French capital is complete without placing a bouquet of flowers on the gravesite.

Pilgrimages to music stores continue as well. Although the format of choice has shifted with the passage of time, from vinyl albums to cassette tapes and then to compact discs and DVDs, admirers have continued to buy recordings of Morrison's music. Yearly sales consistently surpass the one million mark. Why does this singer, who showed no interest in music before he turned twenty-two and then died a mere five years later, continue to engender such a depth of devotion in so many people?

The one-word answer has a mere three letters, as the lead vocalist for The Doors, like no musician before him and few since, oozed *sex*. The handsome young man wrapped his lean physique in tight leather and introduced a theatrical performance style that transformed his singing into an erotic experience. The bad-boy rocker's outrageous off-stage lifestyle and the strong sexual messages in his lyrics have only added to the Morrison mystique.

A daring risk taker, the Lizard King left an indelible mark on American music and, most especially, on the synergistic dynamic between music and sex. The quintessential rock star of the 1960s and early 1970s has proven to be a powerful influence throughout the 1980s, 1990s, and early years of the new millennium. Every musician whose career has benefited from a strong sexual persona—Alice Cooper and David Bowie, Madonna and Britney Spears—owes a sizable debt to Jim Morrison for one or more of the various erotic elements that he introduced—leather costuming, a dynamic stage presence, suggestive lyrics.

The Young Lion's most significant contribution to the concept captured in the phrase *Sex Sells!* may have involved who was buying. *Playboy* magazine and the James Bond films clearly were directed primarily at male consumers who purchased copies of the magazine and tickets to the movie theater. With Jim Morrison, however, the larger segment of the audience was not male but female. There is no question that this sexual provocateur built a fan base consisting largely of throngs of girls and women who bought his records to hear his seductive voice and who fought through the concert crowds to position themselves as close as possible to his pulsating, sweat-drenched body.

All in the Family

Bringing Sex to American Television

IN JANUARY 1971, A NEW SITUATION COMEDY PREMIERED ON CBS. THE initial episode's plotline seemed innocuous enough. A middle-aged husband and wife are about to celebrate twenty-two years of marriage, so their daughter and her husband are planning a surprise anniversary brunch for them. In the first scene, the younger couple is running around the house making sure everything is in place before Mom and Dad return from church.[1]

By the first commercial break, however, viewers learn that this is not television as usual. For the parents arrive home early—the father couldn't stomach the minister's liberal-leaning sermon—to find their daughter and son-in-law on the verge of having intercourse.

Startled when the parents walk in, the son-in-law blurts out, "You're early!"

The father responds, "So are you!" Shaking his head in disgust, the older man tells the younger one, "You ain't supposed to be doin' stuff like that at 11:10 on a Sunday mornin'!"

The son-in-law pauses for a moment to give the audience a chance to laugh and then speaks for the Younger Generation. "Come on, Archie, some things are no different now than they ever were."

This line prompts the older man to deliver a lecture on proper behavior, ending his first line with one of the malapropisms that will soon emerge as his linguistic trademark.

"In my day, we was able to keep things in their proper *suspective,*" he begins. "Take 'keeping company,' for instance. When your mother-in-law and me was goin' around together, there was absolutely nothin'—I mean absolutely nothin'. Not 'til the wedding night."

Then the mother quietly adds an understated line that brings comic relief, "Yeah, and even then. . . ."

More laughter. More wordplay. More debates. And definitely more sex.

One of the most celebrated programs in the history of American television had been launched, and neither the medium nor the nation's sexual self would ever be the same.

All in the Family was the country's top-rated TV program that first season as well as for the next five—a record that remains unmatched to this day. As testimony to the show's unique role in the nation's cultural history, in 1978 the chairs that Archie and Edith Bunker sat in each week were placed on permanent display at the Smithsonian Institution in Washington, D.C.[2]

Although the program's in-your-face treatment of bigotry and its commitment to reflecting timely topics such as women's liberation and opposition to the Vietnam War were factors in its success, the innovative sitcom's most long-lasting contribution may have been bringing sex to the television screen as never before. The initial reception to the libidinous content was mixed, with *Life* magazine condemning it—"All in the Family is a wretched program. Let's clean up this culture!"—and *Newsweek* applauding it—"All in the Family is the hottest sitcom to hit TV in years." In the end, *Good Housekeeping* may have had it right by neither denouncing nor praising the new emphasis on sex but saying of the series: "It has begun to change the very nature of television situation comedies."[3]

Since the industry's birth, television executives had steadfastly avoided any possibility of offending public sensibilities with regard to sex. According to the conventional wisdom that guided the Powers That Be, viewers did not want to have their sexual attitudes challenged by the programs that came into their living rooms.[4]

The force that propelled CBS to add *All in the Family* to this eros-absent milieu at this particular moment was neither a desire to change society

nor an effort to reduce libidinal repression, but the same principle that has driven myriad other media innovations: *Sex Sells!*

In 1969, the network's signature programs were *The Ed Sullivan Show, The Jackie Gleason Show,* and *The Red Skelton Show.* This lineup gave CBS a tight grip on aging viewers from the American Heartland. But as more sophisticated research techniques were beginning to identify demographic factors such as age and education, advertisers were increasingly interested in younger viewers with more schooling—and therefore more potential earning power. (Read: Baby Boomers.) So a small number of creative thinkers began to speculate that if a program could use sexual content to lure the huge population of twenty-something viewers to a particular TV show and the items advertised on it, those men and women would remain faithful to a brand—Breck shampoo, Crest toothpaste, Lay's potato chips—for the rest of their product-buying lives.[5]

In 1970, CBS executives announced that they planned to develop a "young, fresh, new approach to programming," and a year later it was clear that the flagship of that strategy would be a sitcom that revolved around a working-class family in the New York City borough of Queens.[6]

The household at 704 Houser Street was headed by Archie Bunker, a loading-dock foreman with a pot belly and a set of values firmly grounded in the no-sex-we're-American era of the mid-twentieth century. Catering to her husband's every need was stay-at-home wife Edith—*Newsweek* described her as "running around the house like a coolie pulling a rickshaw"—who also was, like Archie, largely bound by the dictates of sexual repression. The couple's miniskirted daughter Gloria Stivic was, by contrast, liberal in her thinking. And Gloria's husband Mike was a full-time graduate student with long hair, a voracious appetite, and an idealistic determination to destroy sexism, racism, and most any other "ism" he encountered.[7]

Some of the show's funniest lines and most insightful social commentary evolved from the fact that the household included two generations. This pivotal aspect of the show was captured in a scene in which the emotionally volatile Gloria, having grown angry at her reactionary father, screams, "You can't even bear the mention of the word *sex!*" Archie in-

stantly yells back, "None of that, little girl. You know I don't allow no *four-letter* words in this house!"[8]

During its triumphant march through TV Land from 1971 to 1979, *All in the Family* explored a long list of sexual subjects that no program had ever so much as mentioned before. The debut episode's depiction of sex during daylight—particularly on a Sunday morning (oh, my!)—was unprecedented, but the program soon showed America that the previously taboo topic was merely the pre-game warm-up in an effort that would change the medium forever.

The liberal magazine *The Nation* dubbed the program the first example of "adult television" and reported that CBS had manned its telephone switchboards with extra operators waiting for a flood of protests after the airing of that first scene involving intercourse—but the calls never materialized. Indeed, the *New York Times* soon reported that millions of people were finding the sexual content on *All in the Family* so enjoyable that they were altering their social calendars to make sure they were home at 8 p.m. Saturday night when the show aired.[9]

The best way to gain a sense of exactly how the program approached sexual topics is to take a close look at the way one plotline unfolded inside the American living room—1970s style.

"He's Stuck in Neutral"

The opening scene shows Mike sitting at the dining room table, surrounded by piles of textbooks, as he studies for final exams. Gloria approaches him and, choosing her words carefully, says, "I just wanted to say that I don't think you should be worried about 'the problem' that's been happening between us lately."[10]

Instantly agitated, Mike lifts up his head so the audience can see that his eyes are wide and his nostrils are flaring. He then screams, his voice several octaves higher than usual, "Worried! Do I look worried!" He is filled with such frenzied emotion that the audience guffaws at the contrast between the words coming out of his mouth and the feelings that he is so obviously trying to hide. "I'm not worried at all!"

Gloria, trying to be supportive, smiles knowingly and says quietly, "I understand."

Her husband reacts in a still more frenetic voice, "No, you don't understand, Gloria!" The words come racing out at such a rapid pace that the audience keeps laughing. "If you understood, you'd know that the last thing I want to hear is that you *understand!*"

Gloria, angry that anything she says seems to be wrong, stomps out of the dining room and into the kitchen.

When Edith, standing at the counter preparing dinner, sees that her daughter is upset, she asks her what's wrong. But Gloria, representing the millions of young people in the television audience who have found themselves in a similar situation, knows that talking about sex with a parent can be highly uncomfortable.

"Ma, you know I can't tell you about a *sexual* problem."

Horror races across Edith's face. Her motherly instincts tell her she needs to help her daughter with her problem, but the sexual repression that has been ingrained into her life tells her to steer clear of this off-limits subject area.

"Se-se-se . . . ," Edith says—try as she may, she can't say the word sex. "I'm your mother," she says, still cringing with anxiety, "and if you have a problem with se-se-se . . . something to do with . . . one of those problems, you can tell me."

Mother and daughter are both conflicted, but they try valiantly to march forward, the audience laughing along with the comical display of their unease.

Gloria continues. "Well, it's Mike. Lately he hasn't been able to . . . "

Edith instantly turns away.

Gloria exclaims, "See, I can't tell you!"

Edith apologizes, Gloria tries again, Edith keeps cringing, Gloria tries to speak in specific terms, Edith retreats to euphemisms—the viewers at home understand, having struggled through similar conversations when trying to talk either to parents or to children about sex.

Edith finally says of Mike's inability to perform in bed, "It's probably just somethin' that's goin' around."

When Archie gets home, even he—a man not known for his sensitivity—feels the tension. He and Edith then struggle through a conversation similar to the one that Edith had with Gloria.

ARCHIE: "What's the problem with them two?"

EDITH: "I just can't tell you. You just don't like to hear about such things."

ARCHIE: "I like to hear about everything that's goin' on in this house. Now what kind of problem have they got?"

EDITH: "Well, it's sexual."

ARCHIE: "Sheesh! You know I don't like to hear nothin' about that there."

Though the discomfort between husband and wife is similar to that portrayed earlier between mother and daughter, the married couple has two decades of experience to draw from. So Edith communicates Mike's unmentionable problem to Archie with an oblique reference to a friend who suffered the same difficulty when he returned from World War II many years earlier.

Archie can't believe that his strapping young son-in-law can't perform his manly duties. "Edith, it can't be. There's nothin' wrong with him like that," Archie says, speaking the same words that other men and women had spoken, or at least thought, when told that a man was sexually impotent—though Archie's words are, of course, funnier. "He's healthy. He's strong. He goes through groceries like an earth remover!"

Next comes another tense conversation between the younger couple. A disciple of the let-it-all-hang-out 1960s, Gloria insists that they confront every issue openly. But Mike is experiencing this particular problem not in the abstract but on a highly personal level. When Gloria tells her husband that she called the family doctor for advice, Mike explodes.

MIKE: "You *what!* This isn't the kind of thing I want spread all over town!"

GLORIA responds facetiously: "I'm glad you're taking such a 'mature' attitude."

MIKE: "Well, Gloria, if the shoe was on the other foot, what would you do?"

GLORIA: "I'd forget my enormous male ego and want to know what the doctor said."

MIKE: "Who cares what the doctor said. Maybe you care, but I don't!"

While Gloria took her questions about impotence to a medical expert, her father turns to the neighborhood bar. As for exactly whose counsel to seek, Archie is driven by one of the many stereotypes that guide his life. He approaches George Jefferson, the first black man to move into the previously all-white neighborhood.

"I've got this friend," Archie begins, "and he's havin' what you call *connubibal* difficulties." Fearful that George might not understand, Archie restates the problem as, "He's stuck in neutral."

Having gotten George's attention, Archie marches forward.

"It's a well-known fact that 'youse people'—I mean the men—when it comes to members of the opposite . . . , you got a special kind of *stamimina*. I hears tell there's somethin' in that soul food you're always eatin' that gives you a lotta moxie."

It's a racial secret all right, George agrees with mock solemnity. He then decides to have a little fun all his own.

"It's the hog jowls," George states authoritatively. "Try a jowl in the morning and a jowl at night, and you'll be just fine."

The scene in the bar ends with Archie having a confused look on his face, unsure what to do with this advice, while George looks highly satisfied with himself, proud of his cleverness.

Meanwhile, back at the Bunker residence, Gloria tells Mike what she has learned from the doctor. Sexual impotence is often caused by anxiety, she informs her husband, such as that experienced by an overtired, overworked student who is cramming for final exams.

Voilà!

The next night, Mike telephones Gloria to tell her that he's passed his exams and is on his way home. Gloria has persuaded her parents to go out so the young couple can have the house to themselves, and she puts on a dress that is pretty but not sexy—she doesn't want to put any added pressure on her husband.

Mike arrives home but is anxious, still worried that he won't be able to perform. Plopping down in a chair, he nervously tells his wife that he wants to see a Japanese monster movie on TV.

Gloria quietly acquiesces to his wishes. But as he watches the film, she stands behind his chair and begins massaging his neck. She gently kneads his shoulders and then works her way down one of his arms. Mike continues to watch the movie, but he is clearly enjoying the caressing. When Gloria reaches his hand, she stops and kneels down beside his chair.

Finally, he turns his face to hers. She gives him a girlish smile. A glint then comes into their eyes and gradually spreads across their faces to become a matched set of shiny-eyed grins. As they kiss, the screen fades to black—the signal to viewers that "the problem" has ended.

The message: Sexual impotence is nothing to be ashamed of. It is usually a temporary physical condition, not unlike the flu or a common cold, that is prompted by specific factors and that will soon pass.

Breaking New Sexual Ground

This detailed description of an *All in the Family* episode provides a concrete example of the kind of sexually themed plotline that the program offered 1970s television viewers, as well as the millions more who have watched—and are still watching, three decades later—reruns of the program. The episode focusing on Mike's sexual impotence succeeded both in entertaining viewers and in educating them about a widely misunderstood medical condition.

Tackling that topic was no small matter. A *Time* magazine cover story reported that some programming executives at CBS had adamantly opposed airing an episode about such a sensitive sexual topic, relenting only after the show's creator, Norman Lear, presented them with an ultimatum: Unless the network approved the segment, Lear would cancel the entire series. Faced with the possibility of losing their most popular program, the executives gave the topic the green light.[11]

That was by no means the last battle that Lear had to fight. He had to make a similar threat before he was allowed to broadcast entertainment television's first-ever segment on homosexuality, and a script about Archie

having lustful feelings for a woman other than his wife went through eight major rewrites and was delayed for a year and a half before it finally made it on the air. "Make no mistake," Lear said of the network officials, "it's sex that really hangs them up," pointing out that he had much less trouble securing approval for episodes about race, class, gender, and politics.[12]

The number of sexual thresholds that the program ultimately crossed during its nine seasons was exhaustive. From infidelity to rape, from menstruation to menopause, from vasectomies to wife-swapping, and from lesbianism to women being more sexually aggressive than their husbands—the Bunkers dealt with them all.[13]

Partly because *All in the Family* was a sexual pioneer, it has become one of the most widely discussed television shows in the history of the medium. At least four books and dozens of articles and essays have been devoted to this single series. One among the legion of scholars who has examined the show wrote that its sexual content placed it "on the cutting edge of TV innovation," while others have said that it "profoundly altered what TV could tackle" and "destroyed the old taboos and opened up new vistas" for bringing sex to prime-time television.[14]

Though it's impossible to produce empirical evidence to prove the program's influence on society, there are indications that at least on some occasions what the fictional Bunker family did on television affected how real Americans were behaving. In 1973, an episode depicted Gloria walking past a construction site when a man grabs her, jams a scarf in her mouth, and begins tearing off her clothes. The would-be rapist lets the young woman go only because she faints and he, fearing that she's dying, flees from the crime scene. After Gloria, on the verge of hysteria, gets home to her parents and husband, Edith takes her into the kitchen. The mother then tells her daughter about the time many years earlier that she had been sexually assaulted. She never told anyone about the incident, Edith says, but she has never stopped wondering how many other women had been attacked by that same man. "In my time," she says ruefully, "we was too scared to talk open." Immediately after that episode aired, law enforcement officials across the country reported a dramatic increase in the number of women who were willing to come forward and file complaints about having been sexually assaulted.[15]

And so there is little doubt that *All in the Family* had an impact on the nation's emerging sexual self. More important still, the groundbreaking program provided the earliest case study to demonstrate how sexual messages could be transported into the American living room via the vehicle that was, by the early 1970s, on its ascendancy to becoming the most powerful medium in the history of communication. As the *New York Times* stated in an article about the program's sexual content: "Television has taken a giant step."[16]

Cosmopolitan Magazine

Celebrating the Sexually Active Woman

"We work in a very casual engineering firm. Each month a
new *Playboy* centerfold went up—and our egos, *down*. But now,
because of you, there is a beautiful centerfold of Burt on our section
of the wall. It hasn't done much for the fellows, but for us *girls*—WOW!"[1]

THE "BURT" IN THIS SAMPLE FROM THE DOZENS OF LAUDATORY LETTERS
that flooded the offices of *Cosmopolitan* magazine was Burt Reynolds, and
the "WOW!" was the nude image of the handsome actor that broke new
sexual ground when it folded out from the center of the magazine in 1972.

More than any other cultural artifact before or since, that photo—
showing the heartthrob's hairy chest and slender torso spread out across
a bearskin rug, his forearm strategically concealing his genitals—marked
the media's public acknowledgment that the American woman deserved
the right to be sexually titillated.

"Men, we reasoned, have been happily eyeing naked women—on calendars, ads, and in 'girly' magazines—for decades," said the copy next to
the image. "Wasn't it time for our women readers to have a naked man
of their own? And so we set out to find just the right attractively virile
fellow who would like to share his charms with a million or so admiring
women."[2]

Burt Reynolds fit the bill perfectly. His well-formed body and rugged
facial features offered readers plenty to fantasize about, while the profiles of him that popped up in other publications—from *Vogue* and

Redbook to *Newsweek* and the *New York Times*—provided *Cosmo* with lots of publicity.[3]

Creating the first male centerfold was the brainchild of Helen Gurley Brown. She had burst onto the nation's radar screen in 1962 by writing the best-selling book *Sex and the Single Girl*. Brown attracted still more attention in 1965 when she was named editor of *Cosmopolitan*. She announced at the time that she had a two-pronged mission: to transform the failing general-interest magazine, with a modest monthly circulation of 700,000, into a successful publishing venture, and to break the American media's long-standing tradition of treating the unmarried woman "like a scarlet-fever victim, a misfit" and, instead, celebrate single womanhood. After Burt Reynolds showed his stuff and *Cosmo*'s circulation shot up to more than two million, no one questioned that Brown had accomplished her mission.[4]

Some of the themes that emerged from the pages of *Cosmo* during the early 1970s were reminiscent of those that *Playboy* had introduced the previous decade, except that now topics such as casual sex and infidelity were being explored not from a man's perspective but from a woman's. Another subject discussed in *Cosmo* moved the media across an entirely new threshold by exposing the male animal as far less than perfect—in bed or otherwise. The most jaw-dropping of all the articles published in the magazine were those that explored the pleasures that women could derive from sex, as *Cosmo* approached the topic with remarkable candor and detail.

Not everyone, however, saw *Cosmo* as a positive force, as a multitude of observers found fault with what the publication was saying to the American woman. Numerous feminists focused, in particular, on two recurring messages. First, the detractors said, the magazine told its female reader that she could not possibly feel fulfilled unless she was attached to a man. Second, the critics continued, *Cosmo* communicated that if a woman hoped to enjoy a satisfying sex life, she first had a long list of flaws she had to "fix."

The Original Cosmo Girl

Helen Gurley was born in rural Arkansas in 1922. Her father, a school-teacher turned state legislator, died when Helen was ten, plunging the family into poverty. Cleo Gurley then moved herself and her two daughters to California, hoping that an uncle would provide financial assistance. That help never materialized, however, and so Helen, despite graduating as valedictorian of her high school class, could not afford to attend college. The young woman also suffered, during her early years, from acne that was so severe that it scarred her face.[5]

With no money or education and only mediocre looks, Gurley recognized that she would have to depend on her own skills and wherewithal to make her way in the world. So she began working for a Los Angeles company as a secretary, the first of seventeen such jobs she would hold during the next dozen or so years. Along the way, Gurley discovered that she had a natural talent for writing in a lively and upbeat style that was well suited to promotional material. So she shifted to the advertising world, working first as a copywriter and then as an account executive.

But Helen Gurley never believed in all work and no play. She lost her virginity as a teenager and dated a series of men during her twenties and early thirties, with "dating" typically extending into the bedroom. Her motto became the slogan stitched into a needlepoint pillow in her apartment: "Good girls go to heaven. Bad girls go everywhere." As Gurley's disposable income rose, she devoted a goodly portion of it to improving her appearance and, simultaneously, to increasing her chances of landing what she would later define as a "good catch" in the husband department. She had her acne scars sanded off, her nose fixed, and her hairline adjusted, while also dieting and exercising so that, standing five feet four inches tall and never weighing more than 100 pounds, she could boast of being a perfect size two.[6]

A landmark in her personal life came in 1959 when she "made the big M," as she later called it, and married motion-picture producer David

Brown, who would go on to finance such lucrative box-office blockbusters as *Jaws, The Sting,* and *Star Wars.* The marriage was a major boost to Helen Gurley Brown's professional life as well, because her husband—she called him, both privately and publicly, "Lambchop"—suggested that she write a book chronicling her experiences as a single woman.[7]

Sex and the Single Girl was a sensation. Reviewers blasted Brown for depending on first-name-only "friends" as her sources, but readers loved the author's breezy style and frank advice. A typical passage: "Theoretically a 'nice' single woman has no sex life. What nonsense! She has a better sex life than most of her married friends. She need never be bored with one man per lifetime. Her choice of partners is endless."[8]

With a best-selling book under her belt, Brown next entered the world of magazine editing by taking over the moribund *Cosmopolitan* and turning it into what ultimately would become her only child: *Cosmo.*[9]

Promoting Casual Sex

In addition to believing that women should be able to ogle a male centerfold, the magazine also insisted that they should enjoy sexual activities that previous generations had seen as the province of men only—and that included casual sex. *Cosmo* writers went far beyond merely reporting on the topic, as they actively promoted it as well. "Women are free to have sex when we choose and with whom we choose," read a typical article. "And if we elect to spend only one night with a man, well, isn't that our privilege?"[10]

The magazine described how casual sex increased the quality of life for hundreds of women. A girl named Erica had enrolled at Indiana University because of its excellent opera program but was soon disappointed in the dearth of suitable men. "And then it hit me," she said. "Who, after all, are the grown-ups on a college campus? Professors, of course. After that revelation, a whole new world opened up to me. I see two or three of them regularly—nothing serious with any of them. I'm not looking for that kind of relationship right now, and neither are they."[11]

Cosmo's stable of writers also made it perfectly clear that some of the best casual sex was of the one-night-stand variety. An article highlighting the carnal adventures of a woman named Linda provided details of her encounter with a man while vacationing in Hawaii. "I was not going to waste the warm, relaxed, sensuous way my body felt," she said. "We only got to spend a day and a night together, but it was fantastic—just sun and sex and play." When the author of the article asked Linda if she felt guilty about having such a brief affair, she was startled by the question. "I would have felt guilty if I *hadn't* slept with Bob," Linda responded. "I would have been cheating myself out of a perfectly marvelous experience."[12]

As with casual sex more generally, *Cosmo* went beyond merely recording women's experiences with single-time sex partners to the point of actively promoting them. An article titled "Brief Encounters," in fact, made it sound like it was a liberated woman's *duty* to invite the occasional stranger into her bed. "A one-night-stand can never own you, never dominate you, never make demands that will interfere with your independence," the article stated. "Even today, most of us chafe under *some* sort of male domination (a demanding lover, tyrannical boss), and the stranger may be the only 'safe' man in our lives."[13]

Glorifying Infidelity

Another frequent topic was one that *Playboy* clearly embraced but did not write about directly. That lack of editorial comment derived from the fact that a married man having intercourse with women other than his wife had been standard practice for so many years that *Playboy* didn't consider the practice worth mentioning. Turning the tables and condoning infidelity by married *women*, however, was a very different matter. For such an activity to become acceptable would require a major readjustment in the nation's sexual mores. *Cosmo* rose to the challenge.

Based on the number of unfaithful women described in the magazine, readers could have assumed that infidelity had become a national pastime. "Joan has been married now for nine years and practically since the hon-

eymoon has managed to keep some other man simmering on the back burner," *Cosmo* reported in a story titled "The Cheaters." The piece went on to tell how Joan firmly believed that her marriage would have ended in divorce long ago if she had forced herself to be faithful to her husband. Another article, this one titled "Creative Infidelity," included details about how an extramarital affair had been just the medicine to cure another mother of the depression that engulfed her when she turned thirty. "Suddenly I felt young again, light and desirable," Beth said. "My infidelity did me more good than two months at a health farm."[14]

It wasn't just unfaithful wives who had glowing words for extramarital sex, as *Cosmo* offered its readers plenty of professional counselors who gave their seal of approval as well. "I have seen infidelity do a wife and her marriage more good than twenty sessions with me," a male psychologist was quoted as saying. A psychotherapist echoed those sentiments. "After marriage, we relegate a woman to just one bed with one man forever, even though we usually expect her husband to slide off the rails occasionally," the man said. "I've often wondered why more women *aren't* unfaithful."[15]

Showcasing female infidelity was such a radical concept that Helen Gurley Brown was repeatedly accused of encouraging single women to become "home wreckers." When the host of a television talk show challenged *Cosmo*'s editor on this point, she insisted that another woman could be a threat to a marriage only if the union was already troubled. "If a wife can't keep her husband at home, she needs to look at what's lacking in her own marriage, not blame it on the other woman."[16]

Putting the American Man Under the Microscope

One of the topics on which *Cosmo* broke entirely new ground involved men. Earlier media enterprises that had fueled the Sexual Revolution had lionized male members of the species—as well as the male member. *Playboy* magazine and the James Bond films, in particular, painted American manhood in decidedly rose-colored hues. But now that a magazine was speaking from the female point of view, a very different picture began to emerge.

An article titled "The Sexually Selfish Lover" cut to the chase vis-à-vis one of man's recurring shortcomings by stating, "Harold is lying contentedly beside Laura, radiating post-coital satisfaction as he drifts away into gratified sleep. Laura, however, is painfully awake." The piece identified the cause of Laura's distress as the fact that her lover was concerned only with his own sexual release. "Laura has just discovered the sexually selfish man. If you haven't been to bed with him, consider yourself fortunate; far too many of us have." The article offered several pointers on how a woman might try to change such a sex partner, but it ultimately ended on a pessimistic note. "What happens when you've tried and tried and you're still wide awake at 3:00 a.m. and hating it/him/yourself because of yet another failure? Look for another man."[17]

Other articles illuminated more male defects. A profile of Hugh Hefner's latest live-in girlfriend—he was forty-seven, she was twenty-two—highlighted a quote from the Playboy of the Western World: "*Sophistication* in women? That's always put me off—it's another of the masks they hide behind." The author of a piece titled "The Sexually Deprived Wife" reported that a huge number of husbands were not living up to their sexual obligation, which *Cosmo* defined as having intercourse at least once a week. Another problem, the magazine stated, was that many 1970s men were not comfortable with the increasing number of women who were being sexually assertive; one woman told how, after their first lovemaking session, the man began interrogating her, "What's wrong with you? Only guys turn on that fast. You a *lesbian?*"[18]

The magazine's men-are-far-from-perfect theme was not limited to editorial content but was also communicated in many of the cartoons that dotted *Cosmo*'s pages. Typical was a drawing set in a nudist camp, with naked women and men in the background playing badminton. The main characters in the cartoon were the couple in the foreground. The woman lying on a chaise lounge was looking directly into the crotch of the naked man standing in front of her. Readers could only see the man from the back, but the cartoon's caption told them all they needed to know about the man's genitalia. The words coming from the woman's mouth read: "Oh, hello Herman. How's every 'little' thing?"[19]

Exploring Female Sexual Pleasure

Cosmo's most significant contribution to helping women become fully evolved sexual beings was its commitment to describing the joys—often with stunning candor—that could be found in various carnal acts. Hugh Hefner had been telling men how to enhance their pleasure quotient since the early 1950s, and Helen Gurley Brown gave female readers comparable guidance in the 1970s.

"Sexual courage starts with the conviction that your body is *worthy* of orgasm and that you deserve sexual gratification as much as anybody else," stated an article called "Why Girls Can't Have Orgasms . . . and What to Do About It." The piece also insisted that achieving sexual gratification is the right of every person: "Ability to have orgasm isn't distributed only to certain women. It's part of your basic equipment." The article went on to acknowledge, though, that it takes most women longer to climax than it takes most men, saying that "anywhere from ten minutes to half an hour" was typical for a woman.[20]

Cosmo also marched boldly forward into uncharted territory with an article titled "Masturbation and Other Pleasures." Social etiquette might dictate that self-produced female orgasms not be discussed, the story said, but the activity is, in fact, the "missing piece in the sexual jigsaw puzzle." Pulling no punches, the author went on to quote a married woman who masturbated every night that her husband was not with her: "While I'm doing it I play with my breasts. And when I finally come, if I pinch the nipples real hard, it feels as if the orgasm is starting right from my toes."[21]

A recurring theme in the articles related to male-female lovemaking was that a woman should not be passive or silent in bed—but assertive and vocal. "A number of us still think that if a man is truly loving, he'll know instinctively what to do," Jeannie said. "We feel it's an insult to him and to the great love between us to take his hand and put it where we want it." In particular, she said, many inexperienced men keep forgetting that neither the breasts nor the vagina is the organ they should be paying the most attention to. "The clitoris, of course, is the critical area to orgasm, and some men need to be reminded and re-reminded it's the push-button of arousal." Another woman agreed, saying of her lover, "He'd

touch me for about two seconds and maybe not get back to the clit for ten minutes, never enough sustained attention." The woman became so frustrated that she finally wrote her lover a note telling him exactly what she wanted him to do in bed. "No, I didn't mail it. I gave it to him," she said. "Reading it turned him on right then and he followed my directions explicitly after that."[22]

Cosmo Draws Its Critics

At the same time that *Cosmo* was advising women on how to liberate their libidos, many other publications were telling their readers that the magazine was not the friend of the American woman, but her enemy.

The most pervasive of the complaints was that, according to *Cosmo's* value system, any woman who did not have a man in her life—or at least in her bed—was not only unhappy and unfulfilled but, in fact, *incomplete*. The *New York Times Magazine* published the definitive piece on the topic, saying that *Cosmo* repeatedly told its readers, "You feel miserable when you don't have a man." The article went on to say that the Cosmo Girl, the magazine's name for its target reader, was consistently discouraged from gaining an education, developing a career, or cultivating friendships with other women. "She's having a face lift, a breast implant, and worrying about how many affairs are good for her. So how can she possibly muster the time, energy and concentration to do anything else?" The article included an interview with Helen Gurley Brown in which the editor confirmed that, in her opinion, a woman without a man—even if she is successful professionally and in her other relationships—is a failure. "A woman," Brown was quoted as saying, "doesn't feel complete or even *alive* unless she has a man."[23]

The second most frequent complaint was best summarized in another withering article, this one in *Esquire*. According to the piece, *Cosmopolitan* portrayed the American woman as a horribly defective creature who faced a daunting list of problems and anxieties. Brown's publication communicated that every woman was plagued with a long list of flaws—from having small breasts to not being thin enough to not knowing how to perform in bed—that she absolutely had to work on, the *Esquire* article contended,

if she had any hope of getting a man to love her. When the author took her criticism to Brown, the original Cosmo Girl not only confirmed this assessment as reality but went on to produce one of the most revealing comments the editor was ever to utter. "A woman cannot sit around like a cupcake asking other people to come and eat her up and discover her great sweetness and charm," Brown said. "She's got to make herself more 'cupcakable' so that she's a better cupcake to be gobbled up."[24]

By the mid-1970s, *Cosmo* had become a lightning rod for editorial attacks. *Time* magazine blasted it for never portraying women as mothers, *Newsweek* complained that it shamelessly promoted the cosmetics companies that advertised in its pages, and the *National Review* condemned *Cosmo* for being too sexual—"It is false and pernicious in its treatment of sex as a casual amusement."[25]

A Girl Joins the Boys' Club

Assessing the role that *Cosmopolitan* played in the evolution of the Sexual Revolution during the 1970s is a challenge. On the one hand, scholars and journalists alike have praised the magazine—because of the Burt Reynolds centerfold as well as the various sexual messages it sent—as making a major contribution. One book credited *Cosmo* with "pioneering the frank discussion of female sexuality," and another said the magazine "became synonymous with young women's sexuality" by telling them they had every right to be sexually active—and not to feel guilty about it.[26]

On the other hand, many of the criticisms of the magazine were valid. Communicating that a woman could not be whole unless she had a man in her bed was certainly not a laudable concept. Nor did it serve women well to tell them that they were fundamentally flawed and, therefore, unlovable unless they undertook significant repair work.

Perhaps such contradictory assessments were inevitable, as Helen Gurley Brown's magazine was a pioneer. And whenever an effort is made to break new ground on behalf of a segment of society that previously has been limited to a narrow and subjugated role, the path is fraught with potential missteps. What's more, it would be naïve to think that any single voice could speak to all members of a group as diverse as American

womanhood. In the final analysis, Brown was selling a new and innovative message, unsatisfactory though it may have been to some critics, to a group of women who otherwise may have continued to depend on old assumptions about their sexuality—or lack of it. In addition, although *Cosmo* and its feminist critics clashed in many respects, they both were promoting the fundamental concept of women controlling their own bodies and their own lives.

And so, regardless of an individual observer's final assessment of *Cosmopolitan,* there is no question that this groundbreaking magazine deserves a place of prominence on the list of media products that fueled the Sexual Revolution. At a time when most provocateurs who were shaping the national libido were looking at sex either from an overtly male perspective—*Playboy,* the James Bond films—or from a viewpoint that could be described as gender neutral—news media coverage of the birth control pill, *All in the Family*—Helen Gurley Brown's publication, by contrast, spoke with a distinctly feminine voice.

The boys' club had, in short, gone co-ed.

Donahue

Talking Sex on Morning TV

IT WAS THE KIND OF COMPLAINT THAT TV PERSONALITIES PRAY FOR.
During a commercial break, the talk show host took a phone call from
the president of the local telephone company, who proceeded to beg him
to end the call-in survey he was conducting. So many viewers were participating in the informal opinion poll, the harried Bell Telephone
Company executive screamed, that if the host didn't *instantly* tell people
to put down their phones, city officials would be forced to commandeer
the phone lines so the police and fire departments could resume their op-
erations.

What vital question of the day had created the crisis?

It all began when the talk show host had held up a brand of doll called
Little Brother, one of the first anatomically complete male dolls available
to American consumers. He then had, with a dramatic flourish, removed
the cloth diaper from the figure to show the viewing audience the tiny
piece of molded plastic that was causing all the fuss. And, finally, the TV
provocateur had called out to the folks at home:

"Good? Bad? Approve? Disapprove? Call in and tell me what you think.
I want to hear from *you*."[1]

Phil Donahue agreed to end that particular call-in survey, but by no
means would it be the last time that the highly animated talk show host
incited controversy. Beginning in 1974 when his five-day-a-week syndicated morning program began to draw a huge national audience, the sil-
ver-haired man with the baby blue eyes demonstrated an uncanny ability

to identify topics that would engage the 200 members of his studio audience as well as the eight and a half million viewers at home. Primary among those topics was sex.[2]

"I want all the topics hot," Donahue told the staff who helped him produce his hour-long show. "Not even lukewarm—*hot!*"[3]

And hot he got. From single women choosing to become pregnant to lesbian couples raising children, from incest victims recounting sexual abuse to men describing the challenge of loving a liberated woman—it all became TV talk. Indeed, the small screen's master showman tackled a topic that was so controversial that even the most daring media, including *All in the Family* and *Cosmo,* had steered clear of it: abortion. A 1978 *TV Guide* cover story clearly nailed the subject on the head when it dubbed Phil Donahue "the man who hit daytime television like a hormone injection." That article was also onto something when it said that Donahue's 235 programs a year proved: "Sex sells. And sex on TV sells very well."[4]

From Altar Boy to Impresario

Phillip John Donahue grew up in a middle-class household in Cleveland, attending Catholic schools and serving as an altar boy in his parish church. His father worked as a furniture salesman, clocking in as many hours of overtime as possible to save enough money to achieve the dream of many an Irish-American father by sending his son to the University of Notre Dame.[5]

The dutiful son majored in business administration, in keeping with Dad's wishes, but was soon seduced by a love not for balance sheets but for broadcasting. By the time the high-energy young man arrived at his morning classes in finance and accounting, he had already spent several hours announcing programs over the air at the campus television station.

After receiving his degree in 1957, Donahue initially followed both the career and personal paths that his parents wanted. He took a job as a bank teller and married his college sweetheart so they could start a family—they had five children in the span of six years.

When Donahue heard about a job at a Cleveland television station, though, he abandoned banking in favor of news reporting. For the next

several years, he chased fires and traffic accidents while reading his share of 5:30 a.m. farm reports about the latest prices for corn and hog bellies. Working harder and waiting longer than many of his colleagues to catch newsmakers for interviews, the affable young man advanced to the point that he was co-anchoring the evening news on the CBS affiliate in Dayton, Ohio.[6]

By 1967, he was looking for a new challenge. Drawing on the college education that had taught him what makes a successful business venture, he went to a competing station and pitched the idea of hosting a new kind of program. The Women's Liberation Movement was gaining momentum, he argued, and so the time was right to create a talk show that focused on feminist issues. He would be the perfect host to do it, he continued, because he offered the novelty of being a man talking about women. The executives at the station were skeptical of the idea, but Donahue talked them into giving him a shot.

The program was an overnight hit, quickly becoming the most-watched local program in Dayton. It clearly was only a matter of time before the visionary broadcaster from Ohio would move to a larger venue.

Reinventing TV Talk

Phil Donahue's career took a major leap forward in 1974 when he packed his wife and kids into his brown Chevy Caprice and moved to Chicago to host the *Donahue* morning program. Now based in one of the country's largest markets, it had the potential to become a national phenomenon. By 1978, the man in the three-piece suit and black wing tip shoes had become the most popular talk show host on daytime television, giving his viewers an experience unlike anything they had ever seen before.[7]

Until Donahue came along, national television talk shows had been based in either Hollywood or New York and had revolved around a host who told a few jokes and sang an occasional song, but mostly sat behind a desk and chatted with an endless stream of actors and actresses talking about the wonders of their latest movie. The shows were filmed before an audience of awestruck fans that a camera panned for about ten sec-

onds each episode, but otherwise they sat like potted plants, with laughter added to the soundtrack before the program aired.

Donahue changed it all.

Not only was the program broadcast live and based in the Midwest, but it included no joke telling, so singing, and no celebrities promoting their work. Even more significantly, Donahue made the audience an essential element of the show. He first introduced the subject of the day, which might involve an expert but often revolved around a "regular person" with experience with the topic, and then bounced around the studio with his microphone in hand, allowing one guest after another to ask a question, make a comment, or add an anecdote from her own life experience.

Donahue's most dramatic change vis-à-vis the talk show—one that media historians would come to label "revolutionary"—was that some 85 percent of his audience members were women. Before the Irish charmer had come to the small screen, much of TV's advertising and programming had been aimed at female viewers, but it had never crossed the minds of the men who ran the networks to ask those women what they *thought*. "The average housewife is bright and inquisitive," Donahue argued, "but television has traditionally treated her like some mental midget. I'm saying there's a lot of women who want something more. Out there in TV land during daytime lies an enormous amount of energy and a lot of curiosity."[8]

And the subject those women were most curious about, according to the man they watched as they stood over their ironing boards or washed the breakfast dishes, was sex.

Showcasing New Sexual Trends

By the mid-1970s, the widespread sexual repression that had dominated 1950s America had been, for many members of society, relegated to the history books. Driven at least partially by the titillating media products that they were reading, viewing, and listening to, more and more people were experimenting with new lifestyles that the Sexual Revolution had helped to make possible. One of the reasons why *Donahue* was such a run-

away success was the host's eagerness to showcase some of those sexual trendsetters on his program.

One controversial trend that Phil Donahue brought into the country's living rooms was the increasing number of single women who were becoming mothers not by accident but by choice. "I always wanted to have a baby, and I knew I'd be an excellent mother," an attractive young woman named Cathy told the television audience. "Getting married sounded OK, too, but that was never as high a priority for me as having a child." So Cathy, in the spirit of the newly independent woman of the era, took the situation into her own hands. She found an attractive and intelligent man, duped him into impregnating her, and then proceeded to raise the child on her own. "I have a good job and plenty of money," she told the audience. "What do I need a man for?"[9]

Single parenting by design was not the only modern-day lifestyle that the king of the television talk show highlighted on his program. One memorable segment featured Burt Reynolds, who had already exposed his body in his *Cosmo* centerfold, baring the details of his long-term relationship with an older woman, and another about sexually active senior citizens had an eighty-year-old woman describing how her octogenarian lover continued to "take her to the stars." Still other segments looked at the rise of surrogate mothers, of sexually promiscuous teenagers, of married women having long-term affairs, and of coed cohabitation—unmarried young men and women sharing the same apartment.[10]

One of the most memorable of the sexual-trend programs was one on which several women guests talked about a topic that *Cosmo* had discussed in print and that *Donahue* now brought to TV: women enjoying the pleasures of sex. Although the former altar boy was fully supportive, he also reminded his audience that he had come of age during a very different era. "Women weren't supposed to enjoy sex. Women were supposed to *tolerate* it," he said, with more than a touch of discomfort in his voice. "Men brought to the marriage relationship a sort of unspoken understanding that there really weren't supposed to be fireworks for you—that this was *my* thing and, 'I'll be through down there in a minute.' Sexual morality really blocked all of us."[11]

Providing a Venue for Sexual Minorities

With only rare exceptions, the pre-*Donahue* mainstream media had sidelined the topic of homosexuality because it was too divisive. That situation changed when the boyish-looking new host arrived on the scene, however, as he was one of the earliest high-profile Americans to advocate gay equality. The liberal host repeatedly challenged audience members with questions such as, "Do you really think, just because you disapprove of what they do, homosexuals should be denied their *rights?*"[12]

Phil Donahue offered gay people a national platform by engaging them in in-depth discussions of such hot-button topics as lesbian couples raising children. "It's not nearly as exotic as you might think," said one mother of six. "Helping with the math homework and staying up all night with the chicken pox is no different, whether you're a mother and a father or two mothers." Whether those activities were exotic or mundane made little difference to several local stations around the country that refused to air the segment, saying they were not in the business of promoting homosexuality.[13]

Despite the firestorm that the pioneering discussion created, lesbians and gay men continued to receive invitations to appear on *Donahue*. One show was devoted to homosexuality and the church, another to parents of gay children, and still another to a highly articulate gay lawyer talking about why sexual minorities deserve equal rights. When a segment became too intense, the host seamlessly inserted some comic relief, with his specialty being humor of the self-deprecating variety. During the call-in portion of one show, a woman said that Donahue was such a strong advocate of gay rights that he must be a homosexual himself. "I could never be gay," he said with a smirk. "I'm a lousy dancer."[14]

Creating a National Confessional

A huge factor in Phil Donahue becoming the most popular talk show host in the history of American television was his ability and his willingness to listen. By the late 1970s, women were waiting up to two years and driv-

ing hundreds of miles to get a seat in his studio audience, many of them eager to do so because the sympathetic host offered them the very real possibility of revealing, for the first time, a sexual secret that neither society nor their own family members had ever allowed them to talk about. "There's nothing too controversial for television," Donahue said. "What's important is the manner in which it is presented."[15]

By far the most frequent confession that women made was that they were victims of the crime of incest. Many of the women who had been sexually abused had kept that information locked deep inside of themselves since childhood. Releasing the details of the incidents produced a flood of heart-wrenching tears, but the host was always there to provide support. "Donahue is an emotional fellow traveler—involved, sympathetic, respectful," the *Washington Post* observed.[16]

Other female guests and audience members brought other confessions to the nation's unofficial parish priest. "He doesn't kiss me anymore," a woman said on a program about wives who felt emotionally abandoned by their husbands; a large bosom is as necessary for career advancement as professional competence, another said during a program on breast augmentation surgery. One show allowed women in the audience to fire questions at a convicted rapist, while another propelled Donahue into investigative journalism, with several women accusing Chicago police officers of fondling them.[17]

On a few occasions, the talk show host switched to the role of confessor. After the woman Donahue had married in 1958 left him in 1975 and he was suddenly single again, he admitted to his television audience that he was terrified by the prospect of entering the dating world. Blaming his career ambitions for the failed marriage, he also told viewers that he felt completely inadequate to advise his four teenage sons—the boys lived with their father while their sister lived with their mother—on romantic relationships.[18]

Exploring Male Sexuality

Another of the unique contributions of *Donahue* evolved from the host's gender and personal circumstances. Although most of his audience mem-

bers were women and he was eager to talk about their concerns, the newly divorced Donahue soon learned that men of the late 1970s also faced troubling issues with regard to sex, and so he explored them on morning TV.

Primary among those anxieties was how the changing role of women was affecting men. In short, as the one gender became more independent and more assertive, in both the boardroom and the bedroom, the other gender struggled to figure out how to respond. "I'm finding that more and more women want to be 'on top' sexually—and, yes, I mean that literally," one male guest said. "And that's just fine by me." But another man on the same program was finding the signals more complicated. "I was dating this one woman who, whenever I started to make a move, the words coming out of her mouth were 'no, no, no,' but her body language was telling me 'yes, yes, yes.'" So the man finally asked the woman, "When you say 'no,' do you really mean it?" She responded, "When I say, 'no,' I absolutely mean 'no.'" But she then gave the man a coy smile and added, "except when I mean 'yes.'" The man shook his head and said, "Phil, I really am a decent guy and I don't want to force myself on any woman, but I ask you: What am I supposed to do with that?"[19]

By 1977 when Donahue began dating actress Marlo Thomas, he frequently contributed comments to the discussion that were clearly drawn from his own life experience. "Can you imagine what it is like," he asked the audience during one program, "to go back to dating after seventeen years of marriage?" Donahue then sat silent for a moment before quietly adding, "I was a virgin when I got married."[20]

Late in the decade, specific sexual topics relating to men ranged from sexual impotence, vasectomies, and penile implants to what single men want in their female sex partners and the toll that a high-pressure work environment takes on a man's performance in the bedroom.[21]

Tackling the Most Controversial Topic of the Era

In January 1973, the U.S. Supreme Court legalized abortion. That landmark decision did not, however, end the debate over whether a woman should be allowed to terminate a pregnancy but, in fact, only added mo-

mentum to one of the most divisive questions in modern times. The vast majority of media decision-makers steadfastly avoided the subject, fearing that they would, no matter which side of the debate they favored, offend huge numbers of their readers or viewers. Phil Donahue, on the other hand, saw abortion as precisely the kind of topic that had made him the number one TV talk show host in the country. "Television's problem isn't controversy," he said. "It's blandness."[22]

Although Donahue described himself as "prudish" in how he lived his own life, it was clear from the guests he invited onto his show—such as single women who chose to become mothers and gay people who sought equal rights—that he leaned toward liberal positions on many social issues. It was no surprise, then, when he publicly supported a woman's right to abort a fetus. "To ban abortion is to ensure that only wealthy women will be able to have an abortion," he told the *Chicago Sun-Times*. "And I, for one, am not interested in having us return to those days."[23]

Some of the abortion-related discussions that aired on *Donahue* reflected the host's pro-choice stance. One program featured a woman who wrote a book with an incendiary title that enraged the Catholic Church: *Abortion Is a Blessing*. The author's appearance on the talk show gave her the chance to defend the title as well as the thesis behind it. "I have conferred in over 12,000 legal abortions, including a twelve-year-old girl and a fifteen-year-old," she told the audience. "I *know* abortion is a blessing."[24]

Phil Donahue's initial career had been in journalism, though, and his treatment of the most contentious topic of the era showed that he placed great value on a fundamental tenet of his original occupation: balance. "I'm not an entertainer, I'm a journalist," he insisted. "My background's been in gathering news, trying to be fair, allowing as many people as possible to have their say." So in his most high-profile segment on abortion, he gave the opposition its due.[25]

For that 1975 segment, the host jettisoned both the studio audience and the portion of the program devoted to viewers calling in by telephone, determined that the emphasis would be on informing viewers rather than entertaining them. The guests included both pro-choice and right-to-life activists, as well as a teenage girl who had an abortion but later regretted it.[26]

But by far the most compelling seven minutes of the most controversial segment that ever aired on *Donahue* were those devoted to a videotape of an actual abortion. The sequence had taken place at the Midwest Family Planning Association in Chicago, and the televised images defined the term "raw." According to one newspaper story that described the tape, "It is graphic. Viewers see the 'birth matter' being deposited in a bottle." But the tape was not sensationalistic, the reporter continued, because "when you're through watching, you KNOW what an abortion is, and from that standpoint I say it's very important."[27]

From a journalistic perspective, Donahue clearly had succeeded, with the *Chicago Tribune* labeling the program "intelligent" and "meaningful." But several of the stations that routinely carried his show refused to air this particular segment. "It's a little touchy," said a spokesperson from WGN-Channel 9 in Chicago. Stations in Milwaukee, Buffalo, Toledo, and Phoenix also refused to broadcast the program.[28]

Talk television's most successful host publicly criticized those stations. "I worked my butt off on that show," Donahue told one reporter, "and I feel that it's an acceptable journalistic treatment of a very volatile issue. Women should have a chance to see it. It's an extremely important program."[29]

Success Creates a New Television Genre

By the end of the 1970s, Phil Donahue was talking not only to the massive audience that watched his show, but to other sizable sectors of the population as well. In 1979, NBC executives recruited him to appear on the *Today* show three times a week, hoping he would boost the morning program's flagging ratings; Donahue kicked off his new gig by interviewing a transsexual, providing exactly the kind of surge in the viewing audience that the network had hoped for and proving once again that *Sex Sells!*[30]

The scope of Donahue's influence also extended to the reading public, thanks to the combination of his best-selling autobiography, *Donahue, My Own Story,* and the legion of magazine and newspaper articles that were published about him, including cover stories in *TV Guide, Newsweek,* and

the *Saturday Evening Post*. The country's most-talked-about bachelor father remained hot property after he and Marlo Thomas married and the media crowned them the perfect modern-day American couple.[31]

And a consistent focus of those stories was how Donahue had succeeded in encouraging the American people to talk openly about what was going on inside their bedrooms. When a critic for the *Los Angeles Times*, for example, took it upon himself to identify exactly what factors had propelled *Donahue* into the most influential program on television, number one on his list was the frequency of sex as a topic—"Nothing is taboo." Many publications also dubbed the dimpled host the country's newest sex symbol. According to *TV Guide*, women all over the country "dreamed of running barefoot through the hair that falls across his forehead like a graying snowdrift," and *People* described him as "cuddly" and "charmingly boyish," while quoting one female viewer as saying, "He can put his slippers under my bed anytime." Donahue demurred at the sex-symbol comments, insisting that he was not good-looking. "Look at my nose. It's too broad," he said. "And my legs are too skinny." He never denied that he had changed the television landscape with regard to sex talk, however, as he proudly accepted the credit. "Boat rockers are the best people," he said. "They get things done and are not sucked in—they retain just a little piece of their souls."[32]

Donahue also received praise from the world of print journalism, which generally did not have kind words for 1970s daytime television programming. The *Washington Post* called him a "tough interviewer and serious commentator" whose talk show was a welcome departure from the "fluff" that otherwise dominated daytime television. *Esquire* magazine wrote admiringly of Donahue as well, saying, "Each day more women are educated about sex and morals by this Notre Dame product than by any other person in the land."[33]

A New Kind of Sexual Provocateur

There is no question that Phil Donahue changed the face of daytime television. Particularly noteworthy was the fact that his program rejected the prevailing concept of using the studio audience as nothing more than a

backdrop and, instead, created a paradigm that not only allowed "regular" people to speak but, in fact, *depended on* those voices as an essential element in a new and highly successful formula built around two-way communication. Perhaps of even more significance was the gender of those audience members, as *Donahue* broke new ground by showcasing the thoughts and concerns of American women.

Nor is there any doubt that this visionary talk show host brought an impressive list of sexual topics into the nation's living room for the first time. From anatomically complete male dolls to gay rights to the traumatic repercussions of incest to the incendiary issue of whether a woman should have the right to abort an unwanted fetus—Donahue provided a venue where they all could be discussed. By so doing, he also helped move many of those topics onto the national radar screen as never before.

With regard to the evolution of the symbiotic relationship between sex and the media, the broadcaster also represented a step forward. During the 1960s, the men who were perceived as being at the forefront of the Sexual Revolution could all be described as "a man's man." Hugh Hefner, James Bond, Jim Morrison—each man had a similar relationship with women. The magazine publisher, the fictional secret agent, the hedonistic rock star—each one used a woman for his sexual gratification and then discarded her before moving on to the next, and the next, and the next.

Phil Donahue was a dramatically different type of sexual provocateur. He didn't exploit women for sexual pleasure; he celebrated women as multifaceted human beings. He wasn't fixated on women's breasts and thighs; he was more interested in their minds. He didn't see male-female interaction solely in terms of its physical dimensions; he delved into the emotional and intellectual aspects of those relationships. He didn't need to prove his machismo; he sought out ways to explore his "feminine side." The talk show host, in short, epitomized a new kind of sexual provocateur: The Sensitive Man.

Three's Company

Adding Jiggle to the Small Screen

THE REV. DONALD WILDMON, A GAUNT MAN WITH ASCETIC WAYS, HAD spent twenty years shepherding his flock on the pathway to Heaven. By the mid-1970s, however, the father of four had become increasingly concerned about the messages that the most powerful medium in the history of humankind was sending into American living rooms. So Rev. Wildmon left his Mississippi pulpit to create the National Federation for Decency in hopes of cleansing television of what he believed to be excessive sexual content. The program that, more than any other, propelled this guardian of morality on his crusade that would grow into one of the country's most high-profile special-interest groups was the same one that debuted the very month—March 1977—that the Methodist minister founded his organization.[1]

The objectionable messages in *Three's Company*, by Rev. Wildmon's account, were numerous. Not only did the ABC sitcom feature a sex-crazed young man living in an apartment with two vulnerable young women, but all three of those main characters talked incessantly about carnal activities. What's more, the young actress who soon emerged as the show's best-known star consistently dressed in provocative clothing and repeatedly jumped and hopped and bounced—movements that caused her abundant cleavage to shake and shimmy in a most unladylike way. And, on top of all this, the young man at the center of the disgraceful *ménage à trois* was portrayed as being, or at least pretending to be, a homosexual.[2]

Many viewers had a very different take on *Three's Company*. They agreed that, yes, the series was a bedroom farce, but they saw it as being

more farce than bedroom. The sitcom revolved around the randy but affable Jack Tripper (played by John Ritter), the dim-witted Christmas "Chrissy" Snow (played by Suzanne Somers), and the sensible Janet Wood (played by Joyce DeWitt). Defenders of the program argued that the likable and highly compatible trio created an endearing mixture of laughter and lunacy, while the sexual undercurrent was of the wink-and-a-nudge variety that offered a half hour of harmless, feel-good escapism.[3]

There is no question that *Three's Company*, regardless of whether it was perceived as salacious or silly, was enormously popular. From its first episode, the program was a major hit, and by the end of the decade it was the number one show on American television, often drawing an audience in excess of fifty million viewers. The series, which aired Tuesday nights at 9, retained its blockbuster status throughout its eight seasons. And in 1980 the program also began its seemingly perpetual life in reruns, ensuring that future generations would receive the same sexual messages as the original viewers.[4]

And, again, whether the program was criticized or praised, it definitely broke new sexual ground. Even though Jack never succeeded in getting either of his roommates into bed, the "hers and hers and his" immortalized in the show's bubbly theme song brought coed cohabitation into the nation's living rooms on a weekly basis during a time when many Americans defined such living arrangements as an invitation to "moral turpitude." Likewise, the sexual references laced into the dialogue took television across a new threshold, while blond bombshell Chrissy traversed a couple more with her revealing outfits and her penchant for bouncing, which made her the epitome of a genre dubbed "jiggle TV." Still another breakthrough of enormous consequence was Jack becoming—up to a point—America's most visible homosexual; he pretended to be gay so the threesome's uptight landlord would allow him to live in an apartment with two women.[5]

Perfecting the Art of Sexual Innuendo

Most initial reviews of *Three's Company* were disparaging. The *New York Times* told its readers that "a blank television screen is better" than the

show, and *The Nation* dismissed the program as the latest example of "video prurience." A few of the critiques, however, praised the series as a standout in one area. *"Three's Company* is a triumph of dialogue," the *Los Angeles Times* declared. "The script is a gem of virtuoso one-liners and double entendres."[6]

Sexual suggestiveness began in the premier episode when Janet and Chrissy throw a party for their departing roommate and awake the next morning to find a guy asleep in the bathtub. Once the girls discover that Jack is a great cook, they are tempted to offer him the now-vacant bedroom in their apartment, but Janet is concerned because the potential new roomie is clearly smitten with Chrissy. The simple-minded blonde assures the down-to-earth brunette that she can resist any come-ons, but Janet is not convinced, voicing her concern by using one of the show's first instances of sexual innuendo. "I know you, Chrissy," Janet says. "You have a very low *melting point*."[7]

With that statement, Janet communicates to the viewing audience that her well-built roommate is sexually vulnerable—though she doesn't use the "S" word. Janet repeats the linguistic technique after she finally agrees to let Jack move in but accompanies the offer with a stern warning. "One false move," she tells him, "and we take you to the vet." This time, viewers understand that Janet is telling Jack that if he so much as touches the virginal Chrissy, they'll have him neutered like the dog he is.

Jack has his share of sexual doublespeak as well. In one early episode, Chrissy is in the shower when Jack comes into the bathroom to shave. She's concerned that he might see her naked body through the shower curtain, but he assures her that he's too depressed to become aroused. When he says, "I'm so down today I couldn't even raise a smile," the audience immediately thinks of another body part that Jack is apparently unable to raise. Another time, Jack and Janet are skeptical when Chrissy tells them she has a date with a guy she met at the supermarket, so she tells them the man is so nice that he even allowed her to go ahead of him at the checkout counter. Jack then quips, "Yeah, so he could get a better look at your *rump* roast."[8]

Chrissy's one-liners often draw huge laughs, too, as they typically are delivered with a look of wide-eyed innocence fully in concert with her

charming naïveté. In one episode, the roommates are in desperate need of $300 to pay their rent. So Chrissy volunteers, "I've only got one thing anybody would want to buy, but I was hoping to save that until I got married." Jack and Janet are shocked that Chrissy would even consider selling her body. Only when she adds the punch line do they—and the audience at home—understand: "My grandmother's wedding ring."[9]

More innuendo comes from the sex-starved Helen Roper, wife of landlord Stanley Roper. In the first episode, when Jack assures the Ropers that his relationship with Janet and Chrissy will be "platonic" but Stanley doesn't know what the word means, Helen explains sarcastically, "Like you and me, Stanley." The husband's sexual shortcomings become a running joke, week after week, with Helen providing an endless stream of double entendres. "Fix the doorbell, Stanley," she says. "It's about time something around here got its *chimes rung*."[10]

Updating the French Farce

More sexual humor evolved from the fact that *Three's Company* was a televised version of a French sexual farce. And like George Feydeau, who originated the genre in the sixteenth century, the writers who created the sitcom often used misunderstandings as comic devices.

One such situation unfolds after Janet and Chrissy have a huge fight, prompting Jack to play peacemaker. He goes into the girls' room, where Janet is lying in bed, and tries to persuade her to forgive Chrissy. Helen Roper then appears at the door and sees Jack and Janet on the bed, overhearing snippets of their conversation that suggest hanky-panky.

JANET to Jack: "No, I just can't."
JACK to Janet: "Will you stop saying 'no'? I want you to do it."

An appalled Helen then storms out of the bedroom. Chrissy, eager to see what all the fuss is about, races into the bedroom and sees Jack and Janet still sitting on the bed together.

JACK pleads: "Come on, Janet, be nice."
CHRISSY—in shock: "So this is what goes on behind my back!"

JACK pats a spot near him on the bed and says: "Chrissy, come over here and join us."

CHRISSY, thinking Jack wants her to join the couple in some sort of kinky three-way, screams: "That's disgusting!"[11]

Other comical scenes include the farcical technique of one person over-hearing—and misinterpreting—a conversation taking place in the next room. In one such situation, Janet is in the living room while Jack and Chrissy are in the kitchen, with the door closed between her and them. They are talking about a puppy they've taken in, but Janet assumes that her roommates are involved in a very different activity.

CHRISSY, in a sweet voice: "Oh, it's so cute."

JACK, cooing: "You are so beautiful."

CHRISSY: "Oh, I love your eyes."

JACK: "Here you go. This is going to make you feel so-o-o good. Ohhhh!"

CHRISSY: "Oh, I could kiss every *inch* of you."

JACK: "Should we do this on the table?"

CHRISSY: "No, on the floor is better."

Janet, determined to bring a halt to the scandalous behavior, then bursts into the kitchen—only to find Jack and Chrissy feeding the puppy on the kitchen floor.[12]

Turning Women's Bodies into Sex Objects

Before *Three's Company*, TV viewers had been given few glimpses of the female body. June Cleaver on *Leave It to Beaver* and Harriet Nelson on *The Adventures of Ozzie and Harriet* had hidden their figures under full skirts and buttoned-to-the-neck blouses. Gloria Stivic on *All in the Family* had dressed somewhat more casually, including in miniskirts, but there is no question that Chrissy Snow was, in matters of provocative apparel, the true revolutionary.

Lustful male viewers didn't even have to wait for the show's weekly plot to begin, as the images accompanying the show's opening credits included a healthy portion of cleavage. As the theme song "Come and Knock on Our Door" puts the audience in a playful mood, Chrissy is shown sunning herself on the apartment balcony. The busty blonde then flips over onto her bottom, smiling broadly into the camera while treating sex-hungry viewers to one of the hundreds of jiggles that soon become a signature element of the show. The action then pauses to offer male eyes a clear view of her ample breasts protruding from the front of her black bathing suit.

Once the weekly stories began, there was plenty more to look at. In the first scene of the debut episode, Chrissy is vacuuming the apartment while dressed in a short nightgown that just barely covers her private parts. The second episode includes a scene with the voluptuous blonde crouching on her hands and knees on her bed; Chrissy's shapely rear end is at the center of the screen as the camera lingers for several seconds to make sure the men at home can enjoy the ruffly panties that she wears under her baby doll nightgown. In another early episode, the TV sex kitten is shown in another provocative piece of lingerie, this one with a slit up the side to reveal a whole lot of tender young thigh.[13]

Jiggling was worked into numerous plotlines. In a typical episode, Jack walks into the apartment to find the girls exercising. When he asks what they're doing, Chrissy tells him they're keeping their bodies firm, and Jack responds, "Don't get too firm. I like to see a little *jiggle* now and then." No problem. The show's writers find plenty of creative ways to keep Chrissy bouncing. One early example comes after Janet decides to apply for a promotion at work, propelling her buxom roommate to show her support by enthusiastically jumping up and down like a cheerleader. Another instance plays out as Jack teaches Chrissy to dance the Charleston—there's no explanation as to why—and her unique version includes not only crisscrossing her arms and legs horizontally, but also jumping vertically. In still another episode, the busty roommate has dinner at a Greek restaurant and mimics the movements of a belly dancer performing there.[14]

Chrissy's wardrobe further enhances the titillation. In the exercising scene, she wears body-hugging leotards; for the cheerleading, she's in a tight sweater and hot pants; for the dance lesson, she dons a low-cut T-shirt and short-short shorts; for the belly dancing, she's in a skimpy halter top—without a bra. Other times she's shown wearing peek-a-boo pajamas or nothing but a bath towel.[15]

While *Three's Company* clearly pushed the envelope regarding sexual images, Rev. Wildmon's crusade led ABC to adopt a strict dress code. "Chrissy and Janet couldn't come out in bras and panties, no matter what," one of the program's producers recalled. "They had to have on a one-piece slip or something, as no bare midriffs were ever allowed." Another hard-and-fast rule forbade either woman from being shown from the rear while bending over, and a third restriction dictated that anytime Jack was shown in his underwear, he had to be wearing boxers—never briefs.[16]

Promoting Coed Cohabitation

Although the program was not overtly political and did not set out to effect social change, it clearly caused many Americans to rethink the prospect of single men and women living under the same roof. The idea of showing three young people of different genders sharing an apartment was so radical in the mid-1970s that CBS and NBC both rejected the program idea when it was proposed to them. ABC executives, by contrast, thought a series that promoted a provocative living arrangement might appeal to a young audience and—in concert with the concept of *Sex Sells!*—become a major profit-maker. In their thinking, the show's statements about coed cohabitation were uniformly positive ones.[17]

The most frequent of the messages played at the beginning of every episode, as the contagious theme song urged viewers to "Come and dance on our floor, take a step that is new." Those words gently challenged the American public to forget its old-fashioned ways and adopt a more modern attitude, at least toward cohabitation.

Individual plotlines sent similarly positive messages. In the second episode, Chrissy's mother arrives for a visit, and the young woman is afraid that Mom and Dad, like most parents of the era, won't allow her

to share an apartment with a man. But the show's writers have the representative of the older generation fully condoning her ditzy daughter's living arrangement. "I'm delighted," Chrissy's mother announces. "With all the terrible things that go on in this town, it's such a relief to know you have a man to protect you." Score one for cohabitation.[18]

An even more persuasive message was the one threaded throughout the series, as Jack never goes to bed with either Chrissy or Janet. Although the program is jam-packed with racy subject matter, titillating images, and enough sexual energy to light up every house in the city of Santa Monica, California, where the sitcom is set, the two girls end their experience with cohabitation as virgins. One scholar of the program had it right when he observed, "Although it often *seemed* sinful, nothing ever happened. It was sexless sexiness!"[19]

Beyond restraining their hormones, the three twenty-something roomies provided an enormous level of support for each other. In one segment, Jack is suspicious of the forty-year-old man Chrissy is dating, even after she assures him that she knows what she's doing. But Jack, like an older brother, takes it upon himself to check out the guy's background. When he discovers that the man is married and has two children, he tells Chrissy, thereby preventing her from getting any further emotionally—or physically—involved with the disreputable cad.[20]

The show's trio of characters soon became national "poster children" for coed cohabitation. In 1979 when *Three's Company* ascended to the vaunted position of TV's most-watched program, the biggest-circulation magazines in the country splashed photos of the three stars all over their covers. From the *Saturday Evening Post* to *TV Guide* and from *People* to *Seventeen* to *Good Housekeeping*, it seemed like every publication in the country was writing about the new lifestyle that the hit program was showcasing.[21]

McCall's even went so far as to report a cause-and-effect relationship between the show and the new trend among American singles. Below a cover photo of the three stars, the venerable women's magazine carried the headline "The Three's Company Life: How Real People Are Imitating TV." The article reported that, "in response to the series, a growing number of single people across the country are making mixed threesomes a way of life."[22]

Raising Gay Visibility

Three's Company also was a pioneer with regard to homosexuality. Although *Donahue* featured gay people on numerous single episodes, Jack pretending to be homosexual kept the topic on the TV screen on a weekly basis. As one writer put it, *"Three's Company* helped pull a forbidden topic out of the closet."[23]

The show's writers knew they were breaking new ground, so they made the most of it by setting up the gay element as the climax of the first episode. The various scenes show how the three young people meet, how the girls ask the attractive student chef to move in, and how Helen and Stanley Roper's sexless marriage is added to the mix. But the lingering question remains: How can the girls persuade the landlord to let a man sleep in the bedroom next to theirs? It isn't until the final scene that the answer finally surfaces. After Jack and Chrissy go into the kitchen for a moment, they return to the living room to find the landlord and his wife smiling. Helen gives Jack's cheek a motherly pinch and says, "We hope you'll be very happy here." Then the Ropers leave and Jack asks Janet what she told them. Her answer becomes the final line of the script, thereby making the crucial word the last one uttered on that historic first episode: "I told them that you are *gay.*"[24]

After that introduction, not a week went by without some mention of Jack's sexuality. At times it comes through Stanley Roper referring to Jack as "Tinkerbell," "the fairy roommate," or "one of the girls"—accompanying each nickname with a smirk. Other times, Jack's presumed sexuality fits into the plotline. In an episode about a bully hassling Chrissy, Stanley taunts Jack—again with a smug smile on his face—by saying, "You could never get into a fight. It would ruin your nails."[25]

The show's creators knew that the comments reinforced stereotypes, so they steeled themselves for criticism from the gay community. But the only complaints came from Rev. Wildmon and his followers, who argued that all depictions of homosexuality, whether positive or negative, should be banned from the airwaves.[26]

Gay America's acceptance of the references, the creators concluded, evolved from the fact that the character in the program who was con-

sistently portrayed as an object of ridicule was Stanley Roper, who came across as a homophobic buffoon. In one episode, Jack is preparing to give the landlord a friendly pat on the back, but Stanley panics and jumps away to avoid being touched by a gay man; another time, Stanley comes to the apartment and finds Jack by himself, so he insists that the gay man keep the door open—the paranoid landlord is afraid of being attacked.[27]

On some occasions, the program consciously broke gay stereotypes. In the second episode, the roommates decide to redecorate their apartment, so Stanley immediately assumes that Jack is in charge of the project. "No, actually not all of us are interior decorators," Jack counters, lowering his voice and adding, "Some of us are boxers." The narrow-minded landlord is stunned, saying, "You'd actually hit another guy?" Jack then moves directly in front of Stanley, cracks his knuckles within inches of the landlord's face, and says firmly, "Only if he makes fun of us." Stanley cringes with fear and runs out of the apartment. In another segment, when a muscle-bound jerk gives Chrissy a hard time, Jack courageously stands up to the guy. Even though the unwanted suitor towers over Jack by six inches and outweighs him by fifty pounds, Chrissy's protector persists until the guy finally backs off.[28]

Actor John Ritter was given considerable leeway in developing his pseudo-gay character. "I didn't want to be a stereotypical lisping, fluttering thing," the actor later said. "I had gay friends who didn't like the stereotype, and I didn't like it either." The executives who were responsible for putting the sitcom on the air had not intended to change how the public viewed homosexuality, but, thanks to Ritter, the program gave millions of viewers an appealing model of how a gay—or a faux-gay—man could look and behave.[29]

Sex Triumphs

By 1980, the war between the Rev. Donald Wildmon and *Three's Company* had been raging for three years. There was no question that the TV show was winning, as the sexy comedy was riding high as the number one program in the country. ABC was further capitalizing on the program's pop-

ularity by airing reruns of the show as part of its daytime lineup, with fans being able to watch eleven different episodes in a single week.

The precise moment when the show was declared the victor may have come when *Newsweek* joined the long list of magazines that placed the stars of the blockbuster program on its cover. The widely respected news weekly did not merely reproduce a mundane group shot of the country's most popular threesome but created an image that was highly titillating in its own right. Suzanne Somers dominated the photo, as she was dressed in—indeed, almost *out of*—a baby blue satin negligee with one strap falling off her voluptuous shoulder to reveal so much cleavage that her right nipple seemed to be on the brink of slipping into full view. The other two stars were in the background, John Ritter leering at his costar's breasts and Joyce DeWitt seeming very much like a third wheel. Emblazoned across the cover was the headline "Sex and TV," and the story inside crowned "dishy Chrissy" the world of television's "most dazzling celestial body" and the undisputed "Queen of Jiggly." *Newsweek*'s editorial stand on the issue of sex on TV was clear not only from the provocative cover image but also from the article's text: "Only incurable prudes would insist that a medium purporting to portray the human condition should draw a curtain over so integral a part of human activity."[30]

During the decades that have passed since *Three's Company* originally aired, numerous scholars have studied the program. One dubbed it the model for giving viewers "titillation in a completely undemanding form," and a second attributed its remarkable popularity "not so much to clever writing or skilled acting but to how Chrissy Snow looked wrapped in a towel or dolled up in a tight top and shorts." A scholar who wrote an entire book about the series concluded that it was one of the most culturally important programs in the history of the medium; more than any other show, the author stated, the fun-loving farce reflected the era's Sexual Revolution and "opened the door for sexier TV."[31]

In addition to its broad significance, the pioneering program also sent a number of specific sexual messages, about individuals as well as relationships, into the American living room. It is impossible to know how much impact those statements ultimately had on television viewers, but the popularity of the program, both in its original form and through the

reruns that have continued to air for more than three decades, suggests that it has been an influential cultural force. Indeed, in 2003 the show still had so many fans that the first season's episodes were released on their own DVD.

Among the several statements that revolve around individual characters, the most blatant involves women as sex objects. For the program clearly joined its predecessors such as *Playboy* and the James Bond films in transforming the female form, particularly that of Suzanne Somers, into an item to be ogled by male viewers. The show's male producers enhanced the objectifying by dressing Chrissy in revealing and tight-fitting outfits and by creating scenes that featured her doing a whole lot of jiggling. The character being portrayed as something less than the sharpest crayon in the box, through the innumerable double entendres that revealed her naïveté, also reinforced the unflattering stereotype of the "dumb blonde" as being so intellectually inferior that her main function in life is to be an object of male sexual desire.

Two other characters who communicate a regrettable message are Helen and Stanley Roper. Their activities in the bedroom are portrayed not only as nonexistent but as a source of continuous frustration for the sex-starved Helen and a subject of unremitting tension in their marriage, which was defined by constant sniping. The ongoing gag produces plenty of laughs, but it also communicates that men and women who age beyond the hormone-rich twenties had best prepare themselves for a life devoid of sexual fulfillment.

The central character in the program, by contrast, sends a much more commendable message. Jack is pivotal to the series as a whole as well as to every plotline, and therefore he fills the role of this particular media product's primary sexual provocateur. And so, John Ritter, both on screen and off, joined Phil Donahue as an example of a Sensitive Man. He liked women and certainly enjoyed physical relationships with them, but when Chrissy and Janet said "No" to his advances, he accepted their decision and was more than willing to get to know them on an emotional level. Indeed, the Jack Tripper character's softness and non-threatening nature were absolutely critical to the program's success, as well as to its impact on the American culture. Not many parents would be eager, in the 1970s

or today, for their virginal daughter to sleep night after night in the bedroom next to Hugh Hefner or Jim Morrison.

Jack also sent positive messages regarding homosexuality. Although the character was not gay, at the time he was as close to it as television executives were willing to show. So he ultimately introduced the viewing public to any number of traits that have continued to be associated with many of the gay characters that have come after him. He was a good cook. He was attractive and physically fit. He was witty and a good conversationalist. He was well liked by everyone except the most foolish of homophobes.

With regard to the sexual messages involving relationships, the most salient one communicated by the ABC hit series was one that did *not* involve sex. In short: Yes, young people of different genders most certainly can live under the same roof without becoming sexually involved with each other. Although it is impossible to know how many young women during the last three decades have uttered one particular sentence when suggesting to their parents that they want to share an apartment with a male roommate, the number must be legion: "The guy's a lot like Jack Tripper."

A second statement about sexual relationships communicated by *Three's Company*, however, is more problematic. The show portrayed Jack in a highly positive light, even though he had innumerable romantic relationships that extended into the bedroom—though none of them seemed to extend beyond a single episode. Throughout the eight-year lifespan of the program, however, Chrissy and Janet both remained virgins. In other words, the series broke new ground vis-à-vis sexual content in many regards, but it perpetuated the sexual double standard that fully condoned sexual promiscuity by single men but frowned on such activity by single women.

Movies of the 1980s

Erasing Sexual Taboos

BEFORE THE STATUESQUE BEAUTY IN THE LOW-CUT EVENING GOWN EVEN removes her mink coat, she has already caught the eye of the handsome young Naval officer who has also just arrived at the Washington, D.C., hotel where an Inaugural Ball is taking place. They have a quick drink and exchange a few lines of flirtatious banter before he suggests, "Let's get out of here." Her initial expression is one of concern, "My date's not going to like that very much." But then she smiles and adds, "But, what the Hell, his wife will be delighted." The setting quickly shifts to the back seat of a limousine. After a kiss or two, she unzips his trousers while he deftly removes her dress to reveal a black bra and lacy garter belt; by the end of the scene, she has also bared her breasts and her buttocks. The driver, meanwhile, cruises past the various sights in the nation's capital— the Washington Monument looking particularly tall and erect. Only in post-coital conversation does the officer introduce himself, "My name is Tom," and she replies, "I'm Susan."

As demonstrated by this steamy sex-at-first-sight segment from the 1987 film *No Way Out*, the carnal content of American movies had escalated dramatically in the two decades since James Bond had begun his on-screen sexual conquests. More than one randy hunk was now adding notches to his belt to keep track of the number of beautiful women he had bedded, and many leading actresses were baring their bodies for anyone willing to buy a ticket. The level of explicitness had risen as well, with films showing men pulling off their Jockey shorts and women sliding out

of their panties to engage in sex acts that extended well beyond the missionary position. In the words of one reviewer, "Virtually all taboos are now taboo."[1]

Observers suggested that the plots had grown more risqué and the images more titillating because the motion picture industry was taking advantage of what a *Time* cover story labeled "the current mood of sexual malaise." In other words, with the cases of AIDS and sexually transmitted diseases soaring to epidemic proportions, casual sex had been transformed into a potentially deadly game of Russian roulette. So the movie industry responded by showing people that it was much safer to play out their libidinous fantasies by watching a film than by taking their chances in real-life encounters. "Sleeping arrangements are seen as a matter of life and death," the news magazine reported. "Folks on dates don't know whether to cross their legs or their fingers. 'So, dear, what's playing at the Cineplex tonight?' Answer: a host of movies that exploit the itch and edginess in right-now relationships."[2]

From the taut dramas *No Way Out* and *Fatal Attraction* to the murder mysteries *Dressed to Kill* and *American Gigolo* to the blockbuster coming-of-age hit *Risky Business* and the soft-porn *9½ Weeks*, sex proliferated in mainstream movies as never before. Indeed, the original versions of these classic celluloid works—all of them rated R—not only pulled viewers into the theaters in record numbers during the 1980s but continue to attract millions of fans via cable television, video, and DVD in the twenty-first century.

As for the themes that dominated the decade's heavy-on-the-sex motion pictures, some were reminiscent of those that had appeared in the media during the 1960s and 1970s—such as marital infidelity and women's bodies being seen as objects. But when morphed onto the movie screen, the specific messages being sent about these familiar topics as well as several new ones—including male dominance, kinky sex, and the connection between sex and violence—felt strikingly fresh and enormously powerful.

These messages clearly had the potential to alter not only how the nation's moviegoers *viewed* sex but also what they actually *did* inside their bedrooms. "Parental lectures, dirty books and friends' tales—none of these compare to the sexual instruction provided on screen," *Mademoiselle*

magazine pointed out. "There's nowhere else we actually see other people making love—a subject of burning curiosity for everyone from adolescence on. In order to satisfy this natural curiosity, we become movie voyeurs, looking to films for lessons in love."[3]

Promoting the Double Standard Through Infidelity

Infidelity had been a recurring subject in the sex-oriented media for decades. Nothing so mundane as a marriage license had stood in the way of James Bond, and *Cosmo* had revisited the theme from a woman's perspective with articles such as "Creative Infidelity." But it was during the 1980s that Hollywood made being unfaithful a staple on the big screen, though with a clear message lurking just below the surface.[4]

In the suspense thriller *Dressed to Kill,* veteran actress Angie Dickinson plays a sophisticated denizen of New York City's Upper East Side who, in the blunt words of one reviewer, "cruises New York to get laid." On the particular day that is the focus of the film, she sends her husband to the office and her son to his private school before putting on her pearls and going to the Metropolitan Museum of Art for a taste of culture. She is soon distracted from the Monets and Bonnards, however, when she exchanges furtive glances with a stranger. The two then proceed to the bedroom of his apartment for some afternoon delight.[5]

Fatal Attraction, one of the most talked about films of the decade, revolves around another frisky Manhattanite with the sexual metabolism of Lady Chatterley. In this plotline, a book editor played by Glenn Close, in a Medusa tangle of blond hair, seduces a married business associate. "Across the restaurant dinner table," one reviewer wrote, "she seems so hungry for him that you can hear her stomach rumble." Michael Douglas plays the man who is perfectly willing to be her midnight snack, while his wife and daughter are out of town. Before the females in his family return to the city, the errant husband finds time to enjoy several sessions of hot sex with his passionate paramour. More than a one-night stand but less than an affair, the adulterous interlude is best characterized, in 1980s parlance, as an "affair-ette."[6]

In *No Way Out,* the lust is of the more sustained variety. The country's Secretary of Defense, played by Gene Hackman, epitomizes the Washington power player by having not only a dutiful wife living in a stately manse but also a youthful and voluptuous mistress, played by Sean Young, conveniently ensconced in her own townhouse. The man responsible for keeping America safe is happy to support his on-call lover so she can devote all her time to preparing for his impromptu visits—morning, noon, or night. Only when the mistress becomes romantically involved with the handsome Naval officer does the arrangement falter.[7]

Although the three instances of infidelity vary in their durations and other dynamics, they share one characteristic that ultimately communicates a clear message regarding marital disloyalty: All three women die. Slashed to a bloody end in *Dressed to Kill,* shot to death in *Fatal Attraction,* and sent flying over a second-story balcony in *No Way Out,* the female adulterers end their respective films no longer breathing—heavy or otherwise. By contrast, when the lights come up in the three theaters after the final scenes, the male sexual betrayers are still going strong. In short, according to the messages sent out by the male producers and directors who dominated the motion picture industry in the 1980s, the sexual double standard, like the philandering male characters, was alive and well.[8]

Using Women's Bodies as Objects

James Bond movies did their part to transform the female form into an ornament by featuring well-endowed actresses in glamorous evening gowns, skimpy swimsuits, and clinging bath towels. Films in the 1980s moved the process forward by removing those various cover-ups to expose the glories that lie beneath, while also finding other ways to suggest that women's bodies often function as mere objects for men to enjoy.[9]

The archetypal example of the female form being used for the erotic pleasure of male filmgoers unfolds in that memorable opening sequence from *No Way Out.* The Sean Young character flirtatiously bats her eyelashes at the Naval officer, played by Kevin Costner, and is as eager as he is to climb into the back seat of the limousine-cum-bedroom. A major difference between how the characters are treated in the sequence emerges,

however, when her body is shown entirely naked, while his remains fully covered. Indeed, viewers who are interested in seeing more of the handsome young Costner are denied so much as a glimpse of the chest that remains concealed under his uniform. As *American Film* magazine commented in 1989, "Male actors continue to keep their private parts strategically covered."[10]

The same gender distinction is made in *Dressed to Kill*. By the end of the first scene, the film's female lead has already exposed her entire body while she is standing naked in the shower. But the male lead, in this instance Michael Caine, remains fully clothed throughout the film. A significant difference with *Dressed to Kill*, however, is that viewers only *think* they are seeing Angie Dickinson's breasts, buttocks, and pubic area. In reality, the moviegoers are only looking at the head of the forty-nine-year-old actress; the anatomical features from the neck down are those of a shapely body double twenty years her junior.[11]

Celebrating Male Dominance

In keeping with the premium that Hollywood has always placed on entertaining its audience, the sexual scenes depicted on 1980s theater screens—as well as the actors and actresses doing the depicting—were generally a pleasure for ticket-holders to watch. Mixed in with the seductive dialogue and the titillating disrobing, however, was a highly disturbing theme. For at the same time that former B-movie actor Ronald Reagan was setting the nation's political agenda, motion pictures were promoting male dominance.[12]

9½ Weeks, one of the most erotic mainstream films in Hollywood history, set the standard. Indeed, critics who reviewed the film called it "smarmy" and "a sleazo movie," shocked that a major studio such as MGM would produce a film that could easily qualify as pornography. "*9½ Weeks* follows the classic porno structure: domineering male and submissive female seen in a variety of sequences with plenty of skin and sleaze," railed *Working Woman* magazine. The dominating ways of the male lead, played by Mickey Rourke, begin when he blindfolds the female lead, played by Kim Basinger, and rubs her face and neck with ice cubes.

His desire to control soon progresses to a series of degrading acts, such as him forcing her to crawl across the floor on all fours to collect the various large-denomination bills he has strewn in front of her. A reviewer had it right when she described the film as "supreme fantasy from a male point of view."[13]

In *No Way Out*, the mistress is the victim of the man's testosterone-driven acts. The nation's Secretary of Defense is perfectly willing to pay the bills to keep a woman half his age at his sexual disposal. But when she begins her hot-blooded affair with the young Naval officer, her lover demands to know, "Who were you with this weekend?" The kept woman tries to break out of her submissive role by talking back, saying, "Why worry? There's plenty left for you," referring to the sexual favors she provides. Gene Hackman's on-screen persona, growing angry, slaps her and again demands to know who she's sleeping with. She refuses to divulge the name, yelling, "He's not a pig like you!" The Hackman character then loses his temper and hits her so hard that she falls backward and crashes through the railing on the upstairs balcony, breaking her neck when she smashes against the floor on the lower level—and paying the supreme price for daring to challenge her lover's dominance.

The sexual roles are turned topsy-turvy in *American Gigolo*. This film was the first of its kind, as it showcases a man who makes his living from women clients who are willing to pay top dollar to spend the night with a suave and virile man who knows how to please the opposite sex. The handsome and physically toned Richard Gere plays the role, with one reviewer writing that he's so attractive "he could seduce a rock." Put another way, this male escort possesses such an abundance of qualifications for the job that he, unlike the typical female mistress, is beholden to no one. The gigolo lives and loves on his own terms, agreeing to have sex only with the women he chooses while rejecting the rest and also refusing to cross the gender line—"I don't do fags," he tells one would-be client. And so, while the Gere character offers moviegoers a type of man they have never seen before, he most definitely retains the familiar Hollywood characteristic of male dominance.[14]

Getting Kinky

During the 1980s, Hollywood took a huge step toward liberating the national libido by bringing, for the first time, a broad range of sexual activities to the motion picture screen. *Vogue* magazine put its well-manicured finger on the phenomenon when it observed, "In contemporary movies, every location has the potential to be an exotic boudoir."[15]

Again, 9 ½ *Weeks* was the benchmark film, with a typical review calling it "a virtual encyclopedia of mutual consent perversions." Reflecting a process that unfolds in many sadomasochistic relationships, Mickey Rourke begins with a playful scene in which he first blindfolds Kim Basinger and then feeds her a series of sweet foods such as cherries and strawberries until she blithely bites into any object he places in her mouth—then he slips in a hot pepper. Later scenes become increasingly uncomfortable for many viewers to watch. When the couple goes to a department store to shop for a new bed, he places her on a mattress and then tells her to "spread your legs for daddy," and late in the film she watches as he makes love to another woman.[16]

Scenes in *Fatal Attraction* also get kinky. Glenn Close and Michael Douglas are depicted as being so aroused on their first night together that they can't even make it into the bedroom; they end up humping madly on the kitchen counter as, in the words of one reviewer, "Dirty dishes clatter under her buttocks and tap water lubricates their lust." Another time, the unfaithful husband and his femme fatale burst into spontaneous sex while riding the elevator in her apartment building.[17]

Risky Business, the coming-of-age classic that captures teenage male fantasy as few movies before or since, includes some edgy sex as well. The main plotline revolves around how a teenager played by Tom Cruise—in his breakthrough role—and a prostitute played by Rebecca DeMornay transform his parents' suburban home into a highly lucrative brothel where several dozen of the boy's high school chums hook up with a bevy of the escort's fellow women of the night. To celebrate their success, she takes him on a commuter train ride he'll never forget; the steamy scene

has her unbuckling his jeans as he slips off her panties, the opening moves on the kind of carnal odyssey that millions of teenage boys dream about.[18]

Connecting Sex with Violence

In numerous 1980s films, the sexual activities involve physical violence. *Newsweek* reported the trend in a story headlined "Blood, Broads and Bucks," saying that the major studios were reaping huge profits by releasing one picture after another that mixed nudity and hot love scenes with equal parts of blood and gore—often including murder. The lead paragraph summarized the phenomenon by stating, "Sex and violence are the bottom line of the movie biz," and the rest of the piece described some of the blockbuster movies that fit the bill.[19]

Although the sex scenes in *Fatal Attraction* define the term "reckless," the monster hit's most memorable moments take place outside the bedroom—or, in this case, outside the kitchen and the elevator. The driving plotline in the film surfaces when, after their second night together, the Glenn Close character says she doesn't want to end the fling after a single weekend. When that message fails to get the response she wants, she turns into an unfaithful husband's worst nightmare. As the Michael Douglas character prepares to leave, she goes into the bathroom and slits her wrists. The bloody image that follows is only the first in a series of them because, as one reviewer succinctly put it, "the sex in *Fatal Attraction* is never far removed from violence." In later scenes, Close changes from temptress to terrorist. She douses her lover's car with acid, causes him tremendous anxiety by kidnapping his daughter for an afternoon, and boils the family's pet rabbit in a stew pot. The rogue husband and his betrayed wife ultimately join in the violence; his weapon of choice is a butcher knife, hers a revolver. By the end of the film, the casualties include one dead femme fatale, one severely damaged marriage, and millions of frightened moviegoers—one review quoted a woman from the Midwest as saying, "I haven't slept right since I saw it."[20]

Other movies that defined Hollywood in the 1980s mix sex and violence, too. *9½ Weeks* contains a series of scenes that a critic described as

showcasing "the borderline between pleasure and pain," including the sadistic male lead taking his female counterpart to a store and trying out a leather riding crop by snapping it within inches of her quivering body. In another sequence, Mickey Rourke becomes so angry with Kim Basinger that he—despite her protests—throws her onto the dining room table, rips off her clothes, and rapes her.[21]

In *Dressed to Kill,* a film that reviewers labeled Hollywood's definitive work on the connections between sex and violence, tools intended for shaving are so prominent that they deserve a mention in the credits. A glistening steel razor first appears in the opening shower scene, foreshadowing the much larger role a similar sharp-edged blade assumes when the female lead is slashed to death, only minutes after having committed adultery, by a faceless stranger. In between that first scene and her murder, she is also shown being physically assaulted from behind by another man. One reviewer commented that throughout the movie, "The violence is pervasive, always threatening to pounce."[22]

Glamorizing Prostitution

Some of the sexual elements in 1980s films—such as the rampant infidelity, nudity, and violence—are explicit, while others meander slightly below the surface. One of the less overt messages is a highly positive view of women and men who earn their livelihood as prostitutes.[23]

Dressed to Kill is unusual in that the best-known actress, Angie Dickinson, is killed early in the film, and then a second female lead emerges. It is with this other woman that the selling of flesh—instead of giving it away—enters the picture. Actress Nancy Allen's character, in her bright red lipstick and nail polish, is not as classy as the murdered adulteress, but viewers gradually come to see that this call girl has numerous qualities other than her looks that are to be admired. First she is shown successfully evading a gang of young hooligans who attempt to rape her while on the subway, next she reveals a highly developed understanding of the stock market, and finally she manages to outsmart the psychopathic psychiatrist who had his eye on her as his next victim. Indeed, by the end

of the movie, as one reviewer pointed out, "the hooker has been transformed into the heroine."[24]

The female lead in *Risky Business* is also a prostitute. In this instance, though, there is no hint of garish lipstick or nail polish. Indeed, the lissome Rebecca DeMornay—with her little-girl bangs, her soft blond hair cascading down her back, and the subtle touches of makeup that enhance her natural beauty—looks more like a fairy-tale princess than a hard-bitten hooker. Nor is it only her appearance that belies the stereotype. As the plot unfolds, DeMornay shows herself to be a clever entrepreneur who sees how she and Tom Cruise can join forces not only to orchestrate a magical evening for their respective friends but also to amass a small fortune. She is clearly no blond bimbo but, as *The New Yorker* magazine observed, both "sensuous" and "sharp."[25]

American Gigolo also looks at the world's oldest profession through decidedly rose-colored glasses, this time showing how a man who sells his body also can be a person worthy of admiration. Indeed, in the words of one reviewer, the film shows "the glamour of prostitution" by successfully making "a Lancelot out of a male whore" and thereby "eliciting both sympathy and respect for the hero." Before this breakthrough motion picture debuted in 1980, the male escort was seen as a greasy and sleazy ne'er-do-well who preyed on wealthy old women. Richard Gere's portrayal, however, shatters that stereotype by showing the new breed of American gigolo to be an Adonis with a slender physique. Most important of all, he prides himself on treating women well; as *The Nation* magazine put it, he "takes his profession seriously as a means of solace for those in need," which often means attractive young wives—the lovely Lauren Hutton stars as one of them—who find themselves trapped in loveless marriages. This gigolo works harder at making his clients feel good about themselves than most husbands do, constantly studying how each woman reacts to his repertoire of sexual techniques and then adapting his skills to her desires. Indeed, the only time that Gere's character encounters problems is when he refuses to physically abuse a client—a request made by the woman's husband.[26]

A Message Not Sent

Major motion pictures of the 1980s communicated a plethora of sexual messages. By celebrating not only casual sex but infidelity—at least for men—they were following in the footsteps of the media products of previous decades. In using women's bodies as sex objects, the films took a huge step—either forward or backward, depending on one's perspective—by uncovering the shapely physical assets of such leading actresses as Academy Award winners Glenn Close and Kim Basinger. On other topics, the decade's movies pushed the envelope in entirely new directions. Most notably, films celebrated men using their physical power to dominate women, showcased various forms of kinky sex, and made a firm connection between sex and violence. Close analysis indicates, in addition, that several films also glamorized prostitution.

With its depictions of these topics, the motion picture industry left other media venues "in the sexual dust," so to speak. TV programs such as *All in the Family, Donahue,* and *Three's Company* had moved the medium far beyond the sexually repressive days of *I Love Lucy* and *The Ed Sullivan Show,* but the small screen was nowhere close to showing the nudity that was such a memorable element in *No Way Out* or the scene from *Risky Business* that depicted public sex on a commuter train. Likewise, *Playboy* and *Cosmo* had crossed any number of libidinous thresholds, but neither magazine dealt with the kind of kinky sex acts that repeatedly occurred during *9½ Weeks* nor the violence that was so central to *Dressed to Kill.* Mainstream newspapers were even more restrictive regarding what sexual topics found space in their pages, with not even the most liberal-leaning journalistic voice reporting on cultural trends such as the emergence of a new kind of male hustler, as *American Gigolo* did, or the consequences of a one-night stand gone bad, as *Fatal Attraction* did.

On one carnal subject of enormous importance during the 1980s, however, Hollywood was silent. For even though the defining dynamic in the lives of sexually active Americans during the decade was the threat of AIDS and sexually transmitted diseases, the individuals responsible for the

content that appeared on theater screens across the country opted not to highlight either why or how sexually active men and women could protect themselves from this public health threat. The half dozen films that have been discussed in this chapter devoted many images and a large chunk of their viewing time to various types of sex—from teenage to extramarital, brutal to illicit, reckless to sadomasochistic. None of the movies, however, made any reference whatsoever to the very real threat of fatal sex or to the prudent path of safe sex. No character had to deal with the horrors of seeing a lesion forming on his calf or feeling a tiny crab crawling through her pubic hair. Not one of the couples swapped sexual résumés before hopping into bed, and not a single condom appeared on screen or merited so much as one line in any of the scripts. When one of Hollywood's hottest producers was asked why the industry was mum on the concept of protection, he responded that no filmmaker would be so foolish as to risk "destroying the moment" by having his star reach for a condom.[27]

The motion picture industry was selling sexual fantasy, not sexual reality.

American Advertising

Pitching with Prurience

THE TREND BEGAN WITH A MERE TEN WORDS. OR, TO BE MORE PRECISE, A nine-word question followed by a titillating one-word answer.

But, then again, the message was definitely not all in the words, as the accompanying image had at least as much impact—probably more.

That memorable TV visual showed a nubile young woman staring directly into the camera as her impressively long legs extended to what seemed like at least six feet. The viewer's eye struggled to decide exactly where to look—on the model's exquisite facial features *or* on the tangle of lustrous dark brown hair framing her face *or* on the blue jeans that clung so tight to her legs and thighs and crotch that they appeared to be painted on.

The teenage temptress smiled seductively as she softly murmured the words in a voice that, feminine but also a tad bit husky, was part innocent little girl and part woman of the world:

"You know what comes between me and my Calvins?"

The pause that followed continued for several seconds, but no one seeing the ad could possibly look away until the mesmerizing young beauty finally arched her eyebrows, lifted her chin, and parted her lusciously full lips as she defiantly answered her own question:

"Nothing."[1]

Actress and model Brooke Shields was a mere fifteen years old when she appeared in that historic 1980 television ad for Calvin Klein jeans that signaled that the world of advertising was crossing a new threshold.

"There is nothing new about using sex to sell," *Time* magazine reported. "What is new is the prurience of the pitch."[2]

Prurience indeed.

After that breakthrough TV commercial and its print counterpart in the country's leading magazines sold more high-priced jeans than even their creator had ever imagined possible, the men and women who hawked products and services to American consumers became obsessed with sexual messages. Calvin Klein was on the vanguard with a continuing series of eye-popping ads that shattered boundaries at a pace that the marketing world has never witnessed before or since.[3]

Not surprisingly, a variety of forces both inside and outside the media tried to halt Madison Avenue's fixation with ads aimed just a few inches below the potential buyer's waist—reminiscent of how the Rev. Donald Wildmon and his National Federation for Decency had attempted to put a stop to sex on television. The ABC, CBS, and NBC stations in New York City all banned the Brooke Shields ad, and an organization called Women Against Pornography denounced it as well. As with the assault on libidinous content in TV Land, however, the now familiar two-word adage *Sex Sells!* ultimately carried the day in Ad Land as well.[4]

And so, sexual content in advertising had, by the mid-1980s, been declared the hands-down winner, with an awestruck *Forbes* magazine saying, "What's amazing is what you can get away with now." The leading publishing voice of American business then went on to predict, "Over the next five years, there will be an even greater use of blatant sexual messages in advertising, because it's become part of our culture."[5]

Even journalists working for publications that focused on public affairs issues felt obliged to make note of the phenomenon. "The art form that probably affects and reflects our culture more than any other—advertising—has become amazingly raunchy," *The New Republic* reported. "Products as everyday as salami, chemicals, and pianos are being sold with a sexual explicitness once reserved for paying customers of soft-core pornography."[6]

The milestones in American advertising's progression into prurience can be traced throughout the 1980s. In the early years of the decade, the Brooke Shields TV commercial opened the door to a plethora of sexy ads

that featured female models exposing increasingly large expanses of skin. By 1983, male bodies had moved to center stage, initially to sell underwear but eventually to peddle a wide range of other products as well. And by the middle of the decade, the big story became an innovative movement toward ads being built around provocative images, with the products themselves often not even being pictured.

Selling Products by Selling Women

To the TV viewer and magazine reader of the twenty-first century, those ten words uttered in 1980 and their accompanying image may seem relatively mild. After all, while the jeans that Brooke Shields wore certainly were snug, her body was almost fully covered, only a few inches of her flat stomach being bared. And yet, a pantheon of publications from the *New York Times* to *Fortune* to *People* all agreed that the ad, rarely mentioned without adjectives such as "sexy" and "scandalous" being attached to it, propelled the marketing world full-tilt into the Sexual Revolution.[7]

The advertisement attracted controversy partly because of the model's "back-story." Three years before Shields posed in the jeans, she had shocked many a moviegoer by starring, at the tender age of twelve, as a prostitute in the film *Pretty Baby*. That the same young woman's alluring pose was now appearing on TV screens and in magazine spreads—and while she was still under the age of consent—prompted critics to charge that she was being exploited and that the image was, as the *Washington Post* called it, "an above-ground representation of child pornography."[8]

The man who had designed the jeans added fuel to the fire. Calvin Klein, who has been credited with creating a casual yet chic style that lifted New York fashion onto a par with that of Paris, personally directed the television commercial and oversaw the print ads, labeling the campaign "The Feminist." Soon after it began airing, he appeared on *Donahue* and defended his new approach to selling jeans. "What do people want me to do," he asked, "show my clothes on a clothesline? They're to be worn on the human body, so I'm going to put them on the most beautiful body I can find. People want to see beautiful shapes, bodies, clothes—and new and exciting ways of showing these things." Klein concluded his com-

ments with his most salient observation about his jeans: "The tighter they are, the better they sell."[9]

And no one could deny that the guy was selling a lot of denim. The year before the ad appeared, sales of Calvin Klein jeans had totaled $65 million; the year after the ad appeared, that figure had soared to $200 million.[10]

With those numbers, it came as no surprise that other companies soon jumped on the sexual bandwagon. A Maidenform ad showed an attractive female model posing as a doctor. Her hair was pulled back primly and she held a medical chart in her left hand, a pen in her right. But the most notable feature was that this particular woman had broken with tradition and, instead of wearing a white doctor's coat, was standing in the hospital corridor dressed in a matching set of lacy, magenta-colored bra and panties. The eye-catching image unleashed a torrent of criticism, beginning with a formal condemnation from the American Medical Women's Association. Jean Kilbourne, an author and lecturer, joined in, charging that "It's out of the question that an advertiser would show a male doctor like that." Although the model was being portrayed as a highly educated professional, Kilbourne continued, "Underneath, she is still a sex object." One of the country's leading syndicated newspaper columnists was also outraged by the ad. "We are plunging into the 'successful woman as sex object' syndrome," Ellen Goodman wrote. "The doctor is ordered to strip, literally, her professional cover. She is revealed to be just another woman insecure about her femininity, just another woman in search of sex appeal."[11]

Women's bodies and accompanying sexual innuendo were soon being used to sell items ranging far beyond jeans and lingerie. A Citibank ad featured a woman who had used the company's travelers' checks to find her way to a Japanese bathhouse where she sat in a steamy swimming pool with a gaggle of admiring men ogling her shapely body. Even the California Avocado Commission embraced the shift to pitching prurience, creating an entire marketing campaign to rename its product the "green love fruit"; in the flagship ad, a voluptuous blond model was sprawled across two pages of recipes, with the headline asking in bold letters: "Would this body lie to you?"[12]

Men Become Sex Objects

By 1983, Madison Avenue was crossing another sexual threshold, with Calvin Klein again the provocateur. Having made a fortune of Midas proportions by flogging designer jeans, Klein now set his sights on doing the same with men's underwear. A new ad campaign with a strong erotic undertone would, as with his earlier triumph, be a major element in his formula for success, but this time the icon-in-the-making would not be a young woman but a young man.

In addition to the change in gender, the other major factor that was different with this second marketing campaign was that the model's name would never become as widely known as that of Brooke Shields (for the record, he was Olympic pole vaulter Tom Hintnaus), but at least three other elements would again return in full force: The image would spark a new trend in sex-oriented advertising. The image would garner Klein another mother lode of sales. The image would be absolutely *stunning*.[13]

"Underwear Man," as he soon became known, was lying stretched out on his back as if he were, in the lingo of the era, "catchin' some rays." This clearly was not the model's first venture into the fine art of sunbathing, however, as his well-defined chest, his muscular arms and legs, his flat stomach, and his flawless facial features were all tanned to bronze perfection. Noteworthy as well was the fact that his dark hair was confined to the top of his head; when observers of cultural trends identified when and why the epitome of male virility shifted from the furry chest such as that of James Bond in the 1960s to the hairless torso that had become the ideal by the end of the century, they pointed to Underwear Man as the trendsetter.[14]

And yet, despite the exposed parts of the model's body, the anatomical feature that dominated the viewer's attention was the one concealed under the bright-white, 100-percent-cotton briefs that covered his genitalia. For just below the double-thick patch at the center of his crotch, the viewer could see, was a 1980s version of the same organ that had gotten Jim Morrison into so much trouble when he had exposed it, or had pretended to, a decade earlier. The Underwear Man, though, had the good

sense to keep his penis inside his shorts where it would remain a mystery, leaving his millions of admirers to speculate just exactly what the model, behind those gently closed eyes, was dreaming about to cause his male member to push hard against that soft cotton shield.[15]

The *Washington Post* published the definitive article on the cultural importance of the ad. "The Calvin Klein Underwear Man is the dominant sexual icon in modern-day America," Tom Shales declared in an article on the front page of the newspaper's Style section. The Pulitzer Prize–winning media critic went on to report that everyone was talking about the larger-than-life image that was not only being published as an ad in the nation's leading magazines and appearing at bus stops from coast to coast, but—most noteworthy of all—was dominating Times Square on the multistory billboard that loomed at the busiest intersection in the entire country.[16]

Shales didn't stop at pointing out that the ad was causing Midtown traffic jams, however, as he went on to place the ad at the forefront of the newest advertising trend. "It's a pecs-and-biceps world now," he wrote. "Flashing the flesh is an old Madison Avenue tradition, but it's a new development for men to find out what it is like to have *their* flesh flashed." Shales ended his piece with the comment, "Women are becoming the voyeurs, men the voyeurees."[17]

Another body that lots of women were looking at was that of Jim Palmer. In the early 1980s, the handsome star pitcher for the Baltimore Orioles stripped off his uniform to become a model for Jockey. As a widely respected athlete who was willing to show fans that he wore red or blue briefs, Palmer played a major role in telling the world that men's cotton undershorts could continue to serve their traditional utilitarian function while also making a fashion statement. As a Jockey vice president put it, "Men's underwear, like fancy ladies' lingerie, is a very sensitive subject. When Jim Palmer, an all-American hero, appears in our colored briefs, he's telling consumers that it's all right to wear them."[18]

The fact that Underwear Man and a hunky athlete dressed only in his bare essentials had become sexy male models prompted many people to ask exactly whose pulse the companies were trying to quicken. Executives for Calvin Klein and Jockey both assured the questioners that they were

aiming for the women who bought 70 percent of all men's underwear, but many people still believed that a second target audience was gay men, who were increasingly becoming major buyers of designer fashion.[19]

Regardless of exactly who was looking at them, partially nude men were soon being used to sell a wide range of products. Magazine and newspaper ads included a series of bare-chested beefcake models pitching Listerine mouthwash, and a muscle-bound man clad in little more than shaving cream became the marketing symbol for Swatch watches. Among the TV commercials, one for Wild Musk cologne focused on a slender young man wearing nothing but a loincloth, and another featured a naked-to-the-waist man lathering himself in a shower to advertise Liquid Drano. Ubiquitous ads for Soloflex bodybuilding equipment featured brawny weight lifters flexing their impressive muscles next to the headline "A hard man is good to find"; *Time* quoted the founder of Soloflex as saying that in the new advertising milieu, "There's no way I can sell the product without selling sex."[20]

Image Advertising: From Romantic to Provocative

In 1985, Calvin Klein decided to conquer yet another commercial niche by introducing two new brands of cologne, one for men and one for women. When he named the new fragrance line Obsession, there was no question that the accompanying ad campaign would be memorable. And yet even the most prescient of observers did not anticipate that Klein's new marketing strategy would change the face of American advertising. For this time, the father of the prurient pitch went beyond creating advertisements in which he had female and male models remove their clothes—he also removed the product.

Some of the images in the campaign showcased couples in romantic scenes. One had a shirtless man and a partially nude woman in bed together with him on top of her (the copy read "fragrance for men") and another had the models switch places so the woman was on top of the man (the copy read "fragrance for women"); both were black-and-white ads with the models shot from behind so neither face was visible. But the most striking of the ads was one featuring three completely nude cou-

ples—two of them of mixed genders, and the other composed of two men—posing their perfect bodies around a huge white obelisk that towered above them, all of the models positioned so their flawless physiques were fully visible but their genitals were not. Advertising experts had various interpretations about exactly what message the ads were trying to communicate—one saying the bodies on the perfectly sculpted men and women were paeans to the recent health and fitness craze, another arguing that the obelisk was a phallic symbol and the models were in the preliminary stages of an orgy—but everyone agreed that one distinctive characteristic of all three of the ads was startling: None of them included a cologne bottle.[21]

The campaign created such a buzz in the advertising world that it became a major news story. *Newsweek* reported that the ads signaled a whole new approach to marketing and then quoted Calvin Klein talking about his strategy: "The ads are meant to be ambiguous—to make people stop and think. I don't want women flipping through 600 pages of *Vogue* and not even pausing at my ads." The *New York Times,* in its coverage, coined the term "image advertising" to describe the innovation and then turned to Klein to explain it. "The intention is to create an image of my own," he said. "There are people who understand what I'm doing and people who don't. I don't have a problem with that at all. I'd have more of a problem if no one cared. Then I'd be really upset."[22]

The visionary designer wanted his ads to be, in two words, *noticed* and *remembered.*

Klein sought to make sure, first and foremost, that anyone who was thumbing through the pages of a magazine would stop and look at his ads. Sometimes the image was romantic; other times it could best be described as provocative. But never, ever, *ever* did Klein want to create an image that a consumer could ignore. And even though this new genre of advertisement did not contain a specific product from the company, it always included the words "Calvin Klein" as well as an image that the public gradually came to identify—or, in a phrase that was just beginning to enter the language, "to brand"—as unique to this one particular designer.

Some journalistic voices turned to academics to articulate the concept. "The aim is first to generate attention. How you do it doesn't matter," a

New York University business professor was quoted as saying. "Research suggests that, over time, people separate the source of the material from the content of the message so all you recall, in the end, is the label."[23]

Newsweek may have done the best job of translating the concept into the succinct and straightforward terms of journalism when it wrote: "The strategy is that, while the consumer studies the picture, the designer's name melts into the brain."[24]

And a big part of the message that was melting in was sexual. In the two ads featuring the man and woman in bed, both models were showing plenty of skin; in the ad built around the obelisk, all six models were nude. "Klein's the creative leader of the new eroticism in ads," said the vice president of one of the country's top ad agencies. "He makes the public think about sex and their own sexuality."[25]

Like Klein's previous pioneering techniques, this one was doing its job. In early 1986, *Adweek* magazine reported that the ad featuring the obelisk and six naked models—but no cologne bottle—was the year's most successful advertisement. A month later, Klein announced that Obsession was producing annual sales of $150 million, making its marketing campaign the most successful in the history of the fragrance industry.[26]

As during the two earlier phases of pitching prurience, the success of Calvin Klein's groundbreaking approach spawned a host of imitators. Guess? was the first, promoting its line of designer jeans with a series of sexy ads, each showcasing a voluptuous model wearing a low-cut dress or bikini or tight hotpants—but never jeans. Numerous other major companies soon followed suit; the *New York Times* reported, "Ralph Lauren, Candies, Donna Karan and others all sell images first and specific products second, if at all. Their ads often trade on sex."[27]

A Clear Past, An Uncertain Future

During the 1980s, American advertising had traveled, thanks to Calvin Klein, along a clear continuum. First, the highly suggestive between-me-and-my-Calvins ad and its accompanying image prompted a multitude of advertisers to transform women's bodies into sex objects. Next, the nearly naked Underwear Man led a stampede of men's bodies onto the auction

block as well. And then came the intriguing trend of image advertising that was aimed at causing consumers, whether being shown a romantic scene or a provocative one, to stop and take a look—and then go fill their shopping bags.

But while the route that advertising had followed regarding sexual content was unequivocal, whether the various developments were positive was open to debate.

In the eyes of many critics, "The Feminist" ad campaign violated—at least figuratively—the age of consent. Brooke Shields may have looked like a woman of the world, but the whole country knew, thanks to a glut of newspaper and magazine articles, that the model who was posing so seductively was a mere fifteen years of age. Indeed, many observers suggested that Calvin Klein had chosen the nubile beauty to wear his skintight jeans at least partially because of the controversy that he knew her underage status would provoke.

With the Underwear Man, the model's age wasn't at issue, but his gender most definitely was. More precisely, opinions were split as to whether the well-defined male body becoming a sex object was a positive or a negative development for either feminism or humankind writ large. Some saw the new focus on objectifying men as a sign that the male/female playing field was finally being leveled; others argued that this development meant that the act of transforming a human being into an object no longer afflicted half the population, but all of it.

Image advertising had its disquieting aspects as well. During the early stages of pitching with prurience, the individuals who created ads had found ways to present their product while also sending suggestive sexual messages. Now that the product itself was no longer being pictured, observers asked, would that mean that the sexual content would have to be amplified in order for advertisers to succeed in persuading the casual magazine reader to stop, to notice, and to remember their ad? In other words: Would it no longer be sufficient for an image to be provocative, but would it now have to be *shocking?*

Regardless of exactly where high-voltage advertising would go next, everyone agreed that one man, more than any other, deserved the credit—or the blame—for leading the parade. As *Newsweek* magazine put it, "No

one understands the Madison Avenue dictum that 'sex sells' better than Calvin Klein," while the *Los Angeles Times* made the same point by dubbing Klein "the king of the sexual sell." This one designer had not only pioneered the influential concepts that later had been adopted by the larger advertising world, but he also had built an empire with annual revenues that had, in a single decade, mushroomed from a respectable $65 million to an astonishing $1 billion.[28]

Because of the degree to which the threat of AIDS and sexually transmitted diseases dominated the nation's sex life in the 1980s, it is relevant to ask how the advertising world was dealing with safe sex. The short answer: It wasn't. The issue created headlines late in the decade when Planned Parenthood challenged the long-standing ban on condoms being advertised on television; the organization accused the networks of "sending a dangerous double message" by running hundreds of commercials that promoted sexual activity but refusing to air any ads that promoted the use of protection from pregnancy and disease. ABC, CBS, and NBC responded, according to the *Los Angeles Times,* that "'They have no intention of altering their ban on commercials for contraceptives." Their justification for that decision, the *Times* continued, was that condom use "touched on moral, religious and political sensitivities" that were too complex to be addressed in the short format of a TV ad. A critical observer of the American media might suggest that the more honest answer was that the advertising world had joined Hollywood films in the business of selling sexual fantasy rather than sexual reality.[29]

Madonna

Tackling Sexual Issues Through Music

MEDIA PRODUCTS OF THE 1980S DEALT WITH SOME HIGHLY CONTENTIOUS topics related to the national libido. Films showed more and more nudity while also depicting the disquieting relationship between sex and violence; advertising reflected the trend toward both underage girls and adult men being used as sex objects. But neither of these media genres confronted two subjects that, although they dominated the minds of huge numbers of sexually active men and women, clearly had been deemed too hot to handle: AIDS and abortion.

Acquired Immune Deficiency Syndrome, in the course of the decade, claimed the lives of more than 100,000 Americans but was considered "too much of a downer" for the entertainment world, and the pro-life/pro-choice debate raged with such emotional intensity that media executives feared any mention whatsoever of the topic would guarantee alienating a critical mass of their audience. And so it was left to one individual not only to touch upon these two incendiary issues but to embrace them with uninhibited passion.[1]

From the moment that Madonna burst onto the nation's radar screen in the mid-1980s, she did everything in her power to shock the public, and her efforts paid off in spades. *Newsweek* called her a "tarted-up floozy," *Rolling Stone* said, "What Madonna is really about is sex," and the *Village Voice* accused her of being "imperiously trampy—just walking down the street she seems X-rated."[2]

But while her various statements, whether in the form of words or action, were clearly designed to stir controversy and attract attention, that was not their only purpose. For underpinning every startling set of lyrics, revealing outfit, and head-turning image, whether on stage or in a music video, loomed a substantive message about a sexual topic. "I'm not the best singer or dancer in the world, I know that," said the music-industry powerhouse. "But I'm not interested in that either. I'm interested in pushing buttons."[3]

The first button that the blond bombshell chose to push involved the sexual repression of the Catholic Church. She next set out to educate millions of young people about the dangers of AIDS. And then came explosive statements on abortion, which outraged not the conservatives who previously had condemned her but the liberals who, before this time, had been her allies. The reigning Queen of Pop thrived on the criticism and continued, throughout the decade, to reiterate the most fundamental of her issues by consistently celebrating women's sexual power.

Emergence of a Sex Symbol

Madonna Louise Ciccone was born in 1958 in Bay City, Michigan, to Silvio Ciccone, who worked as an engineer for Chrysler, and his stay-at-home wife, Madonna. A highly traumatic event in the little girl's life came at the age of five when her mother, a loving woman who was devoted to her children, died of breast cancer. Young Madonna, like her seven siblings, attended Catholic schools and was urged to adopt the beliefs of the church as her own.[4]

During high school, Madonna emerged as both an excellent student and a talented dancer, a combination that won her a performing arts scholarship to the University of Michigan. Academe was too confining for the free-spirited young woman, however, and so, after a year, she dropped out of school and headed for the bright lights of New York City. Silvio Ciccone was not happy about his nineteen-year-old daughter giving up her scholarship; he made it clear to her that, when she left Michigan in 1978, she was on her own.

Martin Burgoyne changed that. The gay designer was, like Madonna, still in his teens when he arrived in the Big Apple with an abundance of talent but an absence of financial resources. So the high-energy twosome pooled their meager incomes—his from bartending, hers from checking hats at a nightclub—to rent a small apartment on Manhattan's tough Lower East Side. At night, they both lived in the sexual fast lane, sleeping with any number of men, while during daytime hours they each pursued the elusive "big break."

Madonna initially focused on ballet, connecting with the prestigious choreographer Alvin Ailey. After a year or so, though, the five-foot-four-inch dancer decided that the road to stardom by way of tights and toe shoes was longer than the one she had in mind. "I wasn't willing to wait five years for a break," she would later tell *Teen* magazine. For a time, she dabbled in movies by starring in a low-budget film about a dominatrix, and next she took off her clothes to pose as a model for artists—years later, the photos surfaced in *Playboy* and *Penthouse*.[5]

It was also during her early years in New York that Madonna suffered several setbacks in her personal life that she has mentioned in interviews but has refused to discuss at length. One incident involved sexual assault. "I have been raped," she has said, "and it is not an experience I would ever glamorize." When she's been asked to provide details about the attack, she has been evasive, saying only, "I was very young, very trusting of people." Her response to questions about abortion has been similar. The generally candid star has stated that she ended three pregnancies, but she's declined to give dates or specifics regarding the circumstances. She has only said that, on each painful occasion, she turned to her roommate for emotional comfort, bringing her and Martin Burgoyne even closer to each other.[6]

By 1980, Madonna's career aspirations had shifted to singing. Within a year, she was performing in small New York nightspots; by 1982, she had a recording contract; and a year after that, her debut album broke into the Top Ten.

Fate then played its hand, as the flaxen-haired sensation entered the entertainment world at the same moment that music videos did. After MTV was founded in 1981, no one mastered the new art form better than

Madonna. She began with her nightclub act but added generous portions of titillation and exhibitionism to create a provocative image that was both unique and compelling. Observers were soon dubbing her the country's most innovative music-video star, with *People* magazine going so far as to suggest that MTV should be renamed "The Madonna Show." When asked to describe her future plans, she announced with characteristic immodesty: "I want to rule the world!"[7]

Attacking the Catholic Church

Madonna's big break came in 1984 when she was chosen to perform on the first Video Music Awards program. She used the high-profile event not only to showcase her talent and promote the title track from her second album, "Like a Virgin"—which overnight shot to number one in the country—but also to launch her attack on the world's most powerful religion.

During an era when most female stars appeared on televised awards shows in floor-length evening gowns, Madonna stepped onto the stage wearing a knee-length white lace wedding dress—complete with a sexy corset and garter belt so she appeared to have transformed her underwear into outerwear. Her accessories were eye-popping as well, highlighted by several rosaries strung around her neck and lots and lots of crosses—including a large one hanging among the beads so that, as she writhed and gyrated, it bounced against her breasts.

With heavy makeup and tousled hair, she strutted her buff body with over-the-top attitude and defiance, her chin jutting upward and her chest pushing outward toward the audience. Observers later recalled that "she worked the stage like a panther in heat," crawling seductively on the floor and flirting with the TV cameras that were transmitting her image to her first international audience. Melissa Etheridge, a musician who is not easily shocked, later recalled her reaction to Madonna's performance: "I remember thinking, 'She's wearing a wedding dress, and she's rolling around on the floor. Oh, my God!' It was the most blatant sexual thing I've ever seen on television."[8]

A major part of the statement that the hard-bodied temptress was making about the Catholic Church came with the contradictions that were

embedded in her appearance, her performance style, and the words to the song. Especially unforgettable was the line about her feelings toward a new lover: "You make me feel like a virgin . . . touched for the very first time." So much as uttering the word "virgin" on television was shocking by the prevailing standards of the era, and the combination of painted face, exposed flesh, raunchy dance moves, and gaudy accessories on a young woman who supposedly was innocent to the ways of the world all suggested deceit and falsity—and most definitely an abundance of hypocrisy.[9]

Madonna's "Like a Virgin" video sent the same messages. The star brazenly poses along the canals of Venice, sometimes in a black lace top and tight miniskirt reminiscent of a prostitute and other times in a virginal wedding gown but with her pulsating breasts clearly visible through the lace bodice. She moves like a stripper, undulating and thrusting her body parts at the camera as she weaves her way through the various scenes strewn with carnival masks, a live lion, an anonymous male lover whose face is never visible—all of it mysterious and resolutely erotic.

The anti-Catholic statements that Madonna was making dominated the flood of critiques that followed in the wake of the MTV performance and video. "By wearing Catholic accoutrements, she was a walking billboard for The Fall From Grace," one review stated. "Her image was Catholic in its bounce between the two components of the great dichotomy in the Church: the Virgin (Mary, Mother of God) and the Whore (Mary Magdalene)." The comments kept flowing during her twenty-eight-city tour. "She is both the virginal bride, swathed in white, and the sexual huntress, barely clad in black lace. The mix is thought-provoking and intoxicating, and it has gotten the world talking about Madonna in religious terms."[10]

She also fueled this initial campaign by giving interviews in which she accused her church of being masochistic: "How many millions of Catholics are in therapy, just trying to get over the idea of Original Sin? Do you know what it's like to be told from the day you walk into school for the first time that you are a sinner, that you were born that way?" She often talked personally about the religion's negative impact on her own

psyche: "The church really screwed me up. It caused all kinds of problems, some I probably don't even know about."[11]

Even more inflammatory was her often-repeated statement about the religious icons that she had turned into stage props: "Crucifixes are sexy because there's a naked man on them." The Catholic schoolgirl had, in short, struck back at the church's sexual repression by taking crosses and crucifixes out of the sanctuary and transforming them into fashion accessories—a technique that other rebellious young performers soon mimicked.[12]

Her anti-Catholic campaign created a bonanza of publicity. During 1984 and 1985, sizzling images of the sexy star—often wearing little more than bra, panties, and rosaries—became ubiquitous in the nation's top magazines and newspapers. *Time* ran a "Madonna: Why She's Hot" cover story, *People* tagged her the Marilyn Monroe of the 1980s but with musical talent, and *Rolling Stone* applauded her "raw sex appeal" and "upfront eroticism" before going on to gush that "she's an unqualified success" and "her influence is becoming pervasive."[13]

Educating a Generation about AIDS

Madonna's second campaign was, like the one against the Catholic Church, propelled by her own life experience. Even more important, this particular crusade had an impact on millions of teenagers who, during the early 1980s, represented the bulk of her fans. Indeed, her actions and statements on this topic may well have saved the lives of an untold number of young people.

Madonna's rise to stardom coincided with AIDS becoming the deadliest sexually transmitted disease in history. She began performing in New York clubs in 1981; the first cases were reported in that city the same year. People became so frightened that they refused even to be in the same room with an AIDS patient, and an activity as intimate as kissing a person with the condition was absolutely unthinkable, as the medical community was still uncertain about whether the HIV virus could be spread through saliva.

It was in this climate of mass fear that Madonna's friend Martin Burgoyne told her that he was infected. From that moment in the summer of 1986 until he died late that year, she supported him both emotionally and financially. Even though the ambitious young singer was, during this crucial stage of her career, trying to make the leap from being a star to being a *super*star, she phoned her former roommate at least once a day and visited him several times a week—never hesitating to kiss him on the lips. She also took full responsibility for his expenses, providing more than $100,000 to cover his medical bills and paying the rent on the new apartment where she moved him so he could be closer to his doctor at St. Vincent's Hospital.[14]

Madonna's commitment soon shifted from the private support of a friend to the public role of a dedicated health educator. Her initial step was to become one of the first stars who was willing to talk with reporters about having a relationship with an AIDS patient. "I cried like a baby when Martin told me," one story quoted her as saying. "I still cry when I think about it." But, in her next breath, she went on to insist that—fear and stigma be damned—friends of AIDS patients should stand by them. "I'll stick by Martin no matter what happens," she said. "He was there for me when I needed him, and I'm here for him now that he needs me."[15]

Madonna's unflagging support was particularly challenging because of another man who was playing a major role in her life. She and Sean Penn met in February 1985 and became husband and wife a mere six months later. The marriage was plagued with a variety of problems, including the actor's moodiness and hot temper, and Madonna's commitment to Burgoyne added still more difficulties. "It's ironic that a gay guy has come between macho Sean and his sexy, feminine wife," one friend told a reporter. "It sickens him that Madonna wants to continue her friendship with a gay man who has AIDS." The singer herself was quoted as saying, "Sean is scared I might pick up the virus. He keeps insisting that it's possible because not that much is known about AIDS." She then concluded her quote with the kind of statement no husband wants to read in print: "I tell him to grow up."[16]

Madonna continued to support Burgoyne, even to the point that she purchased experimental drugs from Mexico for him. Her commitment never waned, and she was holding her friend's hand when he died in December 1986, at the age of twenty-three.[17]

In the wake of the death, Madonna focused on a second form of AIDS activism by encouraging her fans to be sexually responsible. One of the innovative features of her 1987 Who's That Girl tour was incorporating multimedia components into the productions in the form of gigantic video screens that towered over her. The most memorable message to flash on those multistory panels came in two dramatic words that no other musician had either the will or the courage to mention, much less communicate so dramatically: "SAFE SEX."[18]

She followed that special-effects extravaganza with other cautionary messages. On dozens of occasions, she gave concert audiences practical advice about avoiding the HIV virus by using condoms, saying—both whimsically and directly—"Hold on, don't be silly / Put a rubber on your willy!" During one Madison Square Garden fund-raising event, she talked emotionally about the disease that killed Martin Burgoyne. And the lyrics she wrote for the ballad "In This Life" expressed her continuing sadness from the loss of her young friend. "He was only twenty-three / Gone before he had his time," she began, then moving into the chorus, "In this life, I loved you most of all / Now you're gone and I have to ask myself / What for?"[19]

While Madonna increased AIDS awareness at a level of public prominence that was matched by only a handful of other celebrities, she also made enormous financial contributions to the effort to fight the disease. It is impossible to know exactly how much money the superstar contributed to the battle for a cure because many of her donations were anonymous, but even a conservative estimate placed the figure, by the end of the decade, at more than $5 million.[20]

Stirring Controversy on Abortion

Given Madonna's penchant for tackling sexual issues, it surprised no one that she soon weighed in on the most divisive topic of the day. But even

those observers who were intimately familiar with the Queen of Pop were taken aback by precisely what she had to say on the subject—and how successfully she rode the tide of controversy that she created.

The "Papa Don't Preach" video includes flashbacks showing a tiny blond girl sitting at the dinner table with her father and then Madonna as a teenager exchanging smiles with a handsome young auto mechanic wearing a leather jacket. The crucial moment in the video comes when the distraught young woman, after much hesitation, finally tells her father that she's pregnant. She also makes it clear that she is keeping the baby and staying with her boyfriend, even though she knows her father disapproves of him. In the chorus, she sings, "Papa don't preach, I'm in trouble deep / Papa don't preach, I've been losing sleep / But I made up my mind, I'm keeping my baby, oh / I'm gonna keep my baby." And in the various verses, the girl pleads with her father, saying, "I need your help" and "What I need right now is some good advice." The story has a happy ending, as the father ultimately opens his arms to his daughter, with the final scene showing them in a loving embrace.[21]

The video prompted a huge public outcry about what Madonna, widely acknowledged by this point as a powerful influence on American youth, was telling her fans to do, with *Newsweek* reporting that she had mothers across the country "wringing their hands." Planned Parenthood was particularly outraged. "The message is that getting pregnant is cool and having a baby is a good thing and don't listen to your parents, the school, anybody who tells you otherwise," protested the organization's spokesman. "The reality is that what Madonna is suggesting to teenagers is a path to permanent poverty."[22]

The most notable voice from the opposite camp was that of Tipper Gore, whose Parents Music Resource Center previously had lambasted the singer as an affront to decency; this time, though, the wife of Senator—soon to be Vice President—Al Gore had nothing but praise. "The song speaks to a serious subject with a sense of urgency and sensitivity," Tipper Gore gushed. "It also speaks to the fact that there's got to be more support and more communication in families about this problem. And anything that fosters that, I applaud." Many music critics agreed with Gore. One from the *Boston Phoenix* wrote, "'Papa Don't Preach' is Madonna's

finest three minutes, not merely because it addresses teen pregnancy but because it suggests that a portion of the blame rests on parents' reluctance to discuss, not lecture about, sex."[23]

The song provoked a firestorm mainly because observers interpreted its message—as Madonna undoubtedly knew they would—in dramatically different ways. Many people saw "Papa Don't Preach" as opposing abortion. This view became particularly widespread when Madonna sang the powerful words, during a concert tour, against a backdrop of huge images of the Pope and President Ronald Reagan hovering above her on video screens.[24]

In public statements, though, Madonna insisted she was reiterating the pro-choice stand she had always espoused—though her definition of "choice" was broader than that of many abortion rights advocates. In the words of one scholar who analyzed the singer's message, she was saying that a pregnant young woman should seek advice from others but that ultimately any decision about her body was hers and hers alone: "That papa she is telling not to preach is her dad, he is the Pope, he is God. The girl is telling them all that she is keeping her baby, which means she's not getting an abortion, but also that she's not breaking up with her boyfriend; the choice belongs to her as an autonomous woman who has the right to do what she wants with her own body, regardless of what any male might think, and regardless of her young age."[25]

Celebrating Women's Sexual Power

Madonna saying that a teenage girl should make her own decision regarding whether or not to have an abortion was very much in keeping with the larger message that, more than any other, dominated her work during the final years of the decade: Women are independent beings.

Through her own career, the savvy businesswoman was a model of female autonomy. She had emerged as one of the first female singers who not only succeeded in the industry but did so on her own terms—and to her own benefit. She wrote her own songs, produced her own albums, directed her own tours, and headed her own $30 million-a-year entertainment corporation. In the words of one scholar, "She was a successful,

controlling woman in what had, until her own emergence in the 1980s, been very much the man's world of the pop business."[26]

When translating the female independence theme to music, she consistently and vociferously placed her emphasis on women's sexual power. An early expression of the message came in her 1985 video "Material Girl." It begins with a movie producer becoming smitten with a young starlet as she performs a lavish dance sequence from the Marilyn Monroe film *Gentlemen Prefer Blondes*. As the voyeur watches the voluptuous beauty in her glamorous pink satin gown, he hears her say that she's not impressed by the expensive gifts that her handsome suitors use to entice her. Heeding her words, the filmmaker understands that the star is not, despite appearances, a gold digger but is actually a down-to-earth woman who is looking for more fundamental characteristics in a lover than she sees in the tuxedo-clad men who are fawning all over her. So he meets her outside the studio driving an old pickup truck and carrying a humble bouquet of daisies to show that he possesses the values that she is looking for in a man. In the final image, they are locked in a passionate kiss.[27]

Although on the surface the video appears to be a statement about the materialistic years when Ronald Reagan was president, it also speaks to women's sexual power. Madonna's character is totally in charge of the scene, rejecting the sycophant millionaires because she is an independent woman who not only knows what she wants but, by the end of the scene, succeeds in getting it. Helen Gurley Brown applauded both the message in "Material Girl" and the woman who sent it. "The thing I love about Madonna is that she loves men," *Cosmo*'s legendary editor said. "She has made them happy, and they have made her happy."[28]

Another of the musical icon's productions that promoted the same message, though in an entirely different way, was the 1986 video "Open Your Heart." This time, Madonna plays a peep-show stripper dressed in a skimpy black corset with cone-shaped breastplates and tassels. The admirers of the dominatrix-style performer are ensconced in a series of booths and include a grinning cowboy and a man who appears to be reassembling his clothes after having masturbated in response to the show. But when the stripper emerges from the theater, her body is covered in baggy clothes that obscure her shapely form, and she leaves behind the rogue

gallery of lust-driven adults and opts for an innocent young boy. After she chastely kisses the lad, they hold hands and go skipping off together like two free spirits in their own idyllic world.[29]

The words of the chorus—"Open your heart to me, baby / I hold the lock and you hold the key"—underscore that the woman's true desires are not what she pretends them to be while on the job. Again, Madonna is telling her fans to reject the artifice that dominates so much of the modern-day world and follow, instead, their genuine feelings that, in this instance, are represented by those of a pure and guileless young boy.[30]

It may be more than coincidental that Madonna's most blatant statements about female sexual power came in 1989, on the heels of her divorce from Sean Penn. In "Express Yourself," the singer encourages her female fans—who, by this point in her career, had expanded to include many feminists—to get what they need from a relationship and not to accept anything less. The lyrics begin, "Come on, girls / Do you believe in love? / 'Cause I got something to say about it." Words in later verses make similar points, "Express yourself / So you can respect yourself" and "You deserve the best in life / So if the time isn't right then move on / Second best is never enough / You'll do much better baby on your own."[31]

The visual images in the video provide a clear depiction of traditional sex roles—but in reverse. Madonna appears in an evening gown that speaks of femininity, but this woman is not just a shapely body but also a world-wise power figure who is single-handedly running a manufacturing plant supported by the sweat of a mass of toiling men. Her eye is drawn to a particularly handsome hunk among the anonymous workers who are completely subservient to her. Some critics called this the most erotic of the siren's videos because of a provocative bondage scene that shows her chained to a bed, her neck in a dog collar—her statement that sexual desire is not always consistent with conventional feminist parameters. A happy ending unfolds when the shirtless hunk enters the woman's bedroom, his tight trousers loosened in anticipation of the raw sex that clearly is about to follow.[32]

To reinforce the message in "Express Yourself" vis-à-vis women's power, Madonna made sure that reporters knew she had been totally in charge of the production, which had cost a stunning $2 million, and that

she had intended the video to make a statement. "Men have always been the aggressors sexually," she said. "Through time immemorial, they've always been in control. So sex is equated with power." But it was time for the roles to shift, she continued, and she was determined to push that process forward. "Plenty of people are getting my message," she boasted.[33]

Ruling the World

By the end of the 1980s, the music video's foremost impresario was, in the view of many observers, nearing the lofty goal that she had set for herself early in the decade; if she was not ruling the world, she was most certainly ruling the entertainment industry.

Time magazine dubbed her "the superstar sex goddess of the video generation" and applauded, in particular, her messages related to AIDS, teen pregnancy, and drugs—Madonna steadfastly avoided ingesting any substances stronger than herbal tea. Other publications had positive assessments of her as well, with *Rolling Stone* dubbing her "the world's most famous woman," the *Times of London* pointing to her as the only one of the ten richest women in the world who had earned the cash by herself, and *People* writing, "Just a good Catholic girl with a song in her heart, a crucifix around her neck and a jiggle in her bustier, Madonna Louise Ciccone has conquered the world with music, sex appeal and steamy videos."[34]

And there were plenty of numbers to support the assertions. With eighteen consecutive singles having soared to the top of the charts and all six of her albums selling more than one million copies, the college dropout had amassed a personal fortune that surpassed $200 million. What's more, there were no signs that either her success or her energy had peaked.[35]

Particularly noteworthy, in the context of the evolution of the relationship between sex and the media, was how the decade's most celebrated sex symbol compared to her predecessor from twenty years earlier. Jim Morrison and Madonna both used sex to their advantage as they rose to the pinnacle of the music world, including developing distinctive styles in

what they wore, in the lyrics they wrote, and in how they behaved both on and off stage. With regard to the differences between the two musical icons, the hard-driving Madonna was more versatile and more commercial. She didn't limit herself to making records and performing at concerts but also starred in films such as *Desperately Seeking Susan* and the Broadway play *Speed-the-Plow,* pioneered in the new art form of the music video, and choreographed and executed electrifying dance routines. She also earned $5 million by performing in a television ad for Pepsi and marketed more posters, T-shirts, jewelry, promotional magazines, and other memorabilia than any artist before her; the author of a book about sex in the twentieth century clearly had it right when he said "no one better than Madonna understands that sex sells."[36]

Another salient difference between Morrison and Madonna was that he was a he and she was a she. The Young Lion had broken new ground with regard to the synergy between sex and music during the late 1960s, opening the door for his female counterpart not merely to follow in his footsteps but to explode in new directions that he had never even imagined possible. *Newsweek* magazine reported on this aspect of the siren's success in 1985, first by characterizing rock music as "one of the most influential strongholds of knee-jerk misogyny" and then by praising Madonna's "sledge-hammer sexuality" for ushering in a new day.[37]

But, in the final analysis, the most important of all the distinctions between the two lust-inducing superstars was their life spans. Jim Morrison died at age twenty-seven; Madonna was still the music world's leading sexual provocateur as she moved into her mid-thirties. How could she have made any stronger statement about women's power—sexual or otherwise?

The Gay Nineties

Adam and Eve + Adam and Steve

THE HAND IS HISTORIC.

Magazine readers who were thumbing through the pages of *Vanity Fair* in September 1992 came upon a two-page advertisement featuring two slender young men who appear to be in their late teens. The highly attractive models are standing on a rooftop with numerous tall buildings behind them. The background is noticeably tilted, while the models and the words "Banana Republic," in the lower right-hand corner, and "free souls," in the upper right, are level. The most important element of the black-and-white ad, though, is not the background or the camera angle or the text—but the hand. For one of the men has the fingers and the palm of his right hand resting, gently and tenderly, on the chest of the other man.[1]

Scholars have identified the image as the first gay-themed ad to be published in a major American magazine.[2]

Beyond being historic in its own right, that hand also is significant because it was an early sign that the decade would become known as The Gay Nineties. During earlier years, homosexuality had occasionally played a role in the evolution of sex and the media—such as Jack Tripper pretending to be gay in *Three's Company* and some of Calvin Klein's sexually oriented ads appearing to have been aimed at potential gay male buyers. But it wasn't until the 1990s that both the quantity and the quality of gay content rose so dramatically that anyone looking at sex in the media could

no longer consider only male-female activities but in good conscience had to look at same-sex activities as well.[3]

In the world of advertising, Banana Republic was soon joined by other companies, Benetton and Abercrombie & Fitch among them, that began targeting well-heeled gay consumers. The blockbuster films *Philadelphia*, *The Birdcage*, and *My Best Friend's Wedding* also reflected the trend, as did the television programs *Ellen*, *Will & Grace*, and *The Real World*. The news media jumped on the bandwagon, too, by making the debate over gays in the military and the murders of Gianni Versace and Matthew Shepard major stories.

Considering the wide range of venues that gave prominence to gay content, the major themes that emerged from across the media spectrum were surprisingly consistent. For one, gay men were invited into the spotlight of public attention much more frequently than were lesbians. Other recurring themes reinforced many long-standing gay male stereotypes, while some new ones were also promoted. In addition, committed male-male relationships were showcased as never before, and media portraits of gay men often were highly flattering. The most important of the themes—one that ultimately saved an untold number of lives—was that the various media products communicated vital information about AIDS. At the same time, though, The Gay Nineties most definitely had their limitations, offering an example of progress that could rightly be described as two steps forward, one step back.

Spotlighting Gay Men, Sidelining Lesbians

Whether the particular media product under scrutiny was from the world of advertising, motion pictures, entertainment television, or journalism, the homosexual who moved into the spotlight during the decade could easily have been named Adam or Steve (or, for that matter, Tom or Dick or Harry)—but not Eve.[4]

After Banana Republic crossed the gay-content threshold with its 1992 "free souls" ad, other clothing companies soon followed. Benetton's contribution two years later was an image of a pair of twenty-something men

wearing brightly colored shirts, their arms intertwined in a cheek-to-cheek embrace that suggested a relationship that extended well beyond casual friendship. Abercrombie & Fitch joined the parade in 1996 by publishing an ad that featured two men, one middle-aged and one much younger, in various romantic poses aboard a sailboat; two years later the company crossed another line by publishing an image of several shirtless young men in a communal shower as they playfully tugged and pulled in their effort to remove the boxer shorts of another young man who was bent over with his butt already partially exposed—but who didn't seem to mind. None of the pioneering ads included images of lesbians.[5]

The motion picture industry was very much in sync with the explosion of gay content, releasing a stream of big-budget, big-star productions with plenty of gay content. The 1993 film *Philadelphia,* which tells the heart-wrenching story of a gay lawyer who sues his firm for firing him because he has AIDS, was not only a box-office success but also an Academy Award winner; Tom Hanks took home an Oscar for best actor and Bruce Springsteen won another for the song "The Streets of Philadelphia." Then in 1996 *The Birdcage* became an immediate comedy classic by telling the story of a flamboyant South Beach gay couple whose pastel tranquility is transformed into a laugh riot when their son's fiancée turns out to be the daughter of an ultraconservative member of the U.S. Senate; the cast was led by Academy Award winners Robin Williams and Gene Hackman. In 1997 *My Best Friend's Wedding* was another huge hit; it features Hollywood sweetheart Julia Roberts and openly gay heartthrob Rupert Everett in one of the most successful romantic comedies of the decade. None of the three films included a single lesbian.[6]

An even more dramatic illustration of the visibility of gay men versus gay women appeared in the medium of television. In April 1997, ABC aired a segment of its popular sitcom *Ellen* in which the main character, Ellen Morgan, announces that she's a lesbian at the same moment that actress Ellen DeGeneres acknowledged her real-life sexual orientation—including a *Time* cover that featured her photo next to the headline "Yep, I'm Gay!" The program was a TV milestone, as it marked the first time that a network featured a gay character in a leading role. But the euphoria was short-lived because, in the succinct words of one reviewer, "After

Ellen DeGeneres came out as a lesbian, her series began to lose viewers."
Accusations quickly arose that *Ellen* placed too much emphasis on homosexuality and thereby became "too gay," but the more accurate phrasing
should have been that it was "too lesbian," and the program was canceled
within a matter of months.[7]

The very next season, NBC followed in its competing network's footsteps by introducing another sitcom with a gay lead, but with two important distinctions: This character was a man rather than a woman, and he
was played by a straight actor rather than a gay one. *Will & Grace* was a
runaway success, becoming a stalwart on the network's must-see lineup
and, during the next several years, carrying home a wheelbarrow full of
Emmy Awards. While the sharp-witted program starred two gay men in
the ensemble cast and often featured others in supporting roles, lesbians
were virtually nonexistent.[8]

News coverage followed the same pattern. The decade's two biggest
spot news stories with significant gay angles were the murders of fashion
designer Gianni Versace in 1997 and college student Matthew Shepard in
1998—both men. Journalists also tended to turn to gay men when selecting sources for the most important ongoing story of the decade, the debate over gays in the military. When the CBS news magazine *60 Minutes*
took a comprehensive look at the failures of the "don't ask, don't tell" policy, correspondent Ed Bradley interviewed three military officials and described the case studies of two other soldiers who had been involved in
the issue; all five were men. Bradley and his producers had chosen to emphasize gay males even though anyone familiar with the history of homosexuals serving in the military knows that a large percentage of those
individuals have been and still are lesbians.[9]

Stereotyping: In with the Old, In with the New

By the 1990s, most Americans had come to associate certain characteristics with gay men. The myriad media products that appeared during the
decade reinforced many of these stereotypes, while at the same time offering up several qualities that painted a very different portrait of what it
meant to be gay and male at the end of the twentieth century.

Perhaps the trait that people had, for many years, most frequently connected to gay men was that they are effeminate; the Nathan Lane character in *The Birdcage* reflected this tendency, as he worked as a drag queen and dressed in women's clothes during much of the film. A second common stereotype was that gay men are promiscuous; Will's best gay friend on *Will & Grace* fit the bill on this topic, with one snippet of dialogue having Jack boast that he is an expert on dating because, "I go on literally thousands of dates per year," prompting Will to respond, "That doesn't make you an *expert*—that makes you an *escort*." A third common perception of gay men that the decade's media reinforced was that they are physically weak and vulnerable to abuse; the profiles of Matthew Shepard that appeared in the wake of his murder reinforced this impression, with a *Time* magazine cover story flatly stating that the twenty-year-old had "fit the gay stereotype" because he had been "short and slight" and "always the littlest kid" in his class.[10]

At the same time that gay-themed media were perpetuating these stereotypes, however, they also were showcasing another type of contemporary gay male. This new poster boy for Gay America is handsome and has a good body. He also is well educated and successful in his career, and he enjoys the best that money and good taste can buy when it comes to his home and wardrobe. Finally, he is so utterly charming, witty, and personable that he is relentlessly popular with women as well as men.

The Rupert Everett character in *My Best Friend's Wedding* defines this new stereotype, as he exhibits all of the traits on the list; one reviewer wrote that the film's most insightful line was, "All the best men are gay." Will on *Will & Grace* and the Tom Hanks character in *Philadelphia*, both successful lawyers, filled the role as well. In real life, profiles of Gianni Versace that appeared after his death showed that he, too, exhibited many of the qualities, as he was described as having been a successful fashion designer and as a man with exquisite taste who had enjoyed the finer things in life. A whole crop of new-gay-men-in-the-making appeared via the models—with their fine facial features and well-sculpted chests—in the ads for Banana Republic, Benetton, and Abercrombie & Fitch.[11]

Television's *Will & Grace* deserves special mention for its achievement in presenting the old and new stereotypes in a single program, showing

viewers two distinct images of gay men. Jack is promiscuous; Will dates only rarely. Jack has no consistent means of support; Will works at a prestigious Manhattan law firm. Jack is flighty, highly excitable, and over-the-top on the swishy scale; Will is so lacking in effeminate mannerisms that focus group members who previewed the pilot episode refused to believe that he was gay. In the words of one scholar, "Will is the 'straight-acting,' responsible gay character who balances out Jack's nellie fits and keeps gay media activists from screaming 'stereotype!' too loudly."[12]

Showcasing Committed Gay Relationships

Before the 1990s, the American media had provided consumers with precious few examples of same-sex relationships. On the rare occasions that two men had been portrayed as a couple, they had been depicted as conforming to the marriage model—one played the husband, the other played the wife. The explosion of gay-themed content at the end of the century, though, offered some strikingly different images of the bond that could exist between two men.

The male-male pairing in *The Birdcage* conforms to many of the stereotypes. Robin Williams plays the traditional husband; he is a successful nightclub owner, he calls the shots at home, and he wears the pants in the family. Nathan Lane fits just as snugly into the role of wife; he makes no business decisions, he dresses in women's clothes, and he consistently refers to himself as a woman.

But other details about the film's two male leads break—indeed *shatter*—the mold. One night some twenty years earlier, the Williams character had fathered a child and, when the mother abandoned the infant, the gay couple raised him. The film's main plotline revolves around the accommodations that the dad and the pseudo mom are willing to make for their son—the *Washington Post* described the Nathan Lane drag queen character trying to "act like a man" as one of the funniest moments in the history of film, comparing it to "an octopus trying to slip into a pair of slacks." The two gay men, in short, are portrayed as responsible and committed, having not only been faithful to each other for more than two decades but also being devoted to their son. At one point in the film, the

young man acknowledges the couple's stability, telling his rock-steady father, "I'm the only guy in my fraternity who doesn't come from a broken home." One reviewer dubbed *The Birdcage* "the loopiest, most hysterical family-values movie ever made."[13]

In *Philadelphia*, the conventional stereotype is nowhere to be seen, as the gay men are equals, neither subservient to the other. The stability of the relationship is severely tested by the Tom Hanks character's illness. His partner did not flee when AIDS entered their lives, however, as the film shows the Antonio Banderas character devoting huge quantities of time and energy to caring for his partner. That commitment is particularly commendable in light of the fact that the Hanks character became infected with HIV during a clandestine sexual encounter at a porn theater. What's more, the Hanks character continued to have sex with the Banderas character after the unsafe sexual liaison, thereby endangering his partner's life. These circumstances would have destroyed many relationships, whether gay or straight, but in *Philadelphia* the wronged partner remains stalwartly loyal even as the illness gradually overwhelms their lives.

In 1994, the challenge of sustaining a gay relationship during the era of AIDS moved from the movie screen to *The Real World*. The innovative MTV program brought seven young strangers together to share a household and have their every move videotaped, edited, and broadcast nationwide. A gay person had been included among the roommates during both of the show's first two seasons, but the circumstances moved to a whole new level in season three when HIV-positive Pedro Zamora joined the cast. The charismatic and handsome Cuban American—some observers said he had the longest eyelashes in TV history—was single when he moved to San Francisco to participate in the program, but by the third episode he was dating Sean Sasser, who also was infected with the virus. On week six, they declared their mutual love; by week nine, they were engaged.[14]

All of these developments were unprecedented, but those shown in episode nineteen were nothing short of extraordinary. During that segment, MTV introduced the program's two million viewers, most of them young people, to the concept of substantive gay relationships by airing Zamora and Sasser's commitment ceremony. That event included the two

men exchanging rings, cutting a wedding cake, and vowing their undying love for each other, with Sasser saying, "Show me your vision / Share the love / Take me with you / I love you." Perhaps most remarkable of all, the viewing audience witnessed the two men kissing each other—not once, but *seven* times.[15]

Celebrating Gay Heroes

Scholars who have studied how the American media have depicted sexual minorities over time have observed that before the 1990s the vast majority of homosexuals fit into one of two categories: villains and victims. The villains were evil and self-indulgent predators who attacked innocent young heterosexuals; the victims were pathetic and self-loathing misfits who hung their heads in shame that they were degenerates.[16]

Then the new gays arrived.

Reviews of *My Best Friend's Wedding* described Rupert Everett as playing a role that no openly gay actor—there hadn't been many—had ever heard before: a "quasi-romantic lead." Everett's character is handsome, firm-bodied, well educated, and exquisitely dressed. He also has a great job, as he is the Julia Roberts character's editor; overseeing the work of the movie world's reigning sweetheart clearly places him in the ideal position of every red-blooded American male. And yet Everett's primary job in this high-spirited comedy is that of devoted friend. He is the altruistic counselor for the commitment-shy Roberts, repeatedly urging her to stop playing games with the man she wants to marry and tell him, honestly and unambiguously, that she loves him. When the woman foolishly rejects this wise advice and loses her man, the Everett character races to her side not to say "I told you so" but to help her pick up the pieces, including gliding gracefully across the dance floor with Roberts in the film's final scene—making her the envy of every woman at the wedding. For millions of female moviegoers, the best phrase to describe this epitome of the new gay man was "My hero."[17]

Perhaps the most surprising of the male characters who rises to heroic stature is one who, on the surface, appears to embody many of the traditional gay stereotypes. Jack on *Will & Grace* is effeminate, promiscuous,

permanently unemployed, and resolutely narcissistic. And yet, as the series evolved, Jack repeatedly stood tall against gay oppression. When he
hears about an "ex-gay" organization, he seeks out and confronts its members; by the end of the episode, Jack has caused the group to disband. In
another segment, a program on NBC boasts that it's about to make history by airing a male-to-male kiss, but when the camera cuts away before
showing the two men's lips touching, Jack screeches, "They're sending a
clear message that the way I live my life is offensive!"; Will pooh-poohs
the point, but Jack marches down to the studio to protest and then takes
his campaign to a live broadcast of the *Today* show—Jack ultimately triumphs as a national television audience witnesses his and Will's impromptu, though non-romantic, kiss.[18]

A real-life hero arose from coverage of the gay-oriented story that
made headlines throughout the decade. U.S. Representative Barney
Frank received some attention in 1987 when he became the first member of Congress in history to disclose his homosexuality to the public,
but it was the gays in the military debate that catapulted him onto the
national radar screen. During Bill Clinton's presidential campaign, the
liberal candidate had pledged to lift the ban, but he backed off from that
promise once he was elected. When "don't ask, don't tell" emerged as
a compromise, Frank denounced the proposal as "incompatible with the
truth." The Massachusetts Democrat failed to block the policy, but his
outspoken opposition to it established him as a courageous and unapologetic spokesman for Gay America. From that point on, no news story
with a gay angle was complete without a comment from Barney Frank.
In 1998 when Matthew Shepard was killed, for example, news organizations across the country reported the congressman's powerful and articulate statement: "A very decent young man was brutally murdered by
two savages. Given the reason that those two mentally and morally de-
formed individuals murdered, it could have been me. Had I, alone and
unarmed, confronted these two thugs, I could have been subjected to
the same brutality that Mr. Shepard was, because his crime was to be a
gay man."[19]

Educating America about AIDS

Advertisements are designed to persuade consumers to buy, buy, buy, while mainstream films and TV programs are made to entertain their viewers. Three gay-themed media products of the 1990s, therefore, should be lauded for not only fulfilling their primary purposes but also for going well beyond the call of duty and educating the American public about the deadly disease that continued, throughout the decade, to cut a devastating swath through the population.

Benetton took the lead in 1992 by releasing a series of eye-catching ads that served the important purpose of raising AIDS awareness and promoting safe sex. One featured a photo of a huge hot pink condom covering all seventy-four feet of the obelisk at the center of the Place de la Concorde in Paris, while another showed the words "H.I.V. POSITIVE" tattooed on various body parts of muscular male models—one ad focused on the biceps, a second on the buttocks, and a third on the groin area. The most controversial of the Benetton ads was titled "Pieta" and showed an emaciated David Kirby on his deathbed, his father cradling the AIDS activist in his arms as the young man took his final breath.[20]

The motion picture industry made a huge contribution to increasing knowledge about the disease in 1993 with the release of *Philadelphia*. In early scenes, Tom Hanks appears healthy and robust. As the movie progresses, however, his body provides a dramatic visual depiction of the physical realities of the illness, with one reviewer describing the man as becoming "a gray, weak, shrunken figure—yellow from liver failure, bald, blind in one eye and barely able to speak." The film communicates public health lessons about the disease as well. When the lawyer who eventually takes the case, played by Denzel Washington, meets the infected man, he is so concerned about having touched a person with AIDS that he races to his doctor's office; by the end of the scene, the physician has clearly and directly told the lawyer—as well as the moviegoers—that an individual can be infected only through direct contact with one of three bodily fluids: blood, semen, or vaginal secretions. This important message

is reinforced when the Hanks character's parents and siblings do not hesitate to kiss him, including on the mouth.[21]

A year after *Philadelphia* educated motion picture audiences about the disease, Pedro Zamora provided even more specific lessons on MTV's *The Real World*. This venue was particularly important because most of the cable channel's viewers were young people who were just becoming sexually active. In his televised conversation with one of his roommates, Zamora clarified the difference between HIV and AIDS; he explained that the HIV virus destroys the white blood cells that protect the body against infections, while AIDS is a larger medical condition that develops when a person's immune system becomes so damaged that it can no longer fight off diseases. Another time, Zamora explained that latex condoms stop the virus but animal-product condoms do not. In still another conversation, the personable young man bluntly stated that oral sex was not safe sex, pointing out that the active participant can be infected, for example, if he has a cut in his mouth from an activity as seemingly innocuous as flossing his teeth.[22]

Like other persons with AIDS, Zamora had no way of knowing how soon the condition would make him seriously ill. So when the twenty-two-year-old's health plummeted during the six months that the program was being videotaped, everyone involved was surprised. "When Pedro became sick on the show, the other roommates were concerned about the crew filming him and thereby exploiting his illness," recalled Jon Murray, executive producer. "It was Pedro who eased their concerns, explaining to them that it was important for the viewers to see both his good days and his bad days." Toward the end, the bad days grew so severe that they were painful for viewers to watch, as the young man who was so articulate during the early episodes was, like many men and women during the final stages of AIDS, virtually incoherent.[23]

That Pedro Zamora was sending these messages—and on a cable channel that many Americans thought only showed music videos—was so astonishing that it caught the attention of the nation's leading news organizations. People all over the country then began following his powerful story by reading articles in such major newspapers as the *Los Angeles*

Times, Wall Street Journal, and *Chicago Sun-Times* and such high-circulation national magazines as *People* and *Life.*[24]

Zamora's work as a public health educator became so widely known that when he died in November 1994, the President of the United States released a tribute to him. "He taught all of us that AIDS is a disease with a human face, and one that affects every American—indeed, every citizen of the world," Bill Clinton told the nation during Zamora's memorial service. "Pedro was particularly instrumental in reaching out to his own generation, where AIDS is striking hard. He taught young people that 'The Real World' includes AIDS and that each of us has the responsibility to protect ourselves and our loved ones."[25]

Two Steps Forward, One Step Back

There is no question that the 1990s marked a watershed in the evolution of gay visibility in the American media. From that historic hand in the Banana Republic ad to box-office bonanzas such as *Philadelphia* and *My Best Friend's Wedding* to the popularity of television's *Will & Grace* to headlines on front pages and stories leading television newscasts, homosexuality not only seemed to be popping up everywhere but generally was being portrayed in a positive light.

But there also were "the buts."

Gay men seemed to be everywhere, *but* lesbians were hard to find. The plethora of gay-themed ads, movies, TV shows, and news stories focused almost exclusively on men. And on the rare occasion that gay women were invited into the media spotlight, they generally conformed to the tired old stereotypes. One of the few episodes of *Will & Grace* that included lesbians showed two women who were resolutely humorless and combative, both of them overweight and neither of them wearing makeup or jewelry, one of them dressed in a plaid flannel shirt and trousers and the other in a baggy, drab-colored dress. When Ellen DeGeneres with her glistening blond hair, pale blue eyes, shapely figure, and affable nature offered a break from the stereotype, ABC canceled her show *toute suite.*[26]

Advertising executives at companies such as Benetton and Abercrombie & Fitch eagerly targeted gay men and their oh-so-desirable expendable incomes, *but* other members of the industry opted for bigotry. A few days before showing the film *Better than Chocolate* in August 1999, a theater in San Diego, California, sent an ad to the local daily newspaper in which the film was described as "One of the best lesbian movies ever!" But the *Union-Tribune's* advertising director refused to run the ad, bluntly stating, "I didn't like the word lesbian."[27]

The news media generally treated gay subjects fairly, *but* not always. One instance of egregious reporting came in the wake of Gianni Versace's 1997 murder. When police identified the Miami Beach fashion designer as the fifth victim of a gay man named Andrew Cunanan, such high-profile journalists as Tom Brokaw of the *NBC Nightly News* sensationalized the story by labeling the alleged killer a "homicidal homosexual," a phrase that suggested that the murders were related to—perhaps even an outgrowth of—Cunanan's sexual orientation. The *New York Post* went even further by turning idle gossip into the kind of shocking headline that the tabloid is known for: "AIDS Fuels His Fury"; the story reported that Cunanan had become a "bloodthirsty gay serial killer" when he had discovered that he was ill with the disease. Within a matter of days, such widely respected newspapers as the *Miami Herald* and *San Diego Union-Tribune* were also reporting that Cunanan was HIV-positive, although their sources for that information were not clear. It was only after Cunanan committed suicide and an autopsy was conducted on his body that readers learned that he had not, in fact, been infected with the virus.[28]

Movies and network TV programs showcased gay characters, *but* a double standard was firmly in place when it came to sex. None of the major films featuring gay content—not *Philadelphia* or *The Birdcage* or *My Best Friend's Wedding*—showed two men's lips touching, even though two of the plotlines involved men in long-term romantic relationships, prompting *Newsweek* to observe that "two men kissing is a box-office no-no." The pattern was the same on *Will & Grace*, where neither sexless Will nor promiscuous Jack shows physical affection for another man, except when

they protest that very issue on national television. The only men who were shown kissing in a romantic way on 1990s television were Pedro Zamora and Sean Sasser—a clear signal that if sexual thresholds were to be crossed in the future of American television, it was likely to be not on the networks but on cable channels.[29]

The Black Nineties

Showcasing African-American Sexuality

WHEN THE TWENTY-SOMETHING MAN RETURNS FROM A TRIP OUT OF TOWN, he discovers that his girlfriend has repainted their apartment and packed away several of his favorite keepsakes, replacing them with some of her own. He expresses his displeasure, she gets angry, and he slams the door as he walks out. By the episode's final scene, though, the guy is standing in the doorway with a bag of popcorn in one hand and her favorite video in the other. She breaks the tension by smiling and saying, "Get in here." Then they embrace, kiss, and coo endearments in each other's ear. As the TV screen fades to black, the audience knows the couple has made up and is on the verge of "gettin' busy" on the living room couch.[1]

The plot of this episode of a 1994 network sitcom does not sound, for its time, like a groundbreaker; it seems like the kind of story line that could have aired on *All in the Family* or *Three's Company* in the 1970s. In fact, however, the segment helped push the small screen across a new threshold because the two lovers were not only attractive, personable, and sexually adventurous. They were also black.[2]

The series that featured the episode, titled *Martin* and starring comedian Martin Lawrence, was one of a cluster of shows that the Fox channel introduced in the early 1990s, thereby showcasing a critical mass of African-American characters for the first time in the history of television. Although the network's primary goal was not to promote racial equality but to find an audience niche not being adequately served by ABC, CBS, or NBC, nevertheless the author of a book documenting the phenome-

non—*Color by Fox: The Fox Network and the Revolution in Black Television*—had it right when she wrote, "Fox changed the course of black television."[3]

Some of the network's new programs—such as *Martin* and *Living Single*, which starred Queen Latifah—featured African Americans in every major role, while others—such as *Ally McBeal*—placed one or more persons of color in a predominately white cast. But no matter exactly what racial mix was chosen for a particular program, it was clear that by the final decade of the twentieth century, Fox had joined other members of the American media in embracing the credo *Sex Sells!*

The trend toward combining African Americans and sexual content extended well beyond the TV screen. Film studios also discovered that black casts combined with sexual themes could lead to box-office success, with *Jungle Fever* and *The Best Man* ranking among the decade's Hollywood hits. The concept was readily apparent in the music world as well, with rappers such as Ice Cube, 2 Live Crew, and the Geto Boys creating a unique musical genre dubbed "booty rap" that propelled their often vulgar lyrics into the American culture so powerfully that, by 1999, *Time* magazine announced that rap had become the country's top-selling musical format.[4]

Across the broad range of media that showcased African-American sexuality, the underlying themes were much the same—though the rappers expressed them in much harsher terms than did the TV shows or films. One fundamental message was that sex outside of marriage was commonplace. Another recurring statement was that both black men and black women were highly sexual beings. In the category of criticism, the most prominent message was a resounding and unremitting condemnation of sex between the races. Finally, the explosion of media portraying sexual content among Americans of African descent revived a theme that Hollywood films had introduced in the 1980s: Sex is often connected to violence.

Celebrating Extramarital Sex

In the 1970s, the debut of a TV program featuring a sex-crazed young man named Jack Tripper sharing an apartment with two beautiful young women was so objectionable that it propelled the creation of the National

Federation for Decency, even though the guy never made it into bed with either of his comely roommates. But by the 1990s, American mores had changed so dramatically—at least partly because of the media—that TV programs, films, and songs about young people engaging in sexual activity no longer sparked protests, regardless of whether the couple was white or black.

Martin, which began airing in 1992, was primarily a vehicle for popular comedian Martin Lawrence to star in a weekly television program as part of the Fox strategy to lure African-American viewers away from the three major networks. Dialogue often mentioned the main character's job as a radio personality, but the plotlines focused primarily on his personal life with live-in girlfriend Gina. The show routinely showed the couple in bed together—sometimes snuggled in each other's arms, other times casually reading or watching television. Although Martin and Gina eventually became engaged and then married, those milestones in the relationship didn't evolve until long after the twosome had become sexually intimate.[5]

Living Single, which began airing a year after *Martin,* revolved around four upwardly mobile women in their twenties who shared a New York City brownstone. The characters worked in various jobs, but the plotlines centered on their personal lives—with particular emphasis on who they were sleeping with. The premier episode set the tone by focusing on Regine's affair with a handsome man. When she learns that the guy has lied to her and is married, she continues to sleep with him anyway. Other members of the female foursome are also depicted as being sexually active. One of them, Maxine, admits that she's "a woman who thinks of a one-night stand as a long-term commitment" and boasts that she is dating several men while, at the same time, keeping a "boy toy" strictly for sex.[6]

The biggest black films of the decade also condoned sex outside of marriage. *Jungle Fever* tells the story of an affair between an architect and his secretary; when the man, played by Wesley Snipes, tells his best friend that he has something important to say and then goes on to announce that he is cheating on his wife, the friend, played by Spike Lee, shrugs his shoulders and blithely says, "I thought you was gonna drop a bomb or

somethin'." *The Best Man* focuses on half a dozen college friends who, several years after graduating, reunite to participate in the wedding of two members of the group; when one of the women suggests that she and one of the men have sex before the guy's girlfriend arrives the next day, he readily agrees.[7]

Casual sex was also a recurring theme in the decade's rap lyrics. Ice Cube, who began his career as a member of the seminal group N.W.A. (short for Niggaz Wit Attitude), became an instant spokesman for his generation of young African-American men in 1990 when his first album, *AmeriKKKa's Most Wanted,* sold more than a million copies.[8]

The opening lines of the song "It's a Man's World" illustrated the prevailing attitude toward female sex partners:

> *Women they're good for nothing no maybe one thing*
> *To serve needs to my ding-a-ling*
> *I'm a man who loves the one-night stand*
> *Cause after I do ya*
> *Huh I never knew ya.*[9]

During interviews, Ice Cube defended this description of using women for sex and then discarding them. "There is a certain kind of woman," the twenty-one-year-old told the *Chicago Tribune,* "who uses her body to make a man do anything she wants. I've seen lots of guys used up and thrown away once she took all his money." Exploiting women also allows African-American men to assert their manhood, the artist continued, in a society that has denied him the power that white men have consistently wielded.[10]

The African-American Man ~ "Anytime Andy"

While rap lyrics were the media venue of the 1990s that most bluntly communicated the macho attitude of many black men regarding sexual activity, the decade's television programs and motion pictures also consistently portrayed African-American men as highly sexual beings.

Martin episodes often depicted the title character and his two best friends, Tommy and Cole, in pursuit of sexual partners. On one occasion,

Gina goes out of town on a business trip, and as soon as she leaves the apartment, Martin and his buddies get on the phone and start inviting women to a party they are planning for that night. After Tommy ends one call and then says derisively, "Heifer," Martin says, "She ain't comin', is she?" Tommy then responds, "No, but she said she may stop by after her husband goes to sleep." Another time, Martin becomes so aroused when Gina wears a body-hugging dress to a party that the only way she can stop him from pawing her—"I'm telling you, baby, I gots to have it!"—is to agree to go in another room with him for a five-minute quickie. In yet another episode, Martin accepts Gina's challenge to abstain from intercourse for two weeks; after a few days, she discovers that he's succeeding only by wearing an ice pack on his penis—which ultimately still isn't enough to restrain him.[11]

When *Ally McBeal* brought its heavy-on-the-sex plotlines to the Fox lineup in 1997, an African-American attorney soon emerged as one of the most memorable members of the cast. Renee was far more realistic about the ways of the world than most of the quirky characters on the show, and one of the statements that helped her establish that reputation was her characterization of all male members of her race as genetically incapable of sexual fidelity. "Men can't stay attracted to the same female for a long period of time," she tells Ally pointblank. Renee's pessimistic assessment of African-American men is soon reinforced when she runs into a handsome boyfriend from her past and becomes emotionally and physically involved with him—only to discover that he is lying to her and is already married.[12]

The Best Man depicts black men as unreservedly promiscuous. One member of the group of friends had, during college, been a star football player who considered one of the privileges of his celebrity status to be having sex with any number of women—including four with "big ass titties the size of punching bags" after one major game. His sexual appetite grew even more intense when he went pro. Two days before his wedding, he tells his three closest male friends, "I done had all the ass ten men can have," but then adds that his obsession is about to end, saying, "Marriage is a cure for promiscuity." It's clear, though, that his buddies don't believe him—or see any reason why their friend should end his sexual abandon.

"Ain't nothin' natural about no monogamy," one of them says. "God did not intend for us to be with just one person. If he had, he wouldn't have given us all this sperm." When he goes on to conclude with the statement, "You know as well as I do there ain't nothin' better than some pussy, except some new pussy," his pals laugh in hearty agreement.[13]

In the music world, African-American rappers unapologetically communicated that they and their brothers were highly sexual, even though this dimension of their music meant that most radio stations refused to play it, fearful that the content would alienate advertisers. One song on 2 Live Crew's *As Nasty as They Wanna Be* album, "Me So Horny," included the lyrics:[14]

> *I'll play with your heart just like it's a game*
> *I'll be blowing your mind while you're blowing my brains*
> *I'm just like that man they call georgie puddin' pie*
> *I fuck all the girls and i make 'em cry*
> *I'm like a dog in heat, a freak without warning*
> *I have an appetite for sex, 'cause me so horny.*[15]

The African-American Woman ~ "Anytime Annie"

Toward the end of the scene from *The Best Man* in which the four men talk about the joys of promiscuity, one of them argues that black women are just as obsessed with sex as men are—"They're just as scandalous as us niggas, man!"—while the other men nod in agreement. That same message was communicated by numerous of the media products that dealt with African-American sexuality.[16]

Renee on *Ally McBeal* was beautiful as well as extraordinarily buxom, and she readily admitted that she often exploited her sexuality. "Some people tell me I should be ashamed of my sex appeal," she says in one episode. "They say, 'If you use your sexuality, you set the Feminist Movement backward.'" Renee disagrees, arguing that a sexy woman should take advantage of that asset. When she defends a client who is charged with creating a sexually charged work environment, for example, Renee dresses in a skintight suit with no blouse and a plunging neckline

that makes her huge breasts even more prominent than usual. During the trial, she asks the plaintiff, "Am I putting out a sexual signal right now?" Without skipping a beat, she pushes out her chest, leans toward the witness, and asks, in a seductive tone, "What if I said something like, 'I haven't had any for so long—I don't even remember how it goes?'" The befuddled witness then responds, "I doubt if anybody would believe you." Renee wins the case.[17]

Living Single depicted African-American women as so highly sexual that a *Los Angeles Times* review of the program characterized the four female leads as "booty-shaking sugar mamas" who consistently "viewed men as sex objects." The Queen Latifah character's libido is so powerful that it propels her, the publisher of her own magazine, to violate the ethical standards of her profession. On one occasion, she nonchalantly has a sexual relationship with a handsome source, and another time she adds a drop-dead gorgeous writer to her staff without even reading his sample articles or checking his references—and promptly makes a pass at him.[18]

Rappers communicated the same message, as they repeatedly portrayed African-American women as prostitutes. The Geto Boys's track "Let a Ho Be a Ho," for instance, depicted black women as promiscuous and warned black men that they would suffer severely if they fell in love with one of them:

> You knew the ho when she was fucking the whole town
> She fucked you and gave your buddies a blow
> But your trick ass fell in love with the ho
> Tried to change her make her be an angel
> You keep putting your damn life in danger
> Fronting niggas about that slutty ass trifling crow
> You gotta let a ho be a ho.[19]

Condemning Interracial Sex

While some 1990s media sent out occasional warnings about the potential dangers of black men becoming romantically involved with black women, the messages exploded in both number and intensity when the

object of desire shifted to white women. Without an iota of ambiguity, interracial sex was vehemently condemned.

Spike Lee created the definitive film on the topic with *Jungle Fever*. Indeed, the director was so adamant about sending this message that he cast himself in the role of a man who saw it as his duty to do everything within his power to block interracial sex. During the scene in which Wesley Snipes tells his best friend, played by Lee, that he is having an extramarital affair, the friend initially reacts matter of factly—until he learns the woman's race: "White! Man, are you on crack or somethin'!" Viscerally disturbed by his friend's shocking news, Lee completely changes his demeanor as he compares the black/white affair to "nuclear holocaust." The Lee character is so appalled, in fact, that he betrays his lifelong friendship—as well as the black brotherhood—and passes the information on to his wife, knowing full well that she'll tell Snipes's wife.[20]

The interracial affair ultimately destroys Snipes's life. His wife throws him out of the house and severely restricts his contact with their daughter. His parents publicly humiliate his white lover by calling her a whore and a home wrecker. His professional life and emerging relationship with the white woman fall apart as well. And so, by midway through the movie, the successful family man with a high-paying position in a prestigious Manhattan architectural firm is out of a job, alienated from his family, and betrayed by his best friend—all because he had sex outside the race.[21]

Rap musicians also lashed out at interracial sex. "Horny Little Devil," the signature track from Ice Cube's 1991 album *Death Certificate*, begins by disparaging the sexual abilities of white men:

> *Lookin' at my girlfriend's black skin*
> *You wanna jump in, but she don't like white men*
> *She ain't with the pale face*
> *Cause y'all fuck at a snail's pace.*[22]

After that introduction, Ice Cube's lyrics go on to focus specifically on interracial sex. A master at articulating messages through rhyme, he needs only a few lines to suggest why he believes sex between the races is unacceptable—and the penalty that should be exacted for it:

Black women have bodies like goddesses
Sorta like Venus, but put away your penis
Cause the devil is a savage motherfucker
That's why I'm lighter than the average brother
Cause you raped our women and we felt it
But it'll never happen again if I can help it (me neither)
Cause nobody in my neighborhood has caught jungle fever yet
So horny little devil, you better listen
Before your ass comes up missin'.

Ice Cube's threatening words were so incendiary that they provoked *Billboard,* for the first time in its history, to publish an editorial condemning an artist. With the graphic lyrics, the booty rapper had, according to the music industry magazine, "crossed the line that divides art from the advocacy of crime." But the rapper's angry words clearly resonated with many young African Americans, as the album sold more than a million copies.[23]

Connecting Sex and Violence

During the 1980s, the idea of sex sometimes being linked to violence was limited to a few motion pictures such as *Dressed to Kill* and *Fatal Attraction.* But with the 1990s flood of media products featuring African-American sexuality, this disquieting concept received far more emphasis.

In some instances, the sex/violence connection emerged in relation to interracial sex. In *Jungle Fever,* the Wesley Snipes character's betrayed wife throws her husband's clothes out the window; when he arrives home and sees the crowd that has gathered on the street below, his plaintive, "Wait, wait, I can explain" elicits only words of rage from his previously sedate wife—"Explain a fuckin' white bitch! You fuckhead!" Other acts of violence punctuate *Jungle Fever* as well. In one scene, onlookers who see Snipes wrestling playfully with his girlfriend assume that the black man is raping the white woman; in a matter of moments, white police officers are slamming Snipes up against a wall. Another time, a working class white man comments, "Colored women, they like to fuck. They're built

that way. Put a saddle on 'em and you can ride 'em into the sunset—they love it."

The sex/violence connection was ubiquitous in the misogynistic lyrics produced by black rappers. A religious right organization named Focus on the Family said of 2 Live Crew's *As Nasty as They Wanna Be* album, "There has never been an album recorded in our nation's history with this level of explicit sex and degradation." A U.S. District Court judge in Florida agreed, ruling that the lyrics were obscene and therefore that the recording could not be sold, marking the first time in American history that a federal court had found that a musical work had reached that level of indecency. That decision led to multiple arrests of the musicians and various merchants who sold the album, prompting a prolonged legal battle before an appeals court overturned the obscenity ruling.[24]

Although the judge never specified exactly which words he considered to be criminally offensive, it is likely that they were the ones from "Me So Horny" that described the joys a man can derive from damaging a woman's vagina during sex:

> *Girls always ask me why I fuck so much*
> *I say "what's wrong, baby doll, with a quick nut?"*
> *Cause you're the one, and you shouldn't be mad*
> *I won't tell your mama if you don't tell your dad*
> *I know he'll be disgusted when he sees your pussy busted.*[25]

2 Live Crew was by no means the only booty rap group that celebrated sexual violence. The Geto Boys went so far as to describe murdering a woman and then having sex with the dead body. The lyrics for "Mind of a Lunatic" were so offensive that the group's longtime label, Geffen Records, refused to release the track. The musicians soon found another distributor, however, and sent out their message. Even without major-label sponsorship or radio airplay, the album quickly sold a million copies.[26] The shocking lyrics included:

> *Lookin through her window, now my body is warm*
> *She's naked, and i'm a peepin tom*

Her body's beautiful, so i'm thinking rape
Shouldn't have had her curtains open, so that's her fate
Leavin out her house, grabbed the bitch by her mouth
Drug her back in, slammed her down on the couch
Whipped out my knife, said, 'if you scream, i'm cuttin'
Opened her legs and commenced the fuckin
She begged me not to kill her, i gave her a rose
Then slit her throat, and watched her shake till her eyes closed
Had sex with the corpse before i left her
And drew my name on the wall like helter skelter.[27]

Popular, Yes; Responsible . . . ?

The explosion of media depicting African-American sexuality was paradoxical. On the one hand, black men and women were portrayed as being enormously sexually active, as eagerly participating in casual sex, and as being reckless with regard to taking precautions—birth control pills and condoms were rarely mentioned. On the other hand, women did not become pregnant and neither women nor men contracted sexually transmitted diseases.

The fact that HIV and AIDS were not highlighted in the plethora of TV shows, films, and rap lyrics aimed at African Americans was particularly noteworthy because, throughout the 1990s, the epidemic raged ferociously through Black America.[28]

Also relevant, considering that almost half of all black families in the United States were headed by single mothers, was the scarcity of such women in the media. When all of the black females in *Martin, Living Single, Ally McBeal, Jungle Fever*, and *The Best Man* are added together, they total twenty-four. When all of the single mothers in those programs and movies are added together, they total zero.[29]

Of course TV sitcoms and films have no obligation to reflect reality; their mission is to entertain, not inform. And yet, at the same time, these media products have enormous impact on their audiences, particularly because the number of African-American characters in the media is disproportionately small. These factors beg the question: Do entertainment

media that target a historically underrepresented audience—especially one that continues to be economically, socially, and politically oppressed—have a moral responsibility to reflect and/or educate members of that audience about the unique problems they face?

While this key question and the issues underlying it are important, they seem to pale in comparison to the issue of rap music and sexual violence. Right-thinking individuals certainly can disagree on such sex-related issues as whether abortion should be legal or what should be taught in sex education classes. It would be difficult, however, to convince any rational individual that there is any merit whatsoever in depicting—and thereby, at least to some extent, *glamorizing*—either the maiming or the killing of a woman during sexual activity.

Legions of mainstream journalists condemned the sexually violent rap lyrics that emerged during the 1990s. The *Chicago Tribune* called booty rap "sick" and "ugly," while the editorial page of the *New York Times* said, "The music 'plays' at rape and murder in a way that celebrates them." *Newsweek* went even further, using phrasing that suggested a cause-and-effect relationship between young black men listening to misogynistic booty rap and then brutally attacking a woman in Central Park. The news magazine stated, "Fact: Some members of a particular age and social cohort—the one making 2 Live Crew rich—stomped and raped the jogger to the razor edge of death, for the fun of it."[30]

Despite their intensity and abundance, the denunciations of the musical genre offered scant specific suggestions as to how either the number or the power of sexually violent lyrics could be reduced. In a society that values freedom of expression as one of its bedrock principles, the journalists knew that it was unrealistic to believe that any strategy could be devised to prevent rap lyrics from proliferating. In the early 1990s, the American judicial system attempted to prevent the sale of 2 Live Crew's album *As Nasty as They Wanna Be* by labeling the lyrics obscene. Not only did that effort fail when the courts determined that the music was protected by the First Amendment, but the publicity that swirled around the case added significantly to the album's appeal among young music buyers, sending sales soaring to a stunning two million copies.[31]

The better response to sexually violent lyrics clearly was—and would continue to be—education.

Specifically, listeners need to be taught that booty rap is, as one scholar put it, the "lurid fantasies" of the musicians performing it. In other words, it is imperative that young people who are exposed to the lyrics learn that the sexual activities described in the songs are not the actual experiences of the writers or performers but "grandiose and sometimes violent tales."[32]

Although it is probably too complex to explain to a youngster, this dynamic evolved from certain fundamental characteristics that rock 'n' roll shares with rap. Throughout its history, rock music has not been merely the rebellious voice of the younger generation but has been intentionally crafted to *disturb* older generations. Indeed, scholars have argued that if a particular rock piece does not stimulate criticism from older listeners, it does not, in fact, even qualify as bona fide rock 'n' roll. Similarly, an inherent element of rap music is that the lyrics are intended to defy propriety and thereby outrage society's authority figures—which generally means the White Establishment. In the early days of rap, artists such as Ice Cube provoked the requisite reaction by stating, for example, that women were good for nothing but sex or by sprinkling words such as "ding-a-ling" into their lyrics. As time passed, new thresholds of vulgarity had to be crossed in order for booty rap to qualify as shocking, thereby prompting terms such as "ho" and "fuck." It was after this point that rappers began adding descriptions of maiming or killing their sex partners, simultaneously competing with each other to see who could produce the most extreme content.[33]

Young listeners certainly do not have to understand all of these aspects of rap music. What they absolutely need to understand, however, is that many of the lyrics describe fantasies that are not to be imitated. In other words, just as young moviegoers must learn that they should not try to climb the side of a building the way actor Tobey Maguire does in the film *Spider-Man*, young listeners must learn that they should not try to "bust a pussy" or slit a lover's throat the way the artists 2 Live Crew and the Geto Boys do in their music.

In fact, scholars who have studied the impact of sexually violent rap music have found—in direct contrast to the statements of alarm expressed by news organizations—that the vast majority of adolescent and teenage listeners understand that the lyrics are merely flights of the imagination created by the musicians for their shock value. Further, this substantial body of research has concluded that young people have no intention of emulating the horrific activities described in the songs. As one sixteen-year-old told an interviewer: "I like rappers. They cuss and say some crazy things about women, but I pay it no mind. I know I'm not like that."[34]

Semen on the Front Page

Bill Clinton's Sex Life Redefines the News

JACKIE JUDD KNEW THAT ONE PARTICULAR FACT SHE HAD DISCOVERED during her day of reporting was a major scoop, and yet the ABC News correspondent did not mention that detail in the script she wrote for *World News Tonight*, her network's flagship daily newscast, on January 23, 1998. "At that stage, only the third day into the Lewinsky scandal," Judd later explained, "I was still squeamish about putting a story like that on the air. It was all new territory for us."[1]

But the producers at network headquarters in New York knew what Judd had uncovered, and, after reading the script she sent from Washington, they insisted that she rewrite it, arguing that the fact she had opted not to include—though many listeners would find it offensive—ultimately involved forensic proof of President Bill Clinton's guilt or innocence. Judd's revised script marked a journalistic watershed, as two of the sentences read: "Monica Lewinsky says she saved, apparently as some kind of souvenir, a navy blue dress with the president's semen stain on it. If true, this could provide physical evidence of what really happened."[2]

Newspapers across the country published versions of Judd's revelation the next morning, marking the first time in the 300-year history of American journalism that presidential semen became front-page news.[3]

That was only one of numerous thresholds that the news media crossed in their coverage of the sexual goings-on of the forty-second president of the United States. From charges of infidelity and sexual harassment to explicit discussions of oral sex and soiled clothing to bombshell

descriptions of salacious Oval Office encounters, reporting on Clinton's sex life expanded the definition of news in ways that previous generations of journalists could never have imagined.

Sexual wrongdoings by a president were nothing new; reporting them was. Former CBS correspondent Marvin Kalb recalls, for example, a night in 1963 when he witnessed a late-night rendezvous at the Carlyle Hotel in New York City between President John F. Kennedy and a beautiful woman who was not his wife. "Never for one minute did I even consider pursuing and reporting what I had seen," Kalb wrote. "In those days, the possibility of a presidential affair, while titillating, was not considered *news*."[4]

Reporting on Accusations of Adultery

One point at which to begin tracing the coverage of Bill Clinton's sexual adventures is in 1992 when he was seeking his party's nomination for the White House.

In January of that year, in the midst of the New Hampshire primary race, a former lounge singer from Arkansas, where Clinton had served as governor, announced that she and the Democratic front-runner had been involved in an adulterous affair from 1977 to 1989. Most of the country's major news organizations initially kept their distance from the allegations because they first appeared in the *Star* supermarket tabloid, which had paid Gennifer Flowers $100,000 to tell her story.[5]

That situation changed, however, when Ted Koppel devoted a segment of his late-night ABC news program to the topic. *Nightline* approached the infidelity charges not directly but by reporting how the *Star* had faxed copies of its article to TV networks and newspapers in hopes of getting publicity for itself. Other news organizations then followed in Koppel's footsteps. "Allegations about Arkansas Gov. Bill Clinton's sex life achieved front-page status this week," the *Washington Post*'s media reporter wrote. "News executives have insisted they had no choice but to publish Gennifer Flowers's account of a 12-year affair she says she had with Clinton because the issue has taken center stage in his presidential campaign."[6]

To counter the allegations, the candidate and his wife then appeared on the CBS news magazine *60 Minutes* immediately following the Super

Bowl. "I have acknowledged causing pain in my marriage," the wayward husband told fifty million viewers. But even more persuasive were the words that came from the wronged wife. "I love him and I respect him, and I honor what he's been through and what we've been through together," Hillary Rodham Clinton said. "And, you know, if that's not enough for people, then, heck, don't vote for him."[7]

The Clintons contained the damage, and, by continuing to focus on economic issues, the candidate kept his presidential ship afloat. He won the Democratic Party nomination, defeated President George H. W. Bush, and moved into the White House in January 1993.

Covering Sexual Harassment Charges

Next in the series of events that would come to be called Zippergate—a semantic comparison to the Watergate scandal that toppled President Richard Nixon—also involved an incident that allegedly had taken place while Clinton was governor.[8]

At a 1994 press conference, a twenty-seven-year-old Arkansas woman accused Clinton of having sexually harassed her. Specifically, Paula Jones charged that three years earlier, while she was a state employee, the governor had spotted her in the Excelsior Hotel in Little Rock and had summoned her to his suite, where he dropped his trousers and his underwear and told her to perform oral sex on him.[9]

Jones made her allegations to the press during the annual Conservative Political Action Conference, and the right-wing Rutherford Institute supplied her legal counsel. These close affiliations between the accuser and Clinton's political opponents contributed to many news organizations choosing not to cover Jones's charges. The *Washington Post* did not report her press conference, even though the event took place in the nation's capital, and ABC was the only major network to run a story. Another factor in the minimal coverage was that Jones's charges came down to a he-said/she-said stalemate—he the president of the United States, she a big-haired woman who was, in the words of some pundits, "trailer trash."[10]

The coverage increased, however, when the U.S. Supreme Court ruled unanimously that Jones's lawsuit had sufficient merit to proceed toward

trial. That President Clinton was facing sexual harassment charges, regardless of the possible political motivations for them, was a fact that the news media could not ignore. *Newsweek* gave particular prominence to Jones's allegations, including a cover story that advised Clinton to settle the case as soon as possible. "It may require an apology," the magazine acknowledged, "but the alternative seems much worse."[11]

As the number of stories increased, so did American journalism's coverage of oral sex. News organizations previously had considered such a sexually graphic topic to be taboo, but Jones's accusations could not be reported without referring to the specific request that the president allegedly had made of her. And when Jones's lawyers argued that their client was telling the truth because she could identify "distinguishing characteristics" of Clinton's genitalia, newspapers and TV networks again had little choice but to quote the words. Likewise, when the judge hearing the Jones case felt compelled to specify exactly what constituted "sexual relations," newspapers did their job by reporting the definition, word by explicit word: "A person engages in 'sexual relations' when the person knowingly engages in or causes contact with the genitalia, anus, groin, breast, inner thigh, or buttocks of any person with an intent to arouse or gratify sexual desire."[12]

By early 1998, coverage was focused on Kenneth Starr, the independent counsel who was investigating various charges of legal wrongdoing by the president. Unbeknownst to the public at the time, a *Newsweek* reporter had learned that part of Starr's inquiry involved a relationship between Clinton and a former White House intern named Monica Lewinsky. The reporter's sources included Linda Tripp, a forty-eight-year-old friend and coworker of Lewinsky's who had secretly tape recorded telephone conversations in which the younger woman had discussed her affair with the president. The reporter had no proof that Lewinsky was telling the truth, though, and *Newsweek* editors were not willing to print a story that might be inaccurate.[13]

Matt Drudge was. The conservative-leaning dot.com reporter was always on the lookout for juicy items, and he was not the stickler for truth that the news magazine's editors were. So when a Clinton-hating lawyer who had helped the *Newsweek* reporter research his story became frus-

trated that the magazine editors delayed publication, he e-mailed Drudge what he knew, and—Voilà!—the story appeared on the Internet.[14]

When the item was posted on the *Drudge Report* on January 18, 1998, it was labeled "★★World Exclusive★★" and read, in part: "A young woman, 23, sexually involved with the love of her life, the President of the United States, since she was a 21-year-old intern at the White House. She was a frequent visitor to a small study just off the Oval Office where she claims to have indulged the president's sexual preference." The item did not mention Lewinsky by name.[15]

A President Behaving Badly

Three days later, news coverage of Clinton's misbehavior exploded in the mainstream media when the *Washington Post* published a front-page story that raised the scandal to a whole new level. Specifically, the *Post* reported that the former intern had testified before Kenneth Starr as part of his inquiry into the Paula Jones sexual harassment charges and that the independent counsel was investigating the possibility that Bill Clinton had broken the law by encouraging her to lie under oath—which meant the president had obstructed justice.[16]

Monica Lewinsky had begun working at the White House in an unpaid position in 1995, the *Post* reported. Unnamed sources then went on to say that Linda Tripp's tape-recorded telephone conversations included Lewinsky describing her affair with the president that had extended for a year and a half. The sources also stated, however, that Lewinsky and Clinton both had, in their sworn statements to Starr, denied having had such a relationship.[17]

The *Post*'s revelations set off a reporting stampede. Later that day, the story led the newscasts on ABC, CBS, NBC, CNN, and Fox. NBC's *Today* show catapulted Matt Drudge into mainstream journalism by featuring him as an expert; the high-tech rumormonger said unashamedly, "I go where the stink is." Meanwhile, the nation's most prestigious newspapers jumped into overdrive, with the *New York Times*, the *Los Angeles Times*, and *USA Today*, the largest-circulation daily in the country, all publishing stories on the scandal the next day.[18]

The public response to the revelations was so overwhelming that the president felt compelled to make a formal statement on the matter. Clinton told the nation, while sitting at his desk in the Oval Office with his jaw clenched and his finger pointing at the television cameras to emphasize his words: "I did not have sexual relations with *that woman,* Miss Lewinsky. I never told anybody to lie, not a single time—never."[19]

The Most Important Dress in American History

Despite the plethora of stories that filled the nation's airwaves and front pages in the wake of the *Post's* startling revelations and the president's dramatic denial, the scoop that ABC reported on the third day of the scandal stood out from all the rest.

Jackie Judd was the polar opposite of Matt Drudge. A veteran journalist who had begun working for the network in 1974, she was neither a blow-dried bimbo nor a muckraker who sought out sensational stories but, in the words of one scholar, "a solid reporter of reliable, tested judgment." And so, although Judd was sufficiently competitive to do all she could to help ABC take the lead in coverage of the biggest political story to come along in years, she had no intention of reporting inaccurate information.[20]

By the time Judd wrote her script for the January 23 *World News Tonight* broadcast, she had, through her sources, obtained several new pieces of information. First, she knew that Lewinsky had visited the White House on numerous occasions to see the president early on weekend mornings to avoid aides who would have found her presence suspicious. Second, Judd had learned that Clinton had suggested to Lewinsky that she deny having had an affair, as there would be no proof of it if they both said it had not happened. Third, the reporter knew that Kenneth Starr and Lewinsky's attorney were scheduled to meet the next day to discuss the possibility of the former intern receiving immunity from prosecution if she agreed to cooperate in the criminal investigation.

But it was a fourth piece of information that would not only propel Judd and ABC into the lead in the race for details about the Zippergate scandal but that also would push American journalism across a new sexual threshold.

Like any responsible reporter, Judd believed that good taste dictated that certain words were inappropriate to be broadcast on national television—and "semen" was definitely one of them. The producers at network headquarters, however, argued that the fact that the president had ejaculated on a dress that was now in Lewinsky's possession—DNA tests would be able to determine if the semen was Clinton's—proved that he had been involved in a sexual relationship. In addition, the producers insisted, the fact that Clinton had already sworn in his deposition to the independent counsel that he had not had a sexual relationship with Lewinsky proved that he had, in fact, *lied under oath.*[21]

After listening to the producers, Judd concluded that their arguments outweighed her concerns about using a word that she considered in bad taste. "They were right," she later stated. "It was forensic evidence. It was crucial."[22]

The scoop was ABC's alone that first night; by the next morning, it was the world's. The Brahmins of the newspaper world such as the *New York Times* and *Washington Post* reported on the soiled dress, while the United Press International news agency sent an item to its hundreds of clients around the country, putting "semen" on the front pages of such far-flung dailies as the *Miami Herald* and *Seattle Times.*[23]

All Monica, All the Time

Jackie Judd's startling discovery of the dress was followed by a period of several months in which there was a relative paucity of major breakthroughs about Zippergate. A dearth of news did not mean, however, a lack of stories. The media continued to provide their viewers and readers with a banquet of reporting; most of it was accurate, but some of it was not. Many of the items involved the possibility that President Clinton had committed perjury and obstructed justice, but a goodly number also were of a sexual—and highly titillating—nature.

One subject of enormous interest was Monica Lewinsky. The *Washington Post* quoted one of her coworkers at the Pentagon, where she had been transferred after nine months at the White House, as saying that the young woman would "talk about how she wanted to have sex in the

Oval Office, on the desk." Newspapers all over the country reported on a news conference at which the young woman's former high school drama teacher, Andy Bleiler, announced—with his wife standing at his side—that he had been involved in a long-running affair with Lewinsky until the previous year. *Washington Post* executive editor Leonard Downie defended the stories, saying, "Lewinsky's approach to sexual matters is important in evaluating her as the principal witness against the president."[24]

Reporters also tried to shed light on the specifics of the Clinton/Lewinsky relationship. The *Los Angeles Times* stated that the president and the world's most famous intern had engaged in phone sex, and the *Drudge Report* told its readers that the couple sometimes used a cigar as part of their sexual high jinks. After the *Dallas Morning News* announced that a Secret Service agent was prepared to testify that he had been an eyewitness to Clinton and Lewinsky in a "compromising situation," the story became the lead item on ABC's *Nightline* and was sent out to Associated Press clients across the country—until the *Morning News* retracted the story a few hours later.[25]

Another frequent topic of coverage was oral sex. Ted Koppel pioneered in exploring this subject when he devoted a segment of *Nightline* to attempting to answer the question that in previous eras would have been unthinkable but now seemed central to Zippergate: Is oral sex adultery? The question was neither "inappropriate" nor "frivolous," Koppel insisted, because sources in both Little Rock and Washington reported that Clinton believed that only activities involving vaginal penetration were, in fact, "sexual relations"—the term the president used in his public statement. "What sounds, in other words, like a categorical denial [by Clinton] may prove to be something altogether different," Koppel told his audience. The late-night discussion eased the way for the same topic to be explored the next morning on NBC's *Today* show. Matt Lauer began by stating, "New information indicates that the president makes a distinction between having oral sex with a woman and that being considered an adulterous affair." After *Nightline* and *Today* began the discussion, the nation's newspapers joined in.[26]

By February 1998, critics had begun lambasting the news media for "how far this runaway vehicle of a story has careened" from the perjury

and obstruction of justice allegations against Clinton. Number one on the list of objectionable reports, according to the detractors, was Jackie Judd's piece about the soiled dress. The *New York Times* blasted Judd for claiming there were what the newspaper called "phantom semen stains," and the *Los Angeles Times* pointed to her story as the epitome of the media's "sick" performance in covering the scandal, saying, "There was no blue dress and no semen stain, but America's mass media fell for the lurid tales." The strongest of the denunciations came from the man who, perhaps more than any other, defined "muckraker" in the mind of the American public; Geraldo Rivera told listeners on *Rivera Live!*, his talk program on cable channel CNBC, "There is, ladies and gentlemen, absolutely no possibility that a so-called semen-stained dress exists."[27]

Obliterating Sexual Taboos

It is difficult to provide an accurate tally of the number of restrictions on sexual content that the news media wiped away on September 12, 1998, when independent counsel Kenneth Starr's report was released. *Mother Jones*, one of the country's most liberal magazines, called that day "a horrific moment when all of the filters that are present in the world of journalism evaporated and you had raw information suddenly available in the mainstream."[28]

Many major newspapers—including the most respected news organization in the country, the *New York Times*—published all 453 pages verbatim, and hundreds more posted the full report on their Web sites. That meant printing the term "oral sex" ninety-two times, "breasts" sixty-two, "genitalia" thirty-nine, "phone sex" twenty-nine, and "semen" nineteen.[29]

The terms were used in describing ten tawdry sexual encounters, most of them occurring in a windowless hallway connecting the Oval Office and the president's private study. The report detailed nine occasions on which Lewinsky performed oral sex on Clinton, with the president fondling and kissing her bare breasts each time but ejaculating only twice. He never performed oral sex on her, and they did not have intercourse. He stimulated her genitals four times and brought her to orgasm twice.

A *Boston Globe* spokesman explained his paper's decision to reprint the graphic document about the president's unseemly behavior by saying, "For people to make a real informed judgment about this guy and potential perjury, you really needed to have a text of the entire report."[30] Among the highlights:

- "At one point, Ms. Lewinsky and the President talked alone in the Chief of Staff's office," read the description of a meeting early in the relationship. "In the course of flirting with him, she raised her jacket in the back and showed him the straps of her thong underwear."[31]

- "Ms. Lewinsky said, 'We went back over by the bathroom in the hallway, and we kissed. We were kissing and he unbuttoned my dress and fondled my breasts with my bra on, and then took them out of my bra and was kissing them and touching them with his hands and with his mouth. I was touching him in his genital area through his pants, and I think I unbuttoned his shirt and was kissing his chest. And then I wanted to perform oral sex on him and so I did.'"[32]

- "Ms. Lewinsky said, 'He went to go put his hand down my pants, and then I unzipped them because it was easier. And I didn't have any panties on. And so he manually stimulated me.' According to Ms. Lewinsky, 'I wanted him to touch my genitals with his genitals,' and he did so, lightly and without penetration. Then Ms. Lewinsky performed oral sex on him, again until he ejaculated."[33]

- One of the most graphic of all the references involved Clinton placing an object usually belonging in the mouth into a very different orifice of Lewinsky's body: "On one occasion, the President inserted a cigar in her vagina to stimulate her."[34]

Based on these passages and numerous others, it was difficult to argue with the journalist who dubbed the document "the most detailed pornographic government report in history."[35]

Choosing quotations from among the 119,059 words that the *Washington Post* described as "Watergate meets Lolita" presented partic-

ularly difficult problems for television. As soon as correspondents got their hands on the massive report, they immediately went on air live. But then they faced the problem that print and Internet reporters were able to avoid by publishing the entire document: Which details were too sordid and which were not? CNN was the most daring of the networks, with reporters reading passages such as "According to Ms. Lewinsky, the president touched her breasts and genitalia"; CBS was the most squeamish, with Dan Rather at one point stopping a correspondent in mid-sentence and saying, "This is daytime television, and there are children in the audience."[36]

One shocking section of the report that reporters had warned the American public about in advance—thanks first to Jackie Judd and then to newspapers that reported her scoop on their front pages—was the one describing the item that provided the most incriminating evidence: "After reaching an immunity and cooperation agreement with the Office of the Independent Counsel, Ms. Lewinsky turned over a navy blue dress that she said she had worn during a sexual encounter with the President." The report went on to describe the stain on the garment Lewinsky had purchased at a Gap clothing store: "The genetic markers on the semen, which match the President's DNA, are characteristic of one out of 7.87 trillion Caucasians."[37]

Zippergate's Legacy

The September 1998 release of the Starr Report set a series of crucial events in motion.

In November, Clinton agreed to pay Paula Jones $850,000 to drop her lawsuit.[38]

In December, the U.S. House of Representatives voted to impeach the president on two counts; the perjury charge alleged that he had lied under oath about having sexual relations with Monica Lewinsky, and the obstruction of justice charge alleged that he had encouraged Lewinsky to lie under oath.[39]

In January 1999, the U.S. Senate began the impeachment trial—only the second in the nation's history—to determine if Clinton had committed

"high crimes and misdemeanors" and therefore, as stipulated by the Constitution, should be removed from office.[40]

In February, the president was acquitted.[41]

Given these events, it is not surprising that, in the minds of many Americans and other people around the globe, "Bill Clinton" became synonymous with "sex scandal." Indeed, the myriad ramifications of the media's extraordinary coverage of the president's carnal activities are impossible to assess. That every major news organization in the country reported on the nation's highest elected official having adulterous sex with a young woman half his age within a matter of feet from the epicenter of government—not to mention lying about it—clearly had significant influence on the American public's feelings toward not only Clinton and the institution of the presidency but on the country's sense of morality and values writ large.

Despite the uncertainty about the full extent of the scandal's impact, a few specific observations can be made regarding Zippergate and the media's treatment of sex.

Before Paula Jones and Monica Lewinsky moved onto the nation's radar screen, for example, most responsible journalists considered one person's mouth coming into contact with another person's genitals to be far too graphic of an act to be discussed in a general-circulation newspaper. After the scandal propelled oral sex onto America's front pages, however, the subject was there to stay. "Oral sex is an acceptable alternative [to intercourse]," the *Minneapolis Star Tribune* reported in a cultural trend story published in 2003, "and young women absolutely don't consider it to be sex." A similar article about teenagers appeared in Rhode Island's *Providence Journal* the same year, this one stating: "No one uses a condom during oral sex, girls say. 'That would be considered absurd,' says one. Although this generation has had more sex education than any previous one, a sizable number aren't aware that disease can be transmitted by mouth and that condoms reduce that risk."[42]

Revelations about the sexual histories of politicians became another frequent news topic. *Hustler* magazine publisher Larry Flynt hastened this process by offering $1 million to any woman who was willing to go public about her affair with a high-ranking government official. That propo-

sition drew about 2,000 telephone calls, Flynt later said, that private investigators narrowed down to a dozen substantiated cases. The pornographer's biggest prize was Robert Livingston, a Louisiana Republican who was slated to become speaker of the U.S. House of Representatives until he was forced to tell his colleagues, "During my thirty-three-year marriage, I have on occasion strayed," and then to resign. Dan Burton of Indiana and Helen Chenoweth of Idaho, both Republican members of Congress, soon added their names to the list of publicly shamed adulterers. Representative Henry J. Hyde, who had headed the impeachment process, joined the club when the on-line magazine *Salon* disclosed that he had been involved in an extramarital affair during the 1960s; the Illinois Republican didn't resign, though, as he successfully characterized the affair as a "youthful indiscretion"—he had been forty-one at the time. Despite Hyde's success at weathering the story, many people agreed with *USA Today* when the newspaper stated that "an air of Sexual McCarthyism chills the nation's capital."[43]

There is also persuasive evidence that, in the wake of Zippergate, journalists became overly excited about stories that involved the possibility of a sexual relationship between a young woman and a powerful middle-aged man. "From the moment Chandra Levy was linked to Gary Condit, lots of news organizations hit the journalistic accelerator," the *Washington Post* wrote in 2001. "Everyone knew the drill: a love-struck intern from California, an older politician denying an affair." After the twenty-four-year-old Levy disappeared from her Washington, D.C., apartment and her relatives revealed that she had been sexually involved with the fifty-three-year-old congressman, the story exploded onto television newscasts and newspaper front pages across the country with a ferocity that seemed out of proportion to the facts of the case. Many observers believed that the excesses could be attributed, at least partially, to reporters and editors being reminded of the affair between Clinton and Lewinsky.[44]

One final thought related to the scandal's role in the evolution of the relationship between sex and the media involves the public's perception of Bill Clinton. His reckless behavior brought shame and ridicule to the presidency and to the nation, but a critical mass of Americans who read the newspaper accounts and watched the nightly soap opera that played

out through the TV news reports ultimately felt little real hostility toward him. Instead, they continued to regard Clinton as a highly capable and essentially decent man who, because of a regrettable weakness for sex that was hardly unique, had been subjected to a level of scrutiny that few men could endure without embarrassing details being exposed.[45]

Yes, the working-class boy from Arkansas who rose to the pinnacle of political leadership suffered from human frailties and made foolhardy mistakes that were reprehensible.

No, neither his actions nor the lies that he told in a desperate effort to conceal those shameful deeds—to protect himself and his family—posed any real danger to the Constitution or to the long-term stability of the nation.

Although no polls were taken on the topic, perhaps many Americans did not feel animus toward Bill Clinton because, at some level of their consciousness, they acknowledged that he carried the unprecedented burden, after all, of being the first president whose coming of age had coincided with that of the Sexual Revolution.

Youth Media

Shaping Teenage Sexual Values

A TEENAGE BOY LIES ON A BED, KISSING HIS GIRLFRIEND WHILE TRYING TO convince her that the time is right. She thinks about his proposal for a few seconds but then decides that, no, she's not ready to take the big step. So she deftly slides down his slender body and unzips his pants. He is soon writhing and moaning in ecstasy as her head, buried in his crotch, rhythmically bobs up and down. He gives her fair warning before he reaches orgasm, allowing her time to raise her head and see him grab a plastic cup from the nightstand and ejaculate into the beer.

Moments later, the host of the party barges through the door, a girl in tow, and announces that it's his turn to use the bedroom. As the first couple leaves, the second sits on the edge of the bed where boy number two begins his pitch. But the second girl is not as accommodating as the first, and the determined young man soon realizes he'll have to do some fancy talking if he has any hope of scoring. After delivering several cheesy lines, he pauses to refresh himself, reaching for the plastic cup that is now back in its original position on the nightstand.

He takes a big gulp and swallows hard.

An instant later, the boy scowls. Perplexed by the strange taste of the beer, he looks toward the door where the first couple exited. As he puts two and two together, his eyes grow huge and a look of disgust spreads across his face—and he begins gagging fitfully. Moments later, the boy has his head over a toilet bowl, retching desperately in an effort to spit out every drop of the semen he drank.

The primary purpose of the series of scenes is to provide some of the laugh-out-loud humor that turned *American Pie* into a teen film classic—*Rolling Stone* called the movie "two hilarious hours of impure *pow*"—but the sequence, at the same time, contained at least two substantive sexual messages.[1]

Number one: The first girl communicated that having intercourse for the first time is a huge step that a person should think carefully about before taking.

Number two: Many teens do not consider oral sex to be "real sex"—closer to kissing than to having intercourse.

Those messages were part of a libidinous laundry list that young moviegoers and TV viewers were sent in the 1990s. During these years, the media not only continued to provide sexual content for adults but also offered fare that was tailored specifically to teenagers. In the early years of the Sexual Revolution, the media had focused on erotic material for adult men and women, as shown by the content of *Playboy* and *Cosmo*. But gradually, as the decades passed, the target age expanded, at least for such sexual provocateurs as Madonna and booty rappers. And so, by the last decade of the twentieth century, teenagers clearly had become an important focus of the media products that were helping to propel the revolution. As the *Los Angeles Times* put it in 1998, when it came to sexual content in movies and TV shows, "Hollywood has a serious case of Teen Fever."[2]

Joining *American Pie* as youth-oriented media vehicles chock full of sexual content were other films such as *Clueless* and *Election* and hit television programs such as *Dawson's Creek* and *Friends*. Recurring messages, in addition to those about intercourse and oral sex, involved topics such as virginity, cross-generational relationships, the connection between sex and alcohol, and the consequences of unprotected sex.

The content of the films and TV programs was sometimes so bawdy that it created unique challenges for the executives who ran the studios and networks. When the Motion Picture Association of America had a look at the original version of *American Pie,* the film received a rating of NC–17, which meant that no one under the age of seventeen should be allowed to see it. Knowing that the rating would cause most of the coun-

try's major theaters not to show the film, the executives at Universal Studios asked the association what part of the film had been found offensive. Members of the ratings board pointed specifically to a scene in which a teenage boy thrust his erect penis into a warm apple pie five times. The studio's Powers That Be then reduced the number of thrusts to two, and the film was released with an R rating—and became a huge hit among teen viewers.[3]

Planning for the Big Step

In the 1990s, more than 80 percent of young Americans were having intercourse for the first time while in their teens—the average age was sixteen for boys, seventeen for girls. The emotional repercussions of a young person taking such a momentous step were certainly significant on their own, but when combined with the possibility of becoming pregnant or contracting a sexually transmitted disease, this was clearly an activity that demanded careful thought. The decade's film and television offerings aimed at young people provided models for such planning—with the girl consistently being the final decision-maker.[4]

American Pie revolves around four high school boys, all of them virgins, who make a pact that each will have intercourse by the end of prom night, which is three weeks away. Kevin, the boy who ejaculated into the cup of beer, clearly has the inside track on reaching the goal because he and his girlfriend are already having oral sex. Persuading Vicky to move to the next level, though, proves to be a challenge because she has definite ideas about the circumstances for that first time. "It's got to be completely perfect," she says. "I want the right time, the right moment, the right place." Only after several conversations with a more experienced girlfriend does Vicky decide that, in fact, the post-prom party meets all her criteria. She tells Kevin that she'll be ready to take the big step then—but not until then.[5]

Clueless, another teenage film classic, provides an even stronger model of a young woman planning carefully before becoming sexually active. In the 1995 box-office hit, Alicia Silverstone plays a beautiful and popular girl who, despite considerable peer pressure, has made the conscious decision not to have sex until she finds a guy she knows well and really likes. "I'm

just not interested in doing it until I find the right man," Cher tells her girlfriends. "You see how picky I am about my shoes—and they only go on my *feet*." The movie builds to the point that Cher finally finds a guy, a serious and career-minded college student she has known for several years, who meets the high standards of the girl *Time* magazine crowned, because of her sexual restraint, "an icon for her generation."[6]

Dawson's Creek, a program on the WB network that focused on the sexual awakening of American teenagers, showcased several young people who think long and hard before becoming sexually active. Among them is Andie. Her relationship with another sixteen-year-old progresses gradually over a dozen episodes before she begins to consider the possibility of having sex with the guy. Andie then describes the ideal romantic evening, including dinner in a French restaurant and a night in a historic bed and breakfast, that she would want to precede the big event. The boy, in turn, sets out to transform her dream into reality. But even as Andie sees the details unfold before her eyes, her boyfriend makes it clear that he won't push her to do anything she isn't ready for. "I just wanted to give you your fantasy evening," he tells her—and he means it. Even after Andie says she's ready, her boyfriend still asks her several times to make sure that she's thought the decision through before the young couple finally has sex.[7]

Oral Sex as Not Sex

In the distant past and throughout most of the twentieth century, oral sex was widely perceived as an unusual or exotic activity that was practiced by very few couples. Over time, however, the act became commonplace among young people. This shift occurred at least partly because the activity avoided the threat of pregnancy while also dramatically reducing the possibility of contracting the HIV virus. Regardless of the reasons for its increased popularity, oral sex came to be perceived as an activity very different from intercourse. In the 1990s, youth media both reflected the changes and helped to accelerate them.[8]

The most memorable couple to engage in oral sex on the decade's movie screens was the one in *American Pie.* First Kevin squirms and whimpers with delight in the scene immediately before he deposits his semen

in the cup of beer, and then he turns the tables and brings similar pleasure to Vicky—in hopes of moving a step closer to intercourse. *Rolling Stone* considered that second scene worthy of special praise, writing, "We were quite thrilled, as a matter of sexual politics, to see that it wasn't only guys getting off in the movie but girls as well."[9]

Oral sex also plays a role in *Clueless*. Cher's best friend and her boyfriend are shown constantly bickering. As the movie progresses, it becomes clear that the couple's major recurring issue is that she is not as interested in sex as he is. She adamantly refuses to have intercourse, but she is willing—after the guy begs sufficiently—to pleasure him orally. "My man is satisfied," the girl boasts to Cher, "but technically I'm a virgin."[10]

Election, a film that *Newsweek* described as "crisp, edgy and sometimes startlingly raunchy," also portrays an instance of oral sex. The movie revolves around a ferociously overachieving high school student named Tracy, played by Reese Witherspoon, who is determined to be elected student body president. Matthew Broderick plays the civics teacher who makes the mistake of getting in Tracy's way by persuading the star quarterback to run against her. Oral sex enters the quirky comedy when the football player's sister repeatedly tries to kiss one of her female friends. The friend not only refuses the advances but is determined to dispel any suspicion that she might be a lesbian. So she grabs the quarterback, unzips his pants, crouches down in front of him, and begins taking care of business.[11]

Ridiculing Virginity

During a time when eight out of every ten teenagers were experiencing intercourse, numbers nine and ten were often the objects of ridicule. Teen-oriented films and TV programs relentlessly reflected this value, showing how young people routinely mocked the virgins among them.

In *American Pie,* the host of the two major parties depicted in the movie is sexually experienced, and so Steve Stifler is merciless in his verbal abuse of the four boys whose intercourse-by-prom-night pact drives the film. During an early scene, one of the guys boasts about his surefire strategy for succeeding in his quest for sex. Stifler then responds, in his colorful linguistic style, "I got an idea. How 'bout you guys actually *locate* your

dicks, remove the shrink wrap, and *fucking use them!*" The boys also lament their shameful minority status; one of them says to the others, "You know, we're all gonna go to college as virgins. I mean, they probably have special *dorms* for people like us."[12]

Clueless communicates the same message. A new girl in school matter-of-factly assumes that all the attractive and popular students are sexually experienced. When she learns that Cher is not, the girl is shocked, dropping her jaw and whispering—a clear signal that it is something to be ashamed of—"You're a virgin?" Another girl quickly corrects the new one, saying that the word "virgin" is so offensive that a new term has been coined to replace it: "hymenally challenged." Later in the movie, after the newcomer settles in, she begins to consider something Cher says but then changes her mind and dismisses the comment as irrelevant, saying, "Why am I even listening to you? You're a virgin."

Friends, an extremely popular television program that targeted young viewers, revolved around six New Yorkers—the *Los Angeles Times* called them "the sitcom world's sexiest sextet"—who have already completed college. Because all of the highly attractive men and women have been sexually active for years, virginity is not the subject of denigration for this group—conventional sex is. During one episode in the NBC program's 1994 premier season, the various characters compete to see who has had intercourse in the most exotic or dangerous location. Monica takes an early lead by describing the time she had sex on a pool table, but Joey soon outdoes her by boasting that he once had sex in the women's room of a public library. Ross then enters the contest by bragging about the time he and a girlfriend had sex behind one of the rides at Disneyland. Ultimately it's unclear who wins the game, but there's no question who loses. When the best that Rachel can come up with is the time she had sex "at the foot of the bed," the guys mock her by looking stunned and loudly calling out "Step back! We have a winner!"[13]

Crossing the Generational Line

While virginity and conventional sex were objects of ridicule, having intercourse with a much older person definitely was not. Even in instances

when one partner was younger than the legal age of consent—which meant the older partner had committed statutory rape—cross-generational lovemaking was celebrated.

American Pie treats the subject with humor. Despite numerous efforts, by prom night one of the boys appears to have fallen short of his goal of losing his virginity. Paul's fortunes take an unexpected turn during the after-prom party at Stifler's house on the lake, however, when he wanders off to the basement and runs into a va-va-va-voom blonde. The fact that the voluptuous woman is twice his age would, in many circumstances, have created a major impediment, but when she offers him single malt scotch that, she says, "has been aged eighteen years—the way I like it," there's clearly a match. As the song "Mrs. Robinson" plays in the background, the camera focuses on a billiard table that is about to become an impromptu bed. Indeed, Paul both loses his virginity and enjoys sweet revenge, as the mature woman who ushers him into the world of the sexually active is none other than the mother of Steve Stifler, the boy who earlier had taken such joy in ridiculing Paul and his three virgin-plagued buddies.[14]

In two other instances, the partnering is between a high school student and a teacher. In *Election,* Tracy has an affair with her math instructor, who is married and has an infant son; in *Dawson's Creek,* fifteen-year-old Pacey has an affair with his English teacher, who is divorced. The two relationships run a similar course and have similar repercussions. The math teacher is fired from his job, and his wife divorces him; he ultimately leaves town, can't find another teaching job because every potential employer learns about his previous affair, and ends up working in a menial position as a stock clerk in a discount store. The English teacher faces an inquisition by the school board as well as the possibility of being charged with statutory rape until Pacey saves her by lying to authorities and saying he fabricated the affair; the teacher still decides to move to another town and start afresh. Neither Tracy nor Pacey pays any visible price for having an illicit affair.[15]

The cross-generational relationship on *Friends* differs from the other plotlines in that Monica is in her twenties when she falls in love with the recently divorced man, played by Tom Selleck, she had known during

childhood as a friend of her parents. There is initially an element of humor in the pairing, as the younger woman realizes that she's having a sexual relationship with a grandfather who is not only twenty years older than she is but "whose swimming pool I once peed in." Eventually the plotline becomes more serious when Monica learns that the man she is dating doesn't want to have any more children, while she is eager to start a family. Monica then ends the relationship.[16]

Making the Sex–Alcohol Connection

Alcohol can reduce a person's inhibitions and thereby help propel her or him into an unplanned sexual encounter that the individual later regrets. Youth media products of the 1990s frequently depicted this potentially hazardous connection.

In *American Pie*, most of the sex takes place at either a party at Steve Stifler's house in the city or the after-prom party he hosts at the family cabin on the lake. Kevin ejaculates into the beer at the first event; all four boys who made the pact finally lose their virginity at the second. Beer and wine flow freely on both occasions, but the dialogue never specifically speaks to the relationship between sex and alcohol.

Dawson's Creek portrays the link between sex and alcohol on several occasions. The program's most sexually active character, Jen, lived in New York City before moving to Capeside, the small Massachusetts town where the series is set. When she comes to live with her grandparents, she is immediately attracted to Dawson, a fellow fifteen-year-old. In telling him about her past, Jen admits, "I lost my virginity when I was twelve to some older guy who got me drunk." That incident led her into a period when she was highly promiscuous, she continues, saying that alcohol again played a role, "I was drinking a lot and having blackouts." After moving to Capeside, Jen remains celibate for more than a year, including keeping Dawson at bay, until a night when she drinks too much and impulsively sleeps with Chris, a boy she barely knows.[17]

Friends shows that young women are not the only ones whose inhibitions are reduced by alcohol. In one episode, Chandler drinks so much at a party that he fools around with one of Joey's sisters, but the next morn-

ing he can't remember which one. Chandler eventually pays a price for his drunken misconduct, as his friendship with Joey is threatened, the sister he slept with is furious with him, and one of the other sisters—either Gina or Deena or Veronica or Mary Theresa or Cookie—becomes so angry that she knocks him out cold.[18]

Taking Precautions

When the numerous instances of sexual activity in the various 1990s teen-oriented films and TV shows are combined, they constitute an enormous presence in those media products. Scenes showing the characters taking steps to avoid pregnancy and sexually transmitted diseases, by contrast, have only a small presence.

In *American Pie,* the scene in which the four boys pledge to lose their virginity is followed by an image of Kevin placing packages of condoms into the hands of his friends. Another reference comes in one of the final scenes. One member of the foursome, Jim, fails miserably in his efforts to have sex with a buxom Czech exchange student because he becomes what *Rolling Stone* called "the poster boy for premature ejaculation"—his humiliation becomes public when he accidentally broadcasts the scene on the Internet. So Jim ends up going to the prom with a "flute-toting band dork" because she's one of the few students, or so Jim thinks, who didn't see the broadcast. His date turns out, however, to be far more aggressive than he expected. She not only suggests that they have sex, but at the post-prom party she opens her purse and gives Jim his marching orders. "I have two rubbers," the girl says firmly. "Wear them both. It'll desensitize you. I don't want you coming so damned early this time."[19]

Numerous plotlines in *Dawson's Creek* referred to protective measures. Andie and her boyfriend's extended build-up to having intercourse includes him taking an HIV test, at her insistence. Jen mentions cautionary steps when describing her freewheeling sexual past, saying she took birth control pills but didn't always use condoms. That Jen is committed to taking precautions now that she's begun her new, reformed life is apparent when she goes to bed with Chris; when they are shown waking up the next morning, an open condom wrapper lies on the nightstand.[20]

All six of the main characters on *Friends* were portrayed as being sexually active, with one-night stands and other sexual encounters being mentioned frequently. References to safe sex arise occasionally; when the characters muse about what they'd include in a survival kit in case of an emergency, for example, Joey lists two items: candy bars and condoms. But by far the most memorable statement related to protection came during the program's eighth season when Ross and Rachel's on-again/off-again relationship takes a significant turn. One night they drink too much wine and end up having sex, and Rachel soon discovers she's pregnant. She initially thinks the father is her assistant, as she was sleeping with him during the same period, but ultimately she determines that Ross's sperm did the deed. When she tells the dad-to-be about this development, he is stunned because they used a condom. Rachel then points out, "Condoms only work like 97 percent of the time." An overly excited Ross then squeals, "What, what, what? They should put that *on the box!*" When Rachel calmly says, "They do," Ross grabs a box of condoms, reads the small print, and says, his eyes huge and his voice high and squeaky, "Well, they should put it in HUGE BLACK LETTERS!" Ross's over-the-top reaction creates one of the most memorable images in the history of the mega-hit sitcom.[21]

At the same time that condoms occasionally made cameo appearances in movies and on TV shows aimed at American young people, they also made their debut in television advertising. MTV began airing commercials for Ramses Safe Play condoms, the first brand marketed directly to teens, in the early 1990s. The cable channel's breakthrough was followed, late in the decade, by three of the six broadcast networks—Fox, CBS, and NBC—ending their long-standing prohibitions against condom ads. Despite these advances, certain limitations continued, as the broadcast networks only aired the ads late at night, and ABC, UPN, and WB refused to air the commercials at any time whatsoever.[22]

Downplaying the Consequences

Considering the abundance of sexual hookups that occur in the various films and TV programs compared to the relative infrequency of references

to safe sex, it would seem likely that the libidinous denizens of youth media would frequently have found themselves either pregnant or infected with STDs. During the 1990s as well as before and since, however, Hollywood was well aware that viewers find sex much more compelling than sexual consequences.

American Pie, Clueless, and *Election* all take place in high schools where sexual activity is rampant, and yet the movies do not depict even one student becoming pregnant or being infected with a sexually transmitted disease—even though during the 1990s one out of every seven American teenagers suffered from at least one STD. That Tracy in *Election* did not face any consequences is particularly unrealistic. Despite having a sexual relationship with a teacher, she doesn't become pregnant or suffer any public shame or humiliation because of the affair, which is a highly unrealistic turn of events considering that the teacher was fired and that high schools are notoriously fertile ground for gossip. Even more unlikely is that the principal, knowing about Tracy's affair, would have allowed her to run for student body president. In the world of youth media, *The New Yorker* magazine pointed out, adults in cross-generational affairs pay a high price while the teenagers suffer not at all.[23]

Dawson's Creek communicated similar messages. The English teacher has to face charges by the school board as well as law enforcement authorities because of her affair with a fifteen-year-old, but the young man suffers no negative repercussions. She gives up her job and leaves town; he is the envy of every boy in school. That plotline and its accompanying messages prompted criticism on many fronts, including denunciations in *Esquire, Newsweek,* and *Entertainment Weekly.* WB's chief executive, Jamie Kellner, defended the program as reflecting real life, saying, "I don't think there's anything in this program we haven't seen in the news." Kellner was referring to the 1993 case in which Seattle high school teacher Mary Kay Letourneau had a sexual relationship with a thirteen-year-old student. Unlike the teacher in *Dawson's Creek,* however, Letourneau was sent to prison and gave birth to two babies by her young lover—the kind of life-altering consequences that the TV show opted not to depict.[24]

Another *Dawson's Creek* teen who lived a charmed life was Jen. Even though she had sex with numerous men while living in New York City

during her adolescence and early teens, she never became pregnant and apparently never contracted any of the plethora of STDs that were rampant in that urban center during the 1990s. Perhaps even more miraculous, Jen has the will and the wherewithal, at the ripe old age of fifteen, to transform herself and to refrain from having sex with Dawson, even though the two feel a mutual attraction from the moment they meet.

The characters on *Friends* may be the luckiest of all. Joey is an attractive star of a TV soap opera—*People* magazine dubbed him a "hunka hunka"—who's had sex with dozens of women, knowing many of them so briefly that he can't even remember their names, but none of the women ever mentions the possibility of pregnancy or a paternity suit, and he's never infected with an STD. The only time the program deals seriously with sexual consequences is when Rachel gives birth to a daughter. Even then, the repercussions are minimal. The beautiful young woman, played by Jennifer Aniston, is not portrayed as having to shed a single ounce of weight after giving birth, the father of the baby is completely devoted to supporting his child and her mother both financially and emotionally, and Rachel continues her career without interruption. Indeed, the single mother keeps going to clubs and parties exactly as she did before giving birth, none of her suitors so much as batting an eye at the fact that she has a baby to take care of. Baby Emma becomes little more than an occasional prop, in fact, as numerous episodes pass without any reference whatsoever to the child or who is taking care of her.[25]

Good Messages or Bad?

At the same time that media products such as *American Pie, Clueless, Election, Dawson's Creek,* and *Friends* were entertaining their young fans, they also were exerting enormous influence on this highly impressionable audience. Most American young people, during adolescence and their early teens, have no personal experience with sexual activity. And so, such films and TV shows provide them with their only examples of how people engage in sexual activities or navigate sexual relationships. As a *U.S. News & World Report* cover story put it in 1995, "The media are so compelling and so filled with sex, they have become our true sex educators."[26]

Because youth media have such huge potential impact, it's particularly important with this topic to consider the quality of the information that was communicated. Distilled to its most fundamental form, the question is: Were the messages good or bad?

The films and TV programs deserve praise on several counts. Encouraging young people to think about sexual intercourse and to plan that activity before engaging in it, as Cher does in *Clueless,* is an excellent lesson; becoming sexually active has myriad potential consequences—emotionally, physically, socially—and is, therefore, an action that should be preceded by careful thought. Another message that should be lauded is showing the connection between sex and alcohol, as *Dawson's Creek* repeatedly did; hearing how a man getting Jen drunk led her into a life that she later regretted—"I was sexualized way too young," she says in one episode, "and I don't wish that on anybody"—may have helped youthful television viewers avoid going down that same path. A third commendable message evolves from indications that characters depicted in the various youth media, such as *American Pie,* practice safe sex; *Newsweek* described the film as "surprisingly earnest and cautionary" because of scenes such as the one in which Kevin supplies his buddies with condoms.[27]

Other messages are regrettable. When popular media products ridicule virginity, as in *American Pie,* it becomes more difficult for a young person to make a responsible decision regarding when to become sexually active; peer pressure can be a powerful force that is strengthened even more by the content of popular films and TV shows. Also problematic is depicting a teenage girl having intercourse with a much older man, as in *Election;* the message is even more troubling when the man is an authority figure, such as a teacher, and the girl experiences no negative repercussions. Another unfortunate tendency of some youth media is downplaying the consequences of unprotected sex, as in *Friends;* showing a likable young man such as Joey being promiscuous without paying a price and a beautiful young woman such as Rachel having a baby but not having to alter her lifestyle provides misleading information to impressionable young viewers.

As significant as whether a message is good or bad is another question that is virtually impossible to answer, and yet one that should at least be mentioned: Were the messages effective?

Highlighting the context in which just one of the many sexual statements was presented serves to illustrate the complications of assessing not what a particular scene said but how likely it is that the scene had impact. NBC was relentless in promoting the *Friends* segment in which Rachel was to tell Ross that he was the father of her baby. And so, an impressive 20 million viewers ultimately tuned in to hear the beautiful young mother-to-be tell them—and quite correctly—that "Condoms only work like 97 percent of the time." The lesson was an enormously valuable one for sexually active young men and women to hear, as it reminded them that condoms sometimes break during intercourse. Also relevant, though, is the circumstance in which that information was presented. Ross's exaggerated reaction—bulging eyes, perspiring brow, squealing voice—made good television, as viewers all over the country laughed heartily. Less clear is the degree to which that laughter obscured the sex education message. There is no question that millions of young viewers still remember Ross's overly excited and highly humorous reaction to Rachel's news, but it is more difficult to say how many of those viewers still remember the statistic.

One study found, however, that the impact of that scene was substantial. Several days after the episode aired, RAND Corporation researchers asked 500 teenage TV viewers if they recalled learning any sexual lessons from *Friends*. A stunning 65 percent of those young people said they had learned that condoms can fail to prevent pregnancy. "We've always known that teenagers get useful information about sex from factual reporting and advice-oriented media, but now we know they can get this information from entertainment television programs as well," a RAND psychologist said. "That's important because entertainment programs, especially highly rated ones like 'Friends,' reach many more teens."[28]

Paying for Sex (on Cable)

Sex and the City *and* Queer as Folk

Scene 1

The stunning blonde in her late thirties and the virginal college student whiz through the positions as if they're acting out the images in a sex manual—first him on top, then her on top, then doggie style—until the boy finally exhausts himself, flops down on the bed, and announces, "That was awesome. I think I love you." The older, wiser, and infinitely more experienced woman smiles knowingly and responds, "No, Sam, that wasn't love. That was *sex.*"[1]

Scene 2

The twenty-nine-year-old provides words of assurance to the seventeen-year-old by recounting his own first experience with gay sex while he was still in high school. When the older man finishes his description, the awestruck teenager says, "I bet you were really scared." The more knowledgeable man responds softly, "We're all scared the first time," before gently directing the boy, lying naked among the sheets, to lean back and lift his legs up in the air.[2]

Welcome to TV sex in the new millennium.

The two scenes aired on pay-cable channels—the first on HBO's *Sex and the City*, the second on Showtime's *Queer as Folk*. During the early 2000s, these provocative programs are pushing sex on television to places it has never gone before.[3]

Commenting on *Sex and the City*, the *New York Times* has written, "There's never been anything quite like it," while the *Washington Post* has expressed similar sentiments about *Queer as Folk*, dubbing it "the most unapologetic treatment of gay people ever seen on American television."[4]

The reviews that specify what elements set the two shows apart from their less-daring predecessors have consistently mentioned the explicit images and the graphic language. Exposed breasts for women and bare butts for men are commonplace, while full-frontal female nudity occurs occasionally on both programs and full-frontal male nudity makes cameo appearances on *Queer as Folk*. Dialogue routinely includes words such as "fuck," "cock," and "pussy," and one *Sex and the City* plotline was built around repeated use of the word that many Americans consider the most offensive in the English language: "cunt."[5]

TV censors permit the no-holds-barred content partly because the shows don't air until after the kids are in bed—9 p.m. for *Sex*, 10 p.m. for *Queer*—and because each episode is preceded by a warning that the material might not be suitable for children under seventeen. Most important of all, viewers knowingly invite the two channels into their homes by paying a monthly fee, $30 for HBO and another $10 for Showtime, beyond the basic cable charge. Plenty of people are willing to ante up; in 2000, HBO had twenty-five million subscribers and Showtime had twelve million, and those figures rise each year as more and more viewers tune in to the two groundbreaking "sexcoms."[6]

Sex and the City chronicles what the *Los Angeles Times* has called "the erotic and rhapsodically funny mating adventures" of four thirty-something women living in Manhattan. The escapades are seen through the eyes of Carrie, a member of the quartet who writes a newspaper column about sex and is ably played by Sarah Jessica Parker. Her sidekicks are Charlotte, a somewhat naïve art dealer; Miranda, a corporate lawyer; and Samantha, a promiscuous public relations executive—*Newsweek* has dubbed them "a romantic, a careerist and a slut."[7]

Queer as Folk focuses on five men, aged seventeen to the late twenties, who live in a free-spirited section of Pittsburgh that real gay residents of the Steel City can only dream about. Michael, a boy-next-door type who serves as narrator, runs a comic book store, and his best friend Brian, a rapacious demigod who has sex with every hunky gay man in town, makes big bucks by creating advertising campaigns that invariably revolve around sex. The other three main characters are Justin, a teenage art student who falls for Brian; Emmett, a proudly flamboyant party planner; and Ted, an accountant. Two lesbians are also part of the cast, but the plotlines are dominated by the gay men. The program is based on a similar one that aired on English television, and its title is derived from the British saying, "There's nowt so queer as folk," which means there's nothing so strange as people.[8]

Sex and *Queer,* though focusing on different genders and sexual orientations, have several similarities. Most notably, both programs cross any number of sexual thresholds by highlighting subjects that television has never dealt with before. In addition, the two shows both glamorize promiscuity while, at the same time, illuminating a number of substantive sexual issues that network television had assiduously avoided. The shows also communicate that sexually active women and men should take precautions to avoid unwanted pregnancy and disease.

Going Where TV Has Never Gone Before

The two programs take such generous advantage of the freedom available on pay-cable channels that it's a daunting task to communicate the cornucopia of sexual topics they've pioneered. That being said, snapshots of a few plotlines capture some of their distinctive flavor.

- In one *Sex and the City* episode, Carrie's relationship with an attractive politician is moving along nicely until he asks her to urinate on him. Unsure what to do, Carrie talks to her three girlfriends and then decides to turn down the guy's request. He makes it easier for her by announcing that they can no longer be seen together in public because his advisers think her job as a sex columnist is too "seamy" for

the voting public to accept. Carrie gets the last word by publishing an article about the politician titled "To Pee or Not to Pee, That Is the Question."[9]

- Samantha begins dating a handsome, successful, and charming man who appears to be absolutely perfect. Several weeks into the romance, however, the man senses that his hot-blooded girlfriend has grown distant. When she denies there's a problem, he keeps probing, saying, "Sweetheart, there's nothing you can say that can hurt me as long as it's what you are feeling." After still more questioning, Samantha finally blurts out, "Your penis is too small! I need a *big dick!*" Offended beyond words, the man walks quietly away.[10]

- Charlotte is conflicted when the man she's dating asks her to have anal sex with him. She talks to her three girlfriends and hears a range of opinions from Samantha's "go for it" to Miranda's "not on your life." After weighing the pros and cons, Charlotte tells the guy, "I just don't want to be an up-the-butt girl." He then shrugs casually and asks, "Then can we fuck the regular way?" Charlotte smiles sweetly and responds, "Yes, please," as their relationship continues full speed ahead.[11]

- The premier episode of *Queer as Folk* begins with Michael stating: "The first thing you have to know is, it's all about sex. They say men think about sex every twenty-eight seconds. Of course that's straight men. With gay men, it's every nine."[12]

- Later in the first segment, a guy repeatedly tries to pick up Michael at a bar. When his friends point out that the man has a perfectly contoured derriere and a remarkably prominent bulge in his crotch, Michael takes the lad home. But when they undress, it turns out that the guy's two well-formed assets are, in fact, made of molded plastic—he ordered "the butt" and "the bulge" from a catalogue.[13]

- When Justin meets a man at a party who asks him what kind of artistic work he is involved in, the adorable young blond says that most recently he's been manipulating classical form with digital imagery. Impressed, the guy says, "So you're not just a pretty face," and Justin

responds, "No, I've got a pretty big cock as well, and I give one *hel-luva* blow job."[14]

- A potential client says he will do business with Brian's advertising firm only if the handsome hunk has sex with him. Brian has had meaningless encounters with hundreds of men, so he blithely goes to the guy's hotel room and strips off his clothes. Then the phone rings. It's the client's daughter, telling him she broke her arm and needs him to come home as soon as possible. The lustful father is not sympathetic to the girl, saying he'll see her the next day. He then hangs up the phone and prepares to resume his sexual encounter. But Brian turns away, orders a cab to take the guy to the airport, and walks out of the room.[15]

Glamorizing Promiscuity

That *Sex and the City* and *Queer as Folk* are both told from the perspective of a single narrator—Carrie in *Sex,* Michael in *Queer*—doesn't mean that the other characters fade into the woodwork. Indeed, as the two groundbreaking programs gained momentum, it was a lesser member of the cast, in each case, who captured the viewing public's imagination.

Samantha in *Sex* and Brian in *Queer* have a lot in common. Both are highly attractive and have successful careers. Their personal styles are similar, too, as she wears revealing outfits that allow her to disrobe at a moment's notice, and he favors skintight pants that show off his physical assets and yet can also be removed quickly. But the trait that, more than any other, has sparked debate about this hedonistic duo is that both of them consume men as if they're fast food.

Virtually every episode of *Sex* shows Samantha with a new bed partner. From the college student who instantly falls in love with her to a man who earns his livelihood as a dildo model to a wrestling coach she teaches 1,001 sexual positions, the glamorous blonde sometimes worries that she's already slept with every attractive man in Manhattan—which propels her to have an affair with a lesbian. "I don't understand why women are so

obsessed with getting married," Samantha says. "If you're single, the world is your smorgasbord."[16]

Brian in *Queer* is even more promiscuous, having sex with two or more different men in every episode. In the series premiere, he makes eye contact with a handsome young client during a business meeting and then has anal intercourse with the guy in the nearest men's room. Before the end of the segment, Brian also has sex with Justin and another man in the back room of his favorite bar, Babylon. "I don't believe in love, I believe in fucking," Brian says in that first episode. "You get in and out with a maximum of pleasure and a minimum of bullshit."[17]

Illuminating Serious Sexual Issues

Casual observers have dismissed *Sex* and *Queer* as mindless trash. Critics who have taken a closer look, however, know that the programs have tackled many substantive sexual issues. A *New York Times* headline read, "Serious Tone Adds to Success of 'Sex and the City,'" and the cover of the country's leading gay news magazine, *The Advocate*, announced "'Queer as Folk' Gets Serious."[18]

Sex has dealt with heavy-duty topics ranging from abortion to menopause and from infertility and breast cancer to the ever-ticking biological clock, but viewers familiar with the entire series have no doubt which issue—bar none—heads the list: adultery.[19]

During the first two seasons, Carrie was in a relationship with Big, who is divorced, but she broke up with him after he announced that he planned to stay single for the rest of his life. In spite of this statement, in the third season Big married another woman and then, a few episodes later, told Carrie the marriage was a mistake. Big and Carrie then had sex, even though he was married and she was in a serious relationship with another man. All of this background set up what ultimately unfolded as a series of episodes that the *New York Times* praised as the "most moving and superbly acted" depiction of an adulterous affair ever aired on American television.[20]

One segment showed the internal struggle between Carrie's head and heart. "My mind was yelling how angry I was," she recalled after Big

kissed her, "but, oh, my heart, my heart!" Moments later, the couple was shown in bed. A few days after that, she told Big she wouldn't sleep with him a second time. "We gave in to our baser instincts," she said, "but it isn't going to happen again." Big listened to her words and then responded, "But the sex was pretty fucking amazing, wasn't it?"—and Carrie goes to bed with him a second time. The dominant theme during the episodes that chronicled the affair was how profoundly miserable Carrie felt. During one segment, she said, "If only I didn't hate myself," and during another she told herself, "I have one man who loves me and another who wants to leave his wife for me. I should be feeling like I have it all, but I feel like nothing." One of the most poignant scenes came after Charlotte, shortly before her own wedding, found out about the adulterous affair. "I'm getting married in three weeks, and you're my maid of honor," she snapped at Carrie. "How would you feel if someone did this to *me*?"[21]

The infidelity plotline took a dramatic twist the day that Big's wife came home earlier than expected and caught Carrie, dressed in her underwear, in the couple's apartment. That incident ended the affair but not the pain, as Carrie felt compelled to confess her betrayal to her highly sensitive boyfriend. Although Aidan agreed to continue their relationship, the bond of trust clearly had been broken.[22]

Infidelity has been one of the serious sexual issues depicted in *Queer* as well, with Michael speaking for many gay men when he says, "Most of us can't commit to a houseplant, much less a boyfriend." Numerous plotlines have reinforced the point. In one episode, Emmett worked as a maid for a gay couple he idolizes because they've been in a monogamous relationship for eleven years; within a matter of days, however, both men secretly seduce him, prompting Emmett to tell Michael, "One minute I'm starching his collar, the next minute I'm sucking his cock."[23]

Other substantive topics on *Queer* have ranged from becoming addicted to pornography to not being able to have satisfying sex without using drugs. But the most intriguing of the subjects returned to infidelity and explored how a couple can have a committed relationship that is not monogamous. Brian eventually admits that he has feelings for Justin and agrees that they can live together. "But don't get the idea that we're some

married couple," he warns his young lover, saying that he fully intends to continue having sex with other men. "If I'm out late, just assume I'm doing what I want to do—I'm fucking. And when I come home, I'll also be doing exactly what I want to do—coming home to you." The teenager agrees to the rules but also sets some of his own. "You can fuck whoever you want to as long as it's not twice—same for me," Justin stipulates. He also insists that Brian limit himself to anonymous sexual encounters, never asking a man's name or phone number. The couple's other two rules are that they both will always arrive home by 3 a.m. and that neither will kiss another sex partner on the mouth.[24]

Promoting Protection/Cautioning about Consequences

Like the 1990s TV shows *Dawson's Creek* and *Friends,* the two sexcoms of the new millennium focus much of their attention on sexual activities. Unlike the youth-oriented media that premiered the previous decade, however, *Sex and the City* and *Queer as Folk* place a great deal of emphasis on safe sex—rather than passing references—while also highlighting the consequences that people often suffer when they don't take such protective measures.

The four characters on *Sex* not only show how women can avoid becoming pregnant by using the pill but also communicate that women and men should take the additional step of protecting themselves against sexually transmitted diseases. Typical of the scenes sprinkled throughout the series is one in which Samantha, during lunch, flashes her stylish new purse in front of her three friends. Amid the admiring "oohs" and "aahs," Charlotte estimates that the Fendi bag must have cost $3,000, and Samantha boasts, "or $150," and hands the knockoff to her friends for a closer look. When Carrie turns the purse upside down to check the lining, a dozen condoms fall out. That none of the women is surprised at the contents is a subtle reminder that everyone who's sexually active should have protection constantly at the ready. Indeed, the next line from the recently married Charlotte—"I'm so happy to be out of that condom stage"—reinforces the message that protection should be a consistent part of every single woman's life.[25]

Sex communicates that AIDS is another reality that must be dealt with responsibly. In one plotline, Samantha apologizes to her friends for being short-tempered, explaining that she's upset because of the HIV test she's scheduled to have that afternoon. The other women are then instantly sympathetic, saying they get nervous each time they're tested, too—but refusing to let Samantha cancel her appointment.[26]

The HBO program sends even stronger messages about the consequences of a sexually active woman *failing* to protect herself. One episode depicts Charlotte impulsively sleeping with a man without using a condom and then getting a case of crabs, and another has Miranda discovering she contracted an STD years earlier and then having to go through the torturous process of notifying all of her former sex partners—no small number.[27]

By far the most significant statement regarding the price of taking sexual risks unfolds when Miranda becomes pregnant after having unprotected sex, assuming she was safe because her bed partner had only one testicle. She initially plans to abort the fetus, but, after hearing her friends' rueful descriptions of their experiences with abortion, she decides to give birth and raise the child by herself. After Miranda has her baby, she—unlike Rachel on *Friends*—confronts many of the realities involved with parenthood. The most serious of those issues evolves from her efforts to juggle being a single mother and a partner in a law firm. After trying but failing, the Harvard Law School graduate ultimately chooses to put her career on the back burner, a dramatic and yet highly realistic end result of having had unprotected sex.[28]

Queer as Folk, like *Sex and the City*, subtly encourages its viewers to protect themselves against disease. The most closely watched scene in the program's premier episode—the *New York Times*, *Washington Post*, and *Time* all ran stories about it—involved Brian and Justin having sex, as that marked the first time that anal intercourse had been depicted on American television. Just as the older man is about to insert his erect penis into the younger one, Justin looks up at Brian—twelve years his elder—and says, "Wait. In school we have this lecture about safe sex." Without batting an eye, Brian pulls out a condom, flashes a smile, and responds, "Now we're going to have a demonstration." Perfectly willing to accom-

modate Justin's concerns, Brian gently continues, "Put it on me. Go ahead."[29]

Showtime's writers had, in short, placed a non-preachy safe-sex lesson smack dab in the middle of what soon became a classic moment in the gay male culture. Legions of viewers either videotaped that scene off air or later rented or bought the episode at their local video store and have since replayed it numerous times. And Justin's words not only provide viewers, especially young ones who identify with a seventeen-year-old, with an excellent example of responsible sexual behavior, but they also give viewers a two-pronged tutorial on how they should insist upon being treated in a relationship: Say what you need. Don't proceed until you get it.

Queer continually reinforces its potent public health message. When Justin wants to start a gay-straight student alliance at his high school, he catches the attention of the other kids by handing out free condoms. And again when Justin's best friend, Daphne, asks him to be the guy who has sex with her for the first time, he agrees—and provides the condom. Later in the series, after Justin and Brian are living together, the safe-sex issue is again raised. The younger man points out that they've never had intercourse without using a condom but says he'd like to try it. Brian asks, "Do you want me to fuck you bareback?" The lad eagerly responds that he does. But Brian adamantly refuses. "Never let anyone fuck you without a condom," he says sternly. "I want you safe. I want you around for a long time."[30]

The other characters also communicate the importance of taking precautions. Michael prepares for a weekend in the country with his new boyfriend by packing two items: a change of underwear and a box of Trojans. When Ted arrives at a party and discovers men having anal intercourse without using protection, he's so appalled that he immediately turns and walks out. Emmett is so committed to protecting himself that the other characters dub him "the safe-sex poster boy"—he won't even consider having anal sex unless he uses a condom, spermicidal lubricant, and hydrogen peroxide.[31]

That references to taking precautions are sprinkled so liberally through the various *Queer* episodes doesn't mean that all the characters practice

safe sex all the time. Bad boy Brian, in particular, does not protect the hundreds of men he indiscriminately has sex with unless the guy, as Justin did, specifically mentions the topic. When Pittsburgh's narcissistic Lothario had anal sex with the young client in the office bathroom, for example, there was no indication that he stopped to slip on a condom.

Consistent with the risks that many gay men take, *Queer* makes repeated references to guys being infected with STDs such as gonorrhea, crabs, and anal warts. Virtually every episode also at least mentions the pandemic that continues to plague the gay community. Vic, who as Michael's gay uncle appeared in most segments in the first three seasons until he died of AIDS-related complications in the fourth, was suffering from AIDS; in one plotline, Michael's mother collapses from exhaustion because she's working extra shifts as a waitress to pay for her brother's medication. Ben, a gay professor who became a recurring character in the second season, is HIV-positive; when Ben and Michael begin dating, *Queer as Folk* boldly set out to depict the complexities of a person with the virus having a relationship with a guy who doesn't.[32]

Pay Cable as Sex Educator

Sex and the City and *Queer as Folk* both initially endured a barrage of slings and arrows. Detractors called the HBO series "vulgar" and "salacious," while dismissing the Showtime program as "sensation for sensation's sake" and "an assembly line of orgasms." As the shows evolved and their fan base grew, however, they began to attract considerable praise. Indeed, by 2003, numerous reviewers were hailing the two programs as educational television at its best because they were successfully embedding important sexual messages into engaging plotlines that were drawing larger and larger audiences—particularly young people who needed to learn about sex.[33]

The two topics on *Sex* that have received the most accolades are its depiction of the high price that Carrie paid for having an adulterous affair and the difficulties that Miranda faced because of her unplanned pregnancy, while the most-lauded topic on *Queer* has been the safe-sex mes-

sage during the anal intercourse scene between Brian and Justin in the premier episode.[34]

A close analysis of other plotlines demonstrates that, in fact, both pay-cable programs have a great deal to offer a sex education class.

Many parents and teachers would cringe at the thought of introducing teenage girls to urination as a sex act or to anal intercourse. And yet, the manner in which *Sex* treated those two jaw-dropping topics provided young women with an excellent model for how to deal with requests— or demands—from their male partners. In both cases, the female character listens to the man but does not feel the need to respond immediately. Indeed, she not only takes the time to think about the pros and cons of participating in the activity but also consults with her trio of sexually experienced friends. Nor does either woman blithely follow the advice of those peers. Instead, she evaluates the opinions and then—and only then—makes the decision that she believes is right for her. Also worth noting is the fact that in both instances the woman's choice is a firm "No." In other words, first the series provides viewers with a model for how to respond to challenging sexual questions—a model that could easily be adapted to questions about, for example, oral sex or intercourse without a condom—and then it states that an individual involved in a sexual relationship has every right to refuse a partner's request.

It is difficult to imagine a more laudable pair of sexual messages than those two.

Samantha is a more challenging case study. Her casual jumping from bed to bed is difficult for even the most liberated of observers to condone, much less hold up as a model. And yet, this man-eating hedonist sends some valuable messages related to sex and the media. With regard to sex, Samantha conducts her life *on her own terms*. She is no appendage to a man but is an independent woman—sexually and otherwise—who makes her own decisions, right or wrong, and then deals with the consequences, good or bad. With regard to the media, Samantha is an excellent example of the kind of exaggerated character that entertainment television relies on to draw and hold an audience—and keep people talking the next day. In short: That's entertainment! Just as young people must learn that

the dangerous exploits of Spider-Man and the sexual fantasies of 2 Live Crew should not be emulated, they also must learn that the same is true of Samantha's over-the-top promiscuity.

Indeed, one *Sex* episode spoke directly to this point. In the segment, the PR vamp is hired to publicize the bat mitzvah celebration of a wealthy thirteen-year-old who dresses and behaves like she's twenty-one. Samantha is initially jealous that this young girl travels in a limousine and wears designer clothes as expensive as her own. But then she overhears Jenny telling her girlfriends that she expects to have sex with at least three of the band members playing at her party. "Ladies," Samantha says, "aren't you a little *young* for that kind of talk?" Jenny dismisses the older woman, calling her "grandma" and saying blithely, "I've been giving blow jobs since I was twelve." Samantha is appalled. "You have your whole lives to do that sort of thing," she says in a deadly serious tone. "You should enjoy being children."[35]

Again, it is difficult to imagine a more credible messenger for that point than Samantha.

Queer as Folk also communicates important lessons. Michael hooking up with a guy who uses "the butt" and "the bulge" to attract sex partners illustrates that appearance is so highly valued in some segments of the gay community that deceit is commonplace; Brian refusing to have sex with a potential client who is insensitive to his daughter's needs shows that even the most promiscuous gay man has ethical lines he will not cross. Justin and Brian send another powerful message when they say, while negotiating the boundaries of their open relationship, that having sex with another man is acceptable but kissing him on the mouth is not. All of these statements provide a window into male-male relationships that is both revealing and bewildering, especially for young viewers struggling with their own sexual identity: Welcome to a whole new world.

One of the most compelling plotlines on *Queer as Folk* involves the relationship between one character who is HIV-positive and another who is HIV-negative. When Michael learns that Ben is carrying the virus, he immediately seeks the counsel, reminiscent of many *Sex and the City* episodes, of his friends. To a man, they tell him not to have sex with the hunky professor. "You're playing with fire," Ted says. "What happens if a

condom breaks or if he's flossing his teeth and his gums bleed?" Ted then shakes his head, looks his friend straight in the eye, and says firmly, "I wouldn't do it no matter how much I liked the guy." The generally free-wheeling Brian also tells Michael, pointblank, "You should forget Ben." Brian draws on his advertising background to support his argument. "You see those ads for the cocktails with the great-looking guys skiing and mountain climbing like all they have to do is pop a few protease in-hibitors," he says, "but it's tough downhill racing when you've got non-stop diarrhea." Heeding the advice of his friends, Michael ends the relationship.[36]

But the plotline doesn't end there. Michael can't put his feelings for Ben behind him, convinced that he's found the love of his life. The two men then begin talking—in earnest—about what it would take for a relation-ship between them to work. Michael assures Ben that he'll protect him-self. "I know how to be safe. I was putting condoms on cucumbers before I was driving a car." For Ben's part, he insists that Michael know the real-ities of his health status, such as the fact that he takes fifty anti-viral pills a day and that catching a cold, for him, could be fatal. While those details and warnings may have been for Michael, they simultaneously served as a primer on HIV for *Queer* viewers as well.[37]

After several extended conversations and a great deal of thought, the two men finally have sex, beginning a relationship that evolves into a rich and loving one for both of them—as well as the first of its kind ever de-picted on American television.[38]

Cyberporn

Bringing Sex to the World Wide Web

JONATHAN IS A HANDSOME AND PERSONABLE THIRTY-THREE-YEAR-OLD who used his degree from an Ivy League university to secure a responsible position in the sleek offices of a Madison Avenue advertising agency. These days, though, the highlight of his workday is employing the company's high-speed Internet connection not to bring new clients into the company but to masturbate.

"God, it's so fucked up," Jonathan acknowledges, his tone communicating a momentary sense of disgust. But as he continues the description of his daily diversion, his demeanor shifts to one of excitement and exhilaration. "I go into the computer lab, right? And there are these girls all around in their little cubicles, and I want to see if I can reach orgasm right there." Resourceful and accomplished, he consistently succeeds at his mission, smiling proudly as he admits, "Part of the thrill is the danger element."

Jonathan told his story to *New York* magazine as the leading source for a cover story titled "Generation XXX," one of many articles in magazines and newspapers that, during the early years of the new millennium, reported that legions of Internet-savvy porn fans were spending $2 billion a year to view—and sometimes *interact with*—sexually explicit material on a media venue that had not even existed a decade earlier.[1]

Indeed, no less of a voice of The Establishment than the *Wall Street Journal* was among the observers that spoke admiringly of the porn industry's sudden surge in economic success thanks to creative use of the

technological innovation. One front-page story in the business-oriented paper posed the rhetorical question: "How can X-rated fare rack up profits on-line when so many mainstream Web sites focusing on other businesses continue to struggle?" In the next sentence, the *Journal* supplied the two-word answer: "Sex sells."[2]

The newspaper then went on to provide a succinct description of exactly why pornography and the World Wide Web create the ideal marriage. Customers in search of erotic content no longer have to slink into a sleazy bookstore or face the potential embarrassment of having a friend or coworker see them sneak into the "adults only" section in the back of the neighborhood video store, the *Journal* reported, and then added, "Customers can peruse raunchy fare in the privacy of their home—or office." The *New York* magazine article made the same point, stating, "Cyberporn has become the raunchy wallpaper to respectable lives."[3]

Other publications acknowledged pornography's rising fortunes as well. *U.S. News & World Report* wrote, "The sex industry has been transformed from a minor subculture on the fringes of society into a major component of American popular culture." *USA Today* gave prominent play to the phenomenon, too, publishing a cover story that reported the purchase of erotic content accounts for more than 10 percent of all Internet sales, making sex the World Wide Web's number one commodity. The *Boston Globe* added that the billions of dollars people are paying for cyberporn has pushed the annual revenues for the entire sex industry—including magazines, videos, pay-per-view cable, strip clubs, and escort services—to in excess of $10 billion; to put that figure in perspective, the *Globe* went on to say, "That's as much as Americans spend on spectator sports and the movies combined."[4]

In the early 2000s, then, Internet porn sites provide the most recent evidence that the media are continuing to propel the Sexual Revolution as it stretches into a new millennium.

The specific sexual messages that cyberporn is sending include several that are familiar to anyone who has followed the evolution of the symbiotic relationship between sex and the media since the 1960s; they include women being portrayed as sex objects, casual sex and infidelity being glorified, and male/female sexual relationships being depicted not as equal

partnerships but as arrangements in which men dominate. Other prominent themes are unique to the Internet; they include providing Web sites tailored to specific fetishes and, much less laudably, supplying material for users who lust after models who are younger than the age of consent.

The Rise of Internet Sex Sites

Scholars who have studied the history of pornography have traced its beginnings to many centuries ago but say that some of the major milestones in that evolution have occurred during the last fifty years. One came in the 1960s when *Playboy* brought images of naked women into the mainstream, and another followed a decade later with the widespread availability of videocassettes. Even those two breakthroughs, however, pale in comparison to the growth that erupted in the final decade of the twentieth century. In the words of the book *Obscene Profits: The Entrepreneurs of Pornography in the Cyber Age,* "By the middle of the 1990s, pornographers found themselves uniquely positioned to take advantage of the phenomenal production and distribution capabilities of the Internet." As the new millennium began, experts were estimating that the number of adult Web sites surpassed 60,000.[5]

This proliferation was soon having impact on the American culture writ large. Monica on NBC's megahit *Friends* watched Internet porn with her husband Chandler as a Valentine's Day gift to him. Mainstream magazines such as *Esquire* and *FHM* began quoting porn stars as expert sources for their articles on sexual topics. Fully half of all guests at Hilton, Hyatt, and Marriott hotels pay to watch adult films in their rooms. The Showtime cable channel introduced a weekly program called *Family Business* that focuses on a real-life mother and son who earn their livelihood making X-rated videos and operating porn Web sites.[6]

By 2004, Internet pornography has become such a powerful cultural force that several of the country's leading educational institutions officially recognize the phenomenon. Some universities, including UCLA and Vanderbilt, have expanded their curricula to include courses about pornography; others, including American University in Washington, D.C., are using student-activity fees to pay for "pizza and porn nights" during which

students watch cyberporn and then participate in faculty-led discussions of the messages that members of Generation XXX are being sent.[7]

Turning Bodies into Sex Objects

The best way to gain a sense of the degree to which sex-oriented Web sites objectify the female form is to conduct a simple search. Going to Google.com and inserting the word "boobs" produces 1,230,000 items, "breasts" produces 2,120,000 items, and "tits" produces 2,790,000 items. While not all of the six million entries involve erotic content, most of them do.[8]

The first item highlighted by the "tits" search is www.tits-paradise.com, with its narrative description reading: "1000's of Big Tit Pics, High Quality Big Tits Videos." Clicking on that first item takes the searcher to a screen dominated by the image of a voluptuous blonde with lots of mascara, bright red lipstick, and an enticing smile. She's wearing a skimpy outfit consisting of short shorts and a top that she has conveniently unzipped to expose an impressive pair of bare breasts. On one side of the model flash the words "Join Totally Tits Right Now" above icons in the form of eight photos of equally well-endowed models highlighting options such as "mature," "natural," and "ethnic." Clicking on any of the images takes the visitor to a page featuring several more bare-breasted women alongside an order form asking for a name and credit card number. A one-month membership costs $39.99. Even a momentary pause prompts a flurry of pop-up ads attempting to divert the shopper to other Web sites with come-ons such as "Massive Titty Fucking!!!" and "Get Access to 1 Million XXX Images."

Less than a minute after going to the search engine and without providing any proof of being eighteen years of age, the explorer has viewed several dozen pairs of naked breasts.

Glorifying Casual Sex and Infidelity

One highly attractive element of the Internet is that it allows viewers to access motion pictures and videos without leaving the comfort and pri-

vacy of their own home or workplace. This means that the sexual messages that have long been communicated by porn films are now being sent by Web sites as well. And, without question, one of the most frequent of those communiqués is that both casual sex and infidelity are highly enjoyable.

Party Favors is representative of the Internet films, with one reviewer summarizing the plot as "Some good-looking, horny folks get together socially and wind up coupling every which way." The action begins when a husband arrives home from work and persuades his wife to treat him to oral sex. Later in the evening, the couple gives a party for two of the husband's buddies and their girlfriends, plus a single woman. The host soon invites one of the men to join him in having intercourse with his wife, while the other male guest takes another of the women to bed by pretending to be a movie producer in search of a new star. As *Party Favors* revs up, the single woman gets some girl-on-girl action going with the wife and one of the female guests, a scene that the reviewer described as being so hot it "could ignite the flame-retardant curtains."[9]

Celebrating Male Sexual Power

American women have, during the twentieth century and the early years of the twenty-first, made substantial headway toward achieving legal, economic, and political equality. In the porn world, however, male power continues to reign supreme.

One of the most successful innovations related to cybersex is the online strip show. The activity is a form of videoconferencing in which a man in one location watches as a woman in another location, often thousands of miles away, removes her clothes exclusively for him. The show is similar to the performances that have traditionally taken place in strip clubs, but the Internet version shifts much of the control from the woman to the man. In a strip joint, the dancer determines exactly what she'll do and when she'll do it, with beefy bouncers at the ready to protect her from rowdy patrons. In cyberspace, by contrast, the customer directs the woman's every move, with the most popular requests including such denigrating acts as the woman wearing a dog collar as she inserts a dildo in

her vagina. Although women have the option of refusing to comply with a customer's order, most quickly learn to do as they're told. A stripper knows that if she balks at a request, the man will most likely stop visiting her Web site after paying the one-time trial membership fee, typically $5, and take his business to a more accommodating woman who'll be happy to do his bidding in return for an ongoing monthly payment, typically $40.[10]

Catering to Fetishists

The *Wall Street Journal's* laudatory coverage of the cybersex industry had particular praise for on-line entrepreneurs taking advantage of the World Wide Web's ability to aim erotic materials at niche audiences. "Adult sites sharply target their marketing," the newspaper wrote, by developing materials for customers with very specialized "sexual tastes." In other words, Internet innovators recognize that many porn devotees fantasize about unusual images or activities, and they are more than willing to create products that fulfill those dreams.[11]

Head Over Heels is directed, according to its promotional materials, toward men "with a shoe horn and a hard-on." Most of the action takes place inside a women's shoe store and revolves around a painfully shy clerk who secretly videotapes his customers as they try on the merchandise and then watches the tapes for his erotic pleasure. As the plotline unfolds, Dennis acknowledges his foot fetish and approaches one of the beauties, telling her, "I'd crawl through broken glass just to suck your toes." As so often happens in the world of cyberporn, the words are music to the woman's ears. "I like what you're saying," the leggy blonde responds with an appreciative smile. "I like it a lot." The clerk is soon having intercourse with the object of his desire—she's wearing nothing but black leather boots, he's wearing nothing at all. Although the vast majority of Americans would find such a plotline laughable, discovering *Head Over Heels* on the Internet unquestionably has been a dream come true for men who are more than happy to pay $30 to download the film from the www.amazingtails.com Web site without ever stepping out of their foot-fetish closet.[12]

Fetishes are not confined to heterosexuals, and so a number of Internet entrepreneurs have created Web sites that cater specifically to some of the various sexual desires of gay men. A Google search that begins with the words "gay sex" and "bears," for example, quickly takes the viewer to a world inhabited not by buff and clean-shaven hunks in concert with the ideal popularized by the Underwear Man in the early 1980s, but to a wonderland of furry-chested men. Despite the strain of carrying around all that hair, the denizens of www.hardbears.com have plenty of sexual energy, as they most certainly live up to the site's promise that "We have the hairiest, horniest guys on the planet all captured on video," presumably to the delight of the constant stream of visitors who are more than willing to pay $29.95 for a monthly membership.[13]

Gratifying Pedophiles

As the number of sexually oriented Web sites exploded in the final years of the twentieth century, members of the U.S. Congress passed the Child Pornography Prevention Act of 1996. This legislation bans underage models as well as women and men who are older than the age of consent but are made to look younger. Anyone familiar with the world of cyberporn, however, can easily find material that appears to stretch the limits of the law.[14]

Going to the Google search engine and inserting the terms "big boobs" and "pigtails" instantly takes an explorer to the innocent-sounding www.pinkworld.com. The links available on this Web site destroy any hint of purity, with options such as "movies of a few tasty teen girls in action" and "movies of gorgeous blond teens in lesbo action." The images that are used to promote the various choices—which can be viewed by anyone, regardless of age and without paying a fee of any kind—show erect penises being inserted into vaginas, with many of the models wearing their hair in the pigtails that are generally connected with prepubescent girls. Although it is possible that all of the models are eighteen years of age or older, many of them look almost identical to Britney Spears during her adolescent days on the *Mickey Mouse Club*.[15]

Similarly, a search propelled by the words "gay sex" and "boys" takes the Internet traveler to www.boysonly.com and hundreds of young men. Many of the lads appear to have no need for shaving cream or a razor, as the growth on their upper lips looks like peach fuzz. What these slender boys lack in experience at the bathroom sink, however, is more than outweighed by their knowledge in the bedroom, as they are shown eagerly participating in a stunning variety of sex acts involving every orifice known to man. In its effort to prompt visitors to join in the fun for $34.99 a month, the site promises myriad "gay XXX photo categories: anal sex, blow jobs, cumshots, fucking" that feature "barely legal studs caught on film."[16]

Cyberporn: The Good, the Bad, the Future

+ The first word that must be mentioned in a fair-minded assessment of the cyberporn phenomenon is "access." Fans of hardcore pornography traditionally had to go to the booths at seamy adult bookstores or the backrooms of their neighborhood video stores to see the erotica that they desired. But now, through the wonders of the World Wide Web, porn devotees can enjoy that same material without leaving their homes or offices. This shift to a more private and comfortable milieu in which to view this particular form of amusement and stimulation has added greatly to the quality of life of millions of Americans. The *New York* magazine article reporting on Generation XXX quoted a graduate student as saying that renting a porn movie is seedy, but "Being anonymous is very cool. You're watching in the confines of your own home, with your own music playing."[17]

– With regard to negative aspects of cyberporn, topping the list is that the throngs of Internet users who now have convenient access to erotic materials include a sizable number of youngsters. Under the old paradigm, it was relatively easy to bar underage boys from X-rated bookstores or the adults-only sections of video stores. In today's cyberworld, by contrast, many young people are far more adept at navigating the Web than their parents are. Even a simple search can quickly take a sexually curi-

ous minor to sites that are bursting with images of naked couples engaging both in intercourse and in more "exotic" activities such as anal sex and orgies. Parents, teachers, and others concerned about the well-being of the nation's youngsters try to block such content, but a hormone-driven fourteen-year-old with a computer—whether at home, in school, or in a public library—is tough to control.

When it comes to identifying the specific messages being communicated by material available on Internet sex sites, the biggest concern may be that cyberporn promotes reckless behavior. The sexually active men and women depicted on the World Wide Web make no apparent effort to protect themselves from unwanted pregnancy or disease, as words such as "birth control pill" or "condom" simply do not exist in the sparse dialogue that is spoken before or during the abundance of sexual acts that routinely take place. And yet, despite the lack of precautions, the denizens of this fantasy world are not depicted as becoming pregnant or suffering from HIV or any other of the sexually transmitted diseases that plague contemporary America. The message that impressionable viewers receive vis-à-vis consequences of unprotected sex, therefore, is misleading as well as potentially life-threatening.

Another disservice derives from the thousands of video strip shows being performed every hour of every day. These activities perpetuate the idea of male sexual power rather than reflecting the prominence, particularly in recent decades, of gender equality in relationships. Female performers being told to wear a dog collar while performing sexual acts suggests that the Women's Rights Movement has not gained ground on the erotic terrain of cyberspace, thereby misinforming men with regard to the sexual activities that most real women are willing to participate in. *Men's Health* magazine recently reported that two out of every three sexually active couples in the country acknowledge that their sex lives are being adversely affected by Internet porn.[18]

Even the most liberally minded of observers encounters difficulty when attempting to assess whether the cyberporn phenomenon's ability to serve niche audiences rightly deserves to be labeled a plus or a minus. A foot fetishist being able to view a film such as *Head Over Heels* or a gay man who lusts after hairy-chested bears being able to ogle the men of his

dreams seems like a positive—if somewhat kinky—step forward in the pursuit of happiness that the Declaration of Independence guarantees. When the sexual desires cross the line and involve young women or men who appear to be younger than the age of consent, however, most right-thinking Americans condemn the actions and support the perpetrators being prosecuted to the full extent of the law.

Faced with this complicated mix of pros and cons, it may seem like a daunting task to sort out whether the advent of cyberporn is a progressive development or one plagued with so many problems that it should be outlawed. Then again, that question is something of a moot point, as sex-oriented Web sites are clearly positioned to survive and to thrive, regardless of what people think of them, as part of the future of the American media.

The author of one book about X-rated Internet content has concluded: "In their rush to limit the allegedly harmful effects of pornography, Congress has overlooked the role that the pornography industry is playing in making the Internet a faster and more economically viable medium for all businesses. This is not intended to be an argument that illegal businesses should be left alone if they are economically successful; far from it. But any effort to rein in on-line smut should recognize the broader sociological and economic forces that are making the pornography industry an increasingly attractive entrepreneurial opportunity." In other words, in a culture that values free expression as well as successful capitalistic ventures, porn sites have a rosy future.[19]

"A Tempest in a C Cup"

A case study in the power and impact created by the union of sex and the Internet exploded in early 2004. The episode began when singers Janet Jackson and Justin Timberlake decided to add some spice to their performance during the Super Bowl halftime show that was aired live on CBS. As the pair sang the lusty "Rock Your Body," Timberlake reached across Jackson's chest and pulled off one of the cups from the black leather bustier she was wearing—thereby exposing her bare breast to the television audience.[20]

What the two performers disingenuously characterized as a "wardrobe malfunction" quickly took on a life of its own as critics denounced what clearly had been a pre-planned stunt as coarse and vulgar. Public outrage—aided by the news media's trumpeting of it—rose to a fever pitch, prompting an investigation by the Federal Communications Commission. Within a matter of weeks, members of the U.S. Congress voted to increase the fine that a TV or radio station had to pay for broadcasting indecent sexual content—boosting that fee from a modest $27,500 to a stand-up-and-take-notice $500,000.[21]

The Internet played a critical role in transforming the incident into a cause célèbre of major proportions because Jackson's naked body part had appeared on the television screen for only five seconds, but then hundreds of Web masters quickly placed the image on their sites. That meant that curious viewers could have an unobstructed view of the titillating anatomical feature for as long as their hearts—or other body organs—desired. And so, within a matter of days, Jackson's right breast and the silver nipple guard that adorned it became the subject of more searches than any other photo in the entire history of the World Wide Web.[22]

As in the case of cyberporn, an assessment of what CNN dubbed "a tempest in a C cup" includes both positive and negative factors.[23]

+ For the legions of individuals who were distressed by the media's obsession with sexual content, the incident provided reassurance that the public as well as the country's lawmakers continued to identify thresholds that they refused to cross. Indeed, the brouhaha had at least a temporary chilling effect on some media organizations that suddenly began re-evaluating their carnal content to determine if they were willing to take the risk either of paying a hefty fine or of suffering the condemnations that MTV, which had produced the halftime show, was forced to endure. NBC edited an episode of its medical drama ER, for example, so it no longer included a shot of an exposed breast on an eighty-year-old woman who was receiving emergency care.[24]

– That the designed-to-shock antic was televised live and in prime time on a broadcast network during a national sports spectacle that most parents hadn't thought twice about allowing their children to watch placed it in a very different category than the sexual shenanigans that had be-

come commonplace on, for example, the pay-cable programs *Sex and the City* and *Queer as Folk*. Indeed, the fact that one in five American children between the ages of two and eleven had been sitting in front of their televisions when the stunt was carried out gave substantial credence to the accusation published in *USA Today* that the singers had "crassly trampled any remaining sense of decency and decorum, as titillation and exploitation had become the coin of the realm."[25]

– The incident suggested that the irksome double standard was still alive and well. Various media products that had helped to propel the Sexual Revolution had been trying for many decades—*Cosmo* in the 1970s comes to mind—to level the sexual playing field with regard to the roles of men and women. But even though Janet Jackson and Justin Timberlake had collaborated in what the *Washington Post* called the "boob-baring escapade," she paid the higher price. Jackson was summarily "uninvited" to the Grammy Awards Show, on which she had been scheduled to appear, when CBS telecast the event a week after the Super Bowl. Timberlake, by contrast, not only attended the internationally televised program and walked away with two awards, but also managed to put the fiasco of a scant seven days earlier far, far behind him by dressing not in his signature baggy chinos and T-shirt but in a jacket and necktie—some commentators expected him to appear in a Boy Scout uniform—and by praising his date for the evening: "I want to thank the most beautiful woman in the world—my mother."[26]

Reality Television

Crossing New Sexual Thresholds

EVEN THOUGH THE SCENE TOOK PLACE IN THE DARK OF NIGHT, TV VIEWERS HAD no trouble identifying the man and woman who were walking into the woods. Fans of the series had been glued to their sets for six previous weeks, so they recognized the hunky former underwear model and the shapely blonde who'd performed in foot-fetish and bondage films. After the couple disappeared into the trees and bushes, snippets of dialogue began appearing at the bottom of the screen. It wasn't entirely clear which words were his and which were hers, but any viewer with a reasonable imagination quickly got the gist of what the randy twosome was doing.

"They're so on to us. . . . I know. I don't care. . . . He, he, he. . . . Shhh . . . Think it'll go better laying down? . . . Huh, huh, huh, hee. . . . ahhh . . . shhh . . . ahhh . . . (slurp) . . . shhh . . . (slurp) . . . Umh . . . (slurp) . . . Mmmmm. . . . (gulp)"

Observers agreed that the scene pushed American television across a new threshold, but they disagreed about whether that development was a positive one or a negative.

On the plus side, executives at Fox soon had reason to celebrate, as that final episode of the *Joe Millionaire* series attracted a stunning forty million viewers—the largest in the network's history. Members of the audience felt considerable pleasure as well, believing they'd witnessed the first-ever instance of oral sex being performed on network television.

On the minus side, the female member of the couple later accused Fox of having misled viewers into thinking that she'd engaged in an intimate sexual act with her male companion when, in fact, the couple had merely hidden in the woods—barely touching each other—so they could get away from the cameras for a few minutes. "They made it look like I went into the bushes with him so we could hook up," Sarah Kozer said. "And then they put, you know, 'sexual noises' on the bottom of the screen."[1]

Positive or negative? Plus or minus? History or fraud?

Welcome to the latest venue for heavy-on-the-sex programming on the most powerful medium in the history of communication: Reality TV.

This new genre of television not only exploded onto the media landscape at virtually the same moment as cyberporn, but reality shows that feature sexual content also are like X-rated Web sites in trying to arouse lustful feelings in their viewers. Some cultural observers have argued, in fact, that this similarity means that many of the programs—particularly late-night dating shows such as *Blind Date*—qualify as pornography. "Reality television shows are soft-core porn," one of those critics has stated pointblank. "The episodes could be sold at video stores in 'that' section."[2]

The parallels between reality TV and cyberporn extend to several of the messages that the programs send. Many of the shows, for example, portray women as sex objects and also glorify casual sex as well as infidelity. In addition, some of the reality programs—*The Jerry Springer Show* comes to mind—provide material that may or may not be aimed at fetishists, as many Internet sex sites are, but that certainly can be described as *bizarre*.

Reality television also sends some messages that cyberporn does not. Among the positive ones, *Queer Eye for the Straight Guy* has revived the art of creating sexual innuendo and double entendres. Among the negative, *Joe Millionaire* has firmly established a connection between sex and deceit.

The Rise of Reality TV

Media historians trace the roots of reality television to *The Real World*. MTV began bringing seven young strangers together to live under a single roof in 1992, and the program was an instant hit among American

teenagers. Because participants were typically in their early twenties and living in a city where they knew no one except their new housemates, romances developed virtually every season. But it wasn't until the dawning of the new century that sex became a central element in the program.[3]

That shift was no accident, as the men and women responsible for the show used various techniques to encourage frisky behavior. During the process of selecting housemates, interviewers asked applicants about their attitudes toward various sexual activities and then chose the candidates who suited the show's new emphasis. The houses and apartments where the participants lived also were altered to promote intimate contact, with a unisex bathroom and a hot tub—always large enough for the entire cast—becoming standard features. And, finally, the members of the video crew were supplied with infrared cameras so they could capture the libidinous young people's after-the-lights-out antics. The first season of the new century not only contained more sex than any of its predecessors but also attracted the largest audience.[4]

The rise of reality TV was also driven by the same familiar concept that the *Wall Street Journal* had credited with boosting the growth of cyberporn, except that in this case the phrasing was more accurately modified to: *Cheap* sex sells. That is, even a top-of-the-line reality series on a broadcast network, such as *Joe Millionaire* on Fox, only cost about $600,000 an hour to produce, which is half the price of a drama or sitcom. Reality shows don't require a string of expensive sets or a cast of stars who demand $1 million an episode—as each member of the *Friends* sextet did in 2003 when *Joe* aired. And yet Fox found plenty of advertisers that were eager to pay $550,000 to broadcast a thirty-second commercial during that titillating final episode. In short, as the *Washington Post* put it, "Reality shows are a network's dream."[5]

The profit-conscious Powers That Be stretched that dream to its maximum. When corporate executives at General Electric discovered the makeover program *Queer Eye for the Straight Guy* on their Bravo cable channel was a major hit, they didn't merely air episodes multiple times but also broadcast them on the NBC network—Bravo and NBC are both owned by GE. Still not satisfied, the creative executives next aired mini-

marathons by showing two or three episodes back to back and even—as their pièce de résistance—produced a full-fledged marathon consisting of eleven straight hours of *Queer Eye* on New Year's Day 2004.[6]

Turning Bodies into Sex Objects

That reality TV often objectifies women is clearly evident in one of the best known of the myriad dating shows that have burst onto the television landscape, *Blind Date*—the *New York Times* described the archetypal image on the program as "a man cavorting with a bountifully endowed waitress in a hot tub."[7]

The syndicated show, which airs in most markets on UPN at midnight, brings two strangers together for a fantasy adventure that begins in the afternoon and continues late into the night. A camera crew accompanies the couple on the nine-hour date, and the footage is edited down to fifteen minutes. The producing staff then enters the picture, inserting graphic elements and pop-up thought bubbles that appear on the screen at the same time that viewers at home watch the date unfold.[8]

Those added elements play a major role in how *Blind Date* transforms the female member of the couple into a sex object. In a typical episode, a young woman named Leila, who had participated in a previous segment of the show, returns for a second date, this time with a guy named Anthony. As soon as Leila appears, a large red arrow pops up on the screen and points at her breasts alongside the statement, "Breasts 14% larger than last time," followed a minute later by the comment, "Get a load of them melons." Later in the episode, the program's producers further objectify the woman by letting an article of her clothing have its say; a drawing of Leila's blouse pops up on the screen and tells Anthony, "You're two buttons away from heaven."[9]

Glorifying Casual Sex and Infidelity

One of the most memorable of the carnal trailblazers on *The Real World* was Cara. This member of the 2001 cast first distinguished herself for hav-

ing a penchant for wearing top designer outfits to show off her ultrathin body. Soon after arriving in Chicago, she informed her fellow housemates that she had recently broken up with her boyfriend, and by episode three her mission while on the program was clear: the "boy hunt" was on. In a single week, Cara hooked up with and then discarded—like last year's Prada handbag—a muscle boy she found on the beach, a musician she saw perform at a local club, and a friend from home she summoned for yet another one-night stand.[10]

Cara's promiscuous ways were merely a pre-game warm-up, however, for the casual sex and infidelity that dominated the next season of *The Real World*, which was set in Las Vegas. Trishelle and Steven—who was separated from his wife but legally still married—didn't remain strangers for long, as they were soon having sex on a regular basis. By episode six, the program's Web site announced that the couple had already spent more time between the sheets than any other roommates in the show's history. The roller-coaster relationship continued for the rest of the season, highlighted by Steven's immortal line: "Trishelle, you're like a Lay's potato chip. Nobody can have you just once." Few viewers were surprised when, a year after the season ended, the real-life Trishelle Cannatella took it all off for *Playboy* or when, after being asked what celebrity she would most like to sleep with, she asked the interviewer, "You mean one that I haven't *already* had sex with?"[11]

Showcasing the Sexually Bizarre

When it comes to reality TV programs that showcase bizarre sexual circumstances, *The Jerry Springer Show* stands head and shoulders above—or perhaps breasts and butts below—all the rest. The *New York Times* has described the syndicated program as "sexually lurid," the *Los Angeles Times* has dubbed it "road-kill TV," and the *Washington Post* has weighed in with "the freak-show talk show."[12]

The standard cast of a segment hosted by the former mayor of Cincinnati involves either a couple or what might be called a "lust trian-

gle." One person generally appears alone on stage to tell Springer his or her story, and then the other players come on stage, often with fists and vulgarities flying. No matter who appears first or what the specific circumstances, the male member of the couple or group is almost always treated sympathetically.

On an episode titled "Bizarre Betrayals," Eric has been married to Misty enough years to have three children, but for the last several months he's been sleeping with his wife's mother. When the situation is revealed on national TV, Eric isn't embarrassed but boastful, smirking as he tells Misty, "You should be happy. At least I'm keepin' it in the family." The viewers in the studio choose not to condemn the adulterous husband but, instead, aim their wrath at the older of the two women, repeatedly screaming, in unison: "Grandma whore! Grandma whore!"[13]

The studio audience's decision to side with the man is even more surprising in a segment about Jacob having an incestuous relationship with his sister, Rachel. She admits her wrongdoing and promises to stop having sex with her brother; Jacob, by contrast, vehemently asserts that he plans to continue sleeping with his sister—"I'll take her to another state and marry her if she'll do it." Nevertheless, the viewers in the studio still put the blame on Rachel, with each of her several tearful outbursts prompting another round of rebukes: "Incest whore! Incest whore!"[14]

About the only time a man fails to receive support on *The Jerry Springer Show* is when a segment doesn't include one. When Corina announces that lovemaking with her long-time girlfriend has reached such a low point that she has to fake orgasms, the audience calls out "Let's hear!" until the lesbian—or a straight woman playing one on TV—dutifully squeals in make-believe ecstasy. That's only the first of the performances, as the real show begins once Corina's new lust interest, Maria, joins her on stage and the men in the crowd demand "some hot lesbian action." The two highly attractive women then remove their tops and begin kissing passionately while fondling each other's naked breasts. The producers "bleep out" vulgarities and blur any bare bosoms or genitalia—common features on the show—before a segment is broadcast.[15]

Reviving Sexual Innuendo and Double Entendres

During the late 1970s, *Three's Company* broke new ground on American television by bringing sexual repartee to the small screen as never before. A quarter century later, reality television has not only revived this concept but has added a new twist—a gay one.

From the moment *Queer Eye for the Straight Guy* premiered in the summer of 2003, the reality makeover show was a sensation, with an *Entertainment Weekly* cover headline dubbing it an "Outrageous Breakout Hit!" The program not only built a solid base of three million fans on Bravo, making it the most-watched show in the cable channel's quarter of a century on the air, but also pulled in another seven million viewers when episodes were re-broadcast on NBC.[16]

Part of the show's winning formula flows from the unique concept of having five talented gay men help a style-challenged straight guy rework his wardrobe, redecorate his home, cook gourmet food, use upscale grooming products, and come up to speed on cultural trends. But that creative idea never would have caught the public's imagination, reviewers pointed out, without the non-stop sexual references that the Fab Five fire off while they work their magic.[17]

Many of the zingers explode from the mouth of Carson Kressley, the most flamboyant of the *tres gay* quintet. One episode has the fashion Nazi coming upon an elongated stocking cap as he's cleaning out a straight man's closet. He looks at the red wool item, stretches it between his hands, and deadpans, "Oh, look, a penis warmer." At the beginning of another segment, the lifestyle commandos are going over notes on the guy they're preparing to meet—a toupee-wearing lawyer named Richard Miller—when Kressley, with a stoical expression on his face, says, "*Richard* sounds so formal. Let's just say we're lookin' for *dick*." Still another time, the playful fashionista has been sitting on the shoulders of a powerfully built police officer; as Kressley hops to the floor, he wisecracks, "That was quite a dismount. I've never *gotten off* like that before!"[18]

Making the Connection between Sex and Deceit

Joe Millionaire was a benchmark program in the evolution of reality TV not only because it drew a huge audience and offered network viewers a first-of-its-kind depiction of oral sex, but also because the show firmly established that deception often plays a role in sexual relationships—or at least in the new genre of television shows about them.

When the Fox network recruited women to appear on the program, staff members told the potential participants that they'd spend a month living in a chateau to create a French version of *Sex and the City*. Only after the twenty beautiful women left the United States were they informed that, in fact, they'd be competing with each other for a man. The biggest lie of all was still to come, however, as the show's producing staff then added that the object of the women's affection had recently inherited $50 million—even though, in reality, the model turned construction worker had earned a mere $19,000 during the previous year.[19]

The deception continued during the show's videotaping and editing. In one segment, Evan Marriott and one of the women were scheduled to have some private time in a hot tub, but then the producers sent three more bikini-clad hotties into the water to suggest an orgy. Another example of Fox's lack of ethics came when staff members pleaded with Sarah Kozer to dress in a bathrobe and step onto one of the chateau's exterior balconies; the scene was later edited into a segment so it appeared immediately after a shot of Marriott and Kozer in his bedroom at night, thereby suggesting that the couple had slept together—which they had not.[20]

The various deceptions had enormous benefits for Evan Marriott. Not only did he receive $500,000 from Fox at the end of the series, but he also was launched on a lucrative show business career. Marriott chatted on several television talk shows, starred in national ads for Kentucky Fried Chicken, and pulled in $15,000 a pop for dozens of personal appearances in cities from coast to coast—not bad for a guy who, before reality TV, had been hauling dirt for a living. And there was no question that Marriott's celebrity status derived at least partly from the fact that he, un-

like Kozer, would neither confirm nor deny that the gorgeous blonde, who soon appeared on the cover of *Playboy*, had become the first person ever to perform oral sex—or at least appear to—on network television.[21]

Reality TV: More Good, More Bad, More Future

No one knows how many people were surprised when the *New York Times* reported that many of the guests on *The Jerry Springer Show* are paid actors or when the Bravo channel divulged that the women on *Joe Millionaire* had been lied to. Those numbers aren't all that important anyway, as the more illuminating ones are those that came *after* the revelations. Specifically, some seven million viewers continued to watch *Springer* each day, and thirteen million others transformed the Fox network's next reality series—*The Simple Life*, featuring two scantily clad and sexually adventurous Beverly Hills princesses who were relocated to rural Arkansas—into an unqualified hit.[22]

+ The impressive size of the audiences that watched the programs rightly belongs, although many critics would disagree, at the top of the list in an objective assessment of the pluses and minuses of the venue's influence on sexual content in twenty-first-century TV Land.

That reality programming attracts so many viewers speaks to the single greatest triumph of American television, as the medium has an unparalleled record of success in performing a task that is often taken for granted: Entertaining. What the boob tube does best is serve as a form of minimal-effort escapism for a population that very well may work harder and produce more than any other nation in history. Millions of people who turn to their televisions are either not willing or not able to pay full attention to what's taking place on the screen, and so the magical box has repeatedly found new ways to help those viewers relax. Reality TV emerged, in the early 2000s, as the latest of those innovations.

+ A second item in the plus column is that many of the reality programs have become so outrageous that savvy viewers don't look to them for models of how to conduct their sex lives but, in fact, recognize them as

examples of what *not* to do. If college students so much as hear the name "Trishelle" in the same sentence as *The Real World,* spontaneous snickers erupt. Likewise, when denizens of a dormitory gather around a TV set to watch a segment of *Blind Date,* the couple's cheesy dialogue is soon drowned out by the guffaws emanating from the youthful viewers who are far too sophisticated to take their sexual cues from a talking blouse.

Some detractors have criticized *Queer Eye for the Straight Guy* for reinforcing stereotypes about gay men being effeminate. But others have defended the program for helping to reduce a particular kind of homophobia. The program's hunky grooming expert told *The Advocate,* the country's gay and lesbian news magazine, that no one should have to conform to some particular model. "I'm all for guys being butch and guys being men. I identify with that and appreciate that," Kyan Douglas said. "But it's also perfectly OK for a gay guy to be effeminate. If somebody has a problem with that, they need to open up their mind."[23]

Reality television also has its negative aspects.

– Number one on the list is that the programs, similar to their cyberporn counterparts, promote reckless sexual behavior. For even though TV shows such as *The Real World* purport to provide unobstructed windows into how Americans are conducting their lives in the early years of the twenty-first century, they largely fail to communicate that unwanted pregnancies and sexually transmitted diseases are potential threats to the well-being of the men and women who are taking advantage of the liberation that the advanced stages of the media-driven Sexual Revolution offer them. References to condoms, HIV tests, the AIDS epidemic, and the consequences of unprotected sex are consistent elements in *Sex and the City* and *Queer as Folk,* but those realities are virtually unheard of in the world created by *Blind Date, Joe Millionaire, The Simple Life,* and *The Jerry Springer Show.*

– Another concern is the importance that many of the programs place on the physical aspects of relationships. Transforming women's bodies into sex objects is the most salient evidence of this flaw. Shows such as *Blind Date* place enormous emphasis on a woman's anatomy, while paying only

miniscule attention—if any at all—to her intellect, integrity, or personality. Although media-savvy college students may see through the messages that the programs are sending vis-à-vis the female body, not every viewer has such well-developed critical thinking skills.

– Another disquieting element of the new television genre is the emphasis it places on bizarre sexual activities. Every day of the week, millions of Americans tune in to watch Jerry Springer provide a high-profile platform for men who have sex with their mothers-in-law or brothers and sisters who engage in incestuous relationships with each other. Again, consumers who are educated about the tenets of media literacy may laugh at such bizarre situations, but there is no question that some viewers who see programs about these activities consequently find them to be more acceptable—perhaps even intriguing enough to emulate.

– The recurring portrayals of lesbians on *The Jerry Springer Show* are also problematic. Because most genres of the media, including network television, choose not to provide accurate representations of women who love women, these misleading depictions provide many viewers with the only images of gay women they come into contact with. This is a concern not only because the lesbians who appear on the program clearly are paid performers who are pretending to be something they are not, but also because the activities they participate in are orchestrated to titillate male viewers rather than female ones, thereby sending inaccurate messages about lesbians and their sexual desires.

– Less over-the-top reality programs also teach lamentable lessons. *Joe Millionaire* was a major hit for Fox—the final episode drew the largest audience in the history of the network—that spawned any number of similar programs. It is easy to lose sight, amid all of this success, of the fact that the series was based, at its most fundamental level, on *deceit*. The hidden twist that drew so many viewers was that Evan Marriott was portrayed as a multimillionaire even though, in reality, his annual income was minimal. The message? "Hey, guys, if you want a bunch of hot women fighting to spend some time alone with you in a hot tub or to sneak off

into the woods to give you a hummer, make up the biggest lie you can think of!"[24]

As in the case of cyberporn, whether the pluses or the minuses ultimately carry the day is something of a moot point. Tom Shales, the Pulitzer Prize–winning media critic for the *Washington Post*, is among those astute observers who, soon after the new programming genre surfaced, accurately forecast an attractive future for it. "The population explosion in channels and networks means that the demand for cheaply produced entertainment will increase," Shales wrote. "Reality TV shows are not going to go away, and for every one that fails, a couple more pop up on the drawing boards of Hollywood. The race to be more outrageous, more salacious, and more sensational will continue."[25]

In short: *Sex Sells!*

"Sexual Literacy"

Understanding the Media's Sexual Messages

THE ESSAYS IN THIS BOOK CLEARLY SHOW THAT THE SEXUAL CONTENT IN the American media has steadily increased during the last fifty years. Indeed, that growth has been so dramatic that the sexual repression that defined 1950s media products has, by this point, been replaced with sexual obsession. Regardless of how a particular individual judges this sea change in the media's approach to sexual content, there's no reason to believe that it will be abating any time soon.

And so, those who are concerned about the nation's sexual self clearly will find it more productive not to attempt to prevent the media from sending libidinous messages—anyone who favors that exercise in futility should review the judicial system's failed efforts to stop the spread of 2 Live Crew's offensive lyrics in the early 1990s—but to adopt a perspective that has steadily been gaining momentum for more than thirty years.

As early as 1971, a few farsighted observers of American culture suggested that popular media products such as TV sitcoms might be in a position to help educate the public about sexual topics. The *All in the Family* episode on male impotence triggered one of the first such comments; a week after the segment aired, *Newsweek* pointed out that the show was teaching the nation important lessons about sex. Other trailblazers soon followed in the legendary program's footsteps. Phil Donahue and Madonna come to mind as being particularly committed to illuminating sexual issues, while several media products that were part of the Gay Nineties phenomenon should be lauded for helping to raise AIDS aware-

ness—including the film *Philadelphia*, the Benetton ads featuring "H.I.V. POSITIVE" tattoos, and Pedro Zamora's poignant messages on *The Real World*.[1]

When Hollywood exploded with teen-targeted movies and TV shows chock full of sexual content such as *American Pie* and *Dawson's Creek* in the final decade of the twentieth century, the ranks of those who recognized the mass media's potential as public health educators experienced another spurt of growth. A *U.S. News & World Report* cover story observed, "The media are so compelling and so filled with sex, they have become our true sex educators," and a tiny nonprofit organization called the Media Project drew more attention to the concept by giving awards to television programs that communicated positive messages about sexual behavior by American teenagers.[2]

When *Sex and the City* and *Queer as Folk* came on the scene, still more observers—including the *New York Times* and the Associated Press—joined those who touted the instructional benefits of heavy-on-the-sex media products. The boldest statements came in an essay, published in the health journal *Family Planning Perspectives*, titled "Can the Mass Media Be Healthy Sex Educators?" The authors began their article by describing the reality of modern-day America's cultural landscape. "Gone are the 'I Love Lucy' days of single beds and polite pecks on cheeks," they wrote. "Youth today can hear and see sexual talk and portrayals in every form of media." The authors then summarized a research study documenting that when today's teenagers try to find information about sex, they look to the media—especially TV and magazines—just as often as they turn to their parents or their peers. The final paragraph of the essay made it clear where the authors stood on the question they had asked in their title: "The media are important sex educators today and will continue to be in the future."[3]

The most effective response to contemporary media's obsession with sex, then, is to help young people learn how to identify and to understand the libidinous messages that television, film, music, magazines, the news media, and the Internet are sending out each day. Individuals who learn how the communication world works and how specific media products influence the nation's collective values and behavior are far better

equipped to distinguish good messages from bad ones, thereby benefiting from the sex-charged content rather than suffering because of it.

In countries such as Australia and Canada, children at all grade levels are now routinely being taught media literacy skills, largely because of the sex- and violence-filled American movies and TV shows relentlessly marching across their borders. The number of media literacy courses being taught in the United States is growing as well, with many progressive school systems making them a required part of the curriculum.[4]

And so, today may be a propitious moment to adopt the tenets of the media literacy initiative to introduce a concept that might best be labeled "sexual literacy."

The goal of this amalgam of media literacy and sex education would be to help individuals learn how to recognize and to analyze the myriad sexual messages that the various forms of media are routinely communicating. Armed with these skills, media consumers—especially young ones—would be better prepared to navigate today's sexually obsessive media terrain.

This book contains numerous points that could be included in a sexual literacy course or course component. The essay about media coverage of the birth control pill, for instance, illuminates some of the forces that propel news organizations to devote their resources to a particular topic; in this case, those factors included not only the impact and timeliness of the pill but also its potential for selling more newspapers—in concert with the belief that *Sex Sells!* The chapter summarizing news reports about Bill Clinton's sexual escapades reveals another reality that media consumers should be aware of; a single watershed event such as Zippergate can force the nation's leading journalistic voices to revise their standards of news judgment—in this instance, deeming terms such as "semen" and "oral sex" to be acceptable.

Other lessons that could be highlighted as part of sexual literacy instruction come to light not by examining one particular media product or topic but by looking more broadly at themes that have emerged gradually over the last half century.

One such theme is that the sexual content in a particular genre evolves over time, with one pioneer standing on the shoulders of those that came

before it. This process becomes clear by noting the changes in one aspect of the television sitcom. *All in the Family* broke sexual ground, for its time, when Gloria dressed in miniskirts. *Three's Company* pushed the envelope a significant distance further when Chrissy jiggled across the TV screen in revealing bathing suits and baby doll nightgowns complete with ruffled panties—but kept her midriff covered. *Sex and the City* then took television where no program had gone before by showing Samantha in outfits that she could remove in a matter of seconds to showcase full-frontal nudity. Gloria began the striptease; Samantha finished it.

Another broad-based lesson that slices across any number of individual media products is that male sexual provocateurs tend to precede their female counterparts. Hugh Hefner and *Playboy* magazine opened the door that Helen Gurley Brown and *Cosmo* later entered. Likewise, Jim Morrison cleared a path that Madonna followed a decade or so later. And again in the 1990s, it was gay *men* who first stepped into the media spotlight, while lesbians still have not reached a comparable level of visibility. Some feminists may cringe at this men-first notion, but, in fact, it makes perfect sense in light of the sexism that held sway during the second half of the twentieth century. Indeed, that men dominated American society also explains an instance in which a woman broke the sexual barriers first; the Brooke Shields image pushed advertising across new boundaries several years before the Underwear Man did because one of the limited number of roles that society had relegated to women was that of sex object.

Still another lesson that students of sexual literacy could learn by examining media products from the last several decades is that the media have increasingly trivialized sex. The most memorable scene from the 1962 film *Dr. No* was the one showing James Bond's voyeuristic view of Ursula Andress stepping out of the surf. Even though her breasts and genitalia remained fully concealed under her bikini, that classic scene remains one of the most erotic in Hollywood history. That image of a voluptuous, partially clothed beauty being worshipped—by the camera, by the film, by the secret agent, and by the generations of moviegoers who have salivated over it for forty years—stands in dramatic contrast to a man today paying $40 every month to direct an on-line stripper to remove every article of her clothing and then, on command, to insert a huge dildo in her

vagina before the customer moves on to another Web site and another stripper. It is left to the viewer to decide which of the images is ultimately more sensual—and more satisfying.

Janet Jackson and Justin Timberlake's "tempest in a C cup" incident reinforced one final intriguing point about sex and the media. Although the trajectory during the last five decades or so has most definitely been toward a growing quantity of increasingly explicit libidinous content all across the media landscape, sexual provocateurs of different eras have occasionally encountered limitations with regard to thresholds that either public opinion or powerful media decision-makers have determined were not yet ready to be crossed. In 1957, variety show host Ed Sullivan drew the line at allowing Elvis Presley to grind his pelvis on national television. In 1969, law enforcement officials as well as music fans told Jim Morrison to keep his penis inside his leather pants during his on-stage performances. In 1977, ABC executives made it clear to *Three's Company* producers that it was acceptable for two young women to live with a randy young man—but not to expose their midriffs. Two decades later, that same network decided that America was not yet ready to invite either fictitious lesbian Ellen Morgan or her real-life counterpart Ellen DeGeneres into their homes. In 2004, network television's Powers That Be continued to avoid showing two men—even highly popular ones such as a milquetoast lawyer on *Will & Grace*—kissing or otherwise showing physical affection, while the public and the nation's top lawmakers stated loudly and clearly that a televised halftime show of a high-profile sporting event was not the proper venue to educate the nation's children about nipple guards.

Despite the benefits of readers understanding the concepts articulated here, by no means are the lessons relevant to sexual literacy limited to the past. Indeed, the greatest value of this educational initiative is that it enables contemporary media consumers to identify and to understand the messages they are being bombarded with every day.

Throughout the pages of this book, I have attempted to maintain a degree of authorial detachment from the subject at hand, consistently writ-

ing from the third-person perspective and grounding my description and analysis in the observations of other journalists and scholars. In this final essay, however, I want to talk about my own experiences as a college professor who has taught my own version of sexual literacy.

I offered Media and Sexuality for the first time in 2001. The experimental course set out to examine the powerful role that the American media play in shaping society's attitudes toward sex, sexual behavior, and sexual identity, while also at least considering the possibility that the media influence how an individual conducts his or her own sex life. The course was so successful that my colleagues and the administration at American University awarded me a small grant to write materials for the class. So I taught Media and Sexuality in 2002 and again in 2003, and at the same time began the process of researching and writing this book. Each time I taught the course, my students read drafts of the essays that now have morphed—with refinements based on student feedback—into the chapters of this book.

From the outset, the course had a strong historical base that reflected my own background, which includes not only working as a newspaper reporter but also earning a Ph.D. in American history. But as Media and Sexuality has evolved over the last several years, it has paid an increasing amount of attention to helping students learn to "deconstruct" the media products they come into contact with every day. More specifically, in addition to learning about topics such as the Kinsey Report in the 1950s and booty rap in the 1990s, my students also are required to keep individual journals in which they describe sex-laden media products they encounter and then analyze the sexual messages—both overt and subtle—that those products are communicating.

To illustrate the content of these journals while at the same time further illuminating the concept of sexual literacy, I now want to give readers a sampling of the kind of material I ask my students to submit. More specifically, here are three model entries that I wrote and that I give my students at the beginning of the semester—one about a magazine article, one about a film, and one about a song.

Sexual Literacy: Magazines

An article in the September 2003 issue of *Maxim,* a contemporary men's magazine that in many ways parallels *Playboy* in the 1960s, was built around reasons why women are reluctant to provide men with oral sex—and what guys can do to eliminate those obstacles. Specific complaints highlighted in the piece, which was written by a woman, included "It's not romantic" and "I don't like putting dirty things in my mouth."[5]

One sexual message communicated by the article is that oral sex is a highly enjoyable activity that men should partake of as often as possible. The light-hearted tone begins with the article's title: "Sword Swallowing." Word choices reinforce the message; a man's penis is called his "magic wand," his testicles are nicknamed "the boys," and oral sex becomes a woman "traveling south of the border." Indeed, the various phrases serve to portray "getting a hummer" not really as sex so much as a fun, casual activity comparable to kissing or having a massage.

Another clear message is that all five of the women's complaints are frivolous. The author describes them as "minor gripes" and counsels her male readers to "just apply some simple, girl-approved insider strategies and you'll easily overcome her objections." Those strategies portray a woman's reluctance as trivial; one solution for a girlfriend being concerned about "putting dirty things in my mouth" is for the guy to "raid your girl's medicine cabinet for some pre-moistened cleansing cloths and give yourself a quick wipe-down."

Among the most troubling messages is that the article encourages a man to use manipulation and deceit to persuade a woman to acquiesce to his sexual desires. "Lay the butter on thick," *Maxim* tells its readers, "by sweet-talking her with lines like 'Wow, that just completely made my day.' If you can connect her blow jobs to your emotions, you'll score a serious coup." Encouraging men to fabricate "lines" and assuring them that "you'll score a serious coup" are *not* among the steps that lead to a loving relationship built on trust and honesty. Another example of this same disquieting message comes when the female author tells readers another way to dupe women. "We're suckers for romance, so don't be shy about taking advantage of it," she writes. "Convince your girlfriend that getting

head touches you deeply. Once you've conditioned her, she'll be quick to initiate oral action." Again, phrases such as "we're suckers for romance" and "once you've conditioned her" are not found in any guide to creating a long-term and mutually fulfilling bond between a man and a woman.

Another relevant message is one not sent. Although *Maxim* finds plenty of space to describe strategies that a clever man can use to overcome a woman's reluctance to give him sexual service, the magazine doesn't mention that providing oral sex can infect a woman with any number of sexually transmitted diseases—or that using a condom can virtually eliminate this health concern.

Sexual Literacy: Motion Pictures

Chicago was a blockbuster musical with terrific singing, dancing, and film editing that made it a huge Hollywood success; the movie won six Academy Awards, including best picture, and pulled in more than $180 million at theaters and is still making more money through DVD sales and rentals. The film manages to provide a window into the Jazz Era of the 1920s without using nudity or coarse language, so it carries a rating of PG–13.[6]

The sexual messages, however, raise concerns. The central plotline begins with an adulterous wife, played by sweet-faced Renée Zellweger, discovering that her lover does not, in reality, have the business contacts that can make her a showbiz sensation. So, when she realizes the guy has lied to her, she fires three bullets into his chest. The rest of the film shows how she uses her ample sex appeal first to be acquitted of a crime that everyone knows she committed and then to propel her into stardom as a singer and dancer billed as "the scintillating sinner." Zellweger brings the message home in the flashy big-production number that climaxes the box-office smash. "You can like the life you're livin' and live the life you love," the glamorous beauty tells her adoring fans. "Isn't it good! Isn't it grand!" She then gives a sly smile and adds, "You can even marry Harry, and mess around with Ike." The moral of the film: Crime may or may not pay, but *crimes driven by sex* definitely do.

The movie also reiterates the disturbing connection between sex and violence that Hollywood films introduced in the 1980s. *Chicago* showcases

the linkage by having Zellweger kill her deceitful lover mere moments after a lusty roll in the sheets. The second most prominent plotline reinforces the sex/violence theme, with the voluptuous Catherine Zeta-Jones killing her husband and sister immediately after finding them in bed together—but the star is later found innocent. Lesser subplots highlight violence as well. The lovely Lucy Liu plugs her wayward hubby when she catches him having sex with two women at the same time, and a whole chorus line of hotties, dubbed the "merry murderesses of the Cook County Jail," boast about having sex with their mates—and then killing them.

On a somewhat more positive note, another message in the movie strikes a blow to that irksome sexual double standard that has been weakened over time but still refuses to die. When films from twenty years ago depicted adulterous affairs, they consistently had the men survive while the women paid dearly for their philandering—slashed to a bloody end in *Dressed to Kill*, shot to death in *Fatal Attraction*, sent flying over a second-story balcony in *No Way Out*. But the situation plays out very differently in *Chicago*, as the unfaithful women survive—and, in most instances, *thrive*—long after the male adulterers have been killed.

Sexual Literacy: Music

In the song "Can't Hold Us Down," pop princess Christina Aguilera joined forces with African-American rapper Lil' Kim to state, loudly and defiantly, that women should no longer allow men to dominate society. The track from Aguilera's *Stripped* album focuses specifically on attacking society's typical reaction to promiscuous men compared to promiscuous women.[7]

Aguilera begins with the lyrics:

> *If you look back in history*
> *It's a common double standard of society.*
> *The guy gets all the glory the more he can score,*
> *While the girl can do the same and yet you call her a whore.*

Kim then makes the same point:

> *Check it—Here's something I just can't understand.*
> *If the guy have three girls then he's the man*
> *He can either give us some head, sex her off.*
> *If the girl do the same, then she's a whore.*

The lyrics communicate that societal mores respond in opposite ways to men than to women with regard to the quantity of their sexual activity. A guy who has multiple sex partners is celebrated as "the man"; a woman who does the same is condemned as "a whore." The song points out, with the phrase "look back in history," that this inequity has existed for many years. The talented young women clearly have a valid point.

A more questionable sexual message surfaces, however, when Aguilera and Kim identify exactly what action they recommend taking to end this double standard. Specifically, they propose not that men should have *fewer* sex partners, but that women should have *more* of them.

Their lyrics tell female listeners:

> *To all my girls with a man who be tryin' to mack,*
> *Do it right back to him and let that be that.*
> *You need to let him know that his game is whack,*
> *And Lil' Kim and Christina Aguilera got your back.*

Nor do the sexual provocateurs stop with encouraging promiscuity among women as well as men, as they go on to send another sexual message.

This time they target the regrettable practice of women being seen as sex objects. Again, the controversial aspect of "Can't Hold Us Down" isn't the criticism itself, but the specific remedy that Aguilera and Kim propose. They choose not to advocate an end to women being valued by the size of their breasts and other physical features, but for an expansion of the practice so men are judged by the size of their physical attributes as well.

Their lyrics, this time aimed at male listeners, bluntly state:

You're just a little boy
Think you're so cute, so coy.
You must talk so big
To make up for small lil' things.

With these words, the two musicians are demeaning men who are not physically well endowed—a "lil' thing" is clearly a small penis—while presumably judging men with large endowments more positively.

I want to end this book with one last point about sexual literacy.

The concept is attractive primarily because it can help young media consumers develop important critical thinking skills. In recent decades, educators and other people who are concerned about the well-being of the nation's youth have come to believe that it is imperative for adolescents and teenagers to develop such skills, as part of the media literacy initiative, so they are equipped to make vital decisions that can determine the direction of their lives—indeed, in some instances, to *save* their lives. In concert with this belief system, efforts have been made to educate young men and women about the dangers of smoking cigarettes and of using alcohol and other drugs. More recently, comparable materials and educational programs have been developed to illuminate the risks involved in being overweight and the factors that have led to the national epidemic of obesity.

Helping young people develop the skills necessary to understand the messages they are receiving about sex is every bit as important as informing them about the risks involved in using tobacco and drugs or the dangers related to unhealthy weight gain.

As my concluding thought, I want to make a final "pitch" for sexual literacy instruction by pointing out that this particular concept has a unique advantage compared to the other public health initiatives I have mentioned. When educators try to inform teenagers and young adults about topics such as binge drinking and overeating, they face a formidable challenge because the reaction of their audience is often less than enthusiastic. Boys and girls as young as their early teens—but already old enough to consider themselves worldly wise—typically respond to an in-

vitation to participate in such a program first by rolling their eyes and next by trying to come up with some credible reason why their schedule simply will not allow them to attend the sessions.

Not so with sexual literacy.

Based on my experience offering Media and Sexuality, I can absolutely guarantee that when students, regardless of how jaded they are, hear that they'll have the chance to talk about *Playboy* and Madonna, *Three's Company* and Internet porn, James Bond and *Sex and the City*, they will—without question—embrace this new subject area. For this educational concept combines a pair of forces that are without peer both in defining and in fueling the Sexual Revolution as well as the contemporary American culture: sex and media.

Notes

The 1950s

1. William Chafe, *The American Woman: Her Changing Social, Economic, and Political Roles, 1920–1970* (New York: Oxford University Press, 1974), 217. The 1957 birthrate soared to 25.3 per 1,000 women, a huge increase from the Depression-era rate of 18.4 per 1,000 women. The birthrate for third children doubled and for fourth children tripled.

2. Alfred C. Kinsey, *Sexual Behavior in the Human Male* (Philadelphia: W. B. Saunders, 1948).

3. James H. Jones, *Alfred C. Kinsey: A Public/Private Life* (New York: W. W. Norton, 1997), 565.

4. Kinsey, *Human Male*, 499, 513.

5. Kinsey, *Human Male*, 392, 550, 623.

6. Although when the report was released it was attacked mainly because of its findings, researchers since that time have found fault with much of Kinsey's methodology. In particular, they have criticized him for relying on volunteers for his participants, rather than making sure that the survey included a representative sampling of demographic characteristics such as age, race, and level of education. Kinsey never released demographic details about the participants, but some critics have estimated that as many as 86 percent of them were either "criminals or sexual deviants," a term that in the 1950s was applied to homosexuals. See, for example, Judith A. Reisman, *Kinsey: Crimes and Consequences* (Arlington, VA: Institute for Media Education, 1998), 102.

7. "Kinsey—A Professor in Search of Sex," *People*, 19 July 1950, 30; "Kinsey Again," *Catholic Mind*, September 1949, 561; "Must We Change Our Standards?" *Reader's Digest*, June 1948, 4–5.

8. Lewis M. Terman, "Kinsey's 'Sexual Behavior in the Human Male': Some Comments and Criticisms," *Psychological Bulletin*, vol. 45 (September 1948): 444; Lawrence S. Kubie, "Psychiatric Implications of the Kinsey Report," *Psychosomatic Medicine*, vol. 19 (March–April 1948): 96; Margaret Mead, "An Anthropologist Looks at the Report," in *Problems of Sexual Behavior* (New York: American Social Hygiene Association, 1948), 60; "Must We Change Our Standards?" 6.

9. Alfred C. Kinsey, *Sexual Behavior in the Human Female* (Philadelphia: W. B. Saunders, 1953), 142, 286, 416, 454.

10. Kinsey, *Human Female*, 320.

11. Reinhold Niebuhr, "Sex and Religion in the Kinsey Report," *Christianity and Crisis*, 2 November 1953, 138; Karl Menninger, "What the Girls Told," *Saturday Review of Literature*, 26 September 1953, 21, 30, 31 (quotes are on page 30); Billy Graham, "The Bible and Dr. Kinsey," *Moody Monthly*, November 1953, 13.

12. "Postal Ban Urged on Kinsey's Book," *New York Times*, 30 August 1953, 78 (the congressman was Louis B. Heller); Wardell Pomeroy, *Dr. Kinsey and the Institute for Sex Research* (New York: Harper & Row, 1972), 298; James R. Petersen, *The Century of Sex: Playboy's History of the Sexual Revolution, 1900–1999* (New York: Grove, 1999), 228.

13. Evelyn Duvall, *Facts of Life and Love for Teenagers* (New York: Association Press, 1950), 157–158, 285.

14. Steven D. Stark, *Glued to the Set: The 60 Television Shows and Events That Made Us Who We Are Today* (New York: Free Press, 1997), 30; Louis Chunovic, *One Foot on the Floor: The Curious Evolution of Sex on Television from I Love Lucy to South Park* (New York: TV Books, 2000), 34; David Halberstam, *The Fifties* (New York: Villard, 1993), 200.

Notes

15. Elvis Presley, "I Want You, I Need You, I Love You," 1956; Elvis Presley, "Teddy Bear," 1957; Chunovic, *One Foot on the Floor*, 41; Stark, *Glued to the Set*, 61.

16. Gregory D. Black, "Sound Motion Pictures," in Margaret A. Blanchard, ed., *History of the Mass Media in the United States* (Chicago: Fitzroy Dearborn, 1998), 611. (Father Daniel Lord wrote the Motion Picture Production Code, and Joseph I. Breen enforced it. The code was established in 1930 and remained in effect until it was replaced by the ratings system in 1968.) On specifics of the code, see Frank Walsh, *Sin and Censorship: The Catholic Church and the Motion Picture Industry* (New Haven: Yale University Press, 1996), 46–65.

17. Athan Theoharis, *J. Edgar Hoover, Sex, and Crime: An Historical Antidote* (Chicago: Ivan R. Dee, 1995), 101, 103; Colin Spencer, *Homosexuality in History* (New York: Harcourt Brace, 1995), 357; Anthony Summers, *Official and Confidential: The Secret Life of J. Edgar Hoover* (New York: G. P. Putnam's Sons, 1993); Petersen, *Century of Sex*, 216 (the man was Eugene Williams).

18. Fredric Wertham, "The Comics . . . Very Funny!" *Saturday Review of Literature*, 29 May 1948, 6–7, 27–28; Petersen, *Century of Sex*, 219.

19. Les Daniels, *Comix: A History of Comic Books in America* (New York: Outerbridge & Dienstfrey, 1971), 83–90. The quotes are on pages 84, 87, and 90.

20. Petersen, *Century of Sex*, 206, 211, 237.

21. Halberstam, *The Fifties*, 430–441 (the quotes are on page 435).

Chapter One

1. The standard dosage of the birth control pill during the early 1960s was ten milligrams, although that standard dosage was later reduced to one milligram.

2. Ann Marie Cunningham, "The Pill: How It Changed Our Lives," *Ladies' Home Journal*, June 1990, 123.

3. On the original medical purposes of the birth control pill, see Bernard Asbell, *The Pill: A Biography of the Drug That Changed the World* (New York: Random House, 1995), 170–171; Loretta McLaughlin, *The Pill, John Rock, and the Church: The Biography of a Revolution* (Boston: Little, Brown, 1982), 136–139; "The Pills," *Time*, 17 February 1961, 39; "U.S. Approves Pill for Birth Control," *New York Times*, 10 May 1960, 75.

4. On the central role that the media played in celebrating and/or popularizing the birth control pill, see McLaughlin, *The Pill, John Rock, and the Church*, especially 137–139, 154–155, 165–166, 172–173; Elizabeth Siegel Watkins, *On the Pill: A Social History of Oral Contraceptives, 1950–1970* (Baltimore: Johns Hopkins University Press, 1998), especially 6, 35–36, 41–49.

5. On public opposition to contraception, see McLaughlin, *The Pill, John Rock, and the Church*, 133–139.

6. "U.S. Approves Pill for Birth Control," *New York Times*, 10 May 1960, 75.

7. "Contraceptive Pill?" *Time*, 6 May 1957, 83.

8. Robert Sheehan, "The Birth-Control 'Pill,'" *Fortune*, April 1958, 154–155.

9. "The Remarkable Pill," *Newsweek*, 30 January 1961, 71; J. D. Ratcliff, "An End to Woman's 'Bad Days'?" *Reader's Digest*, December 1962, 73; Jane E. Brody, "The Pill: Revolution in Birth Control," *New York Times*, 31 May 1966, A1.

10. Alan F. Guttmacher, "How Safe Are Birth Control Pills?" *Ebony*, April 1962, 123, 127–128.

11. "The Better Way," *Good Housekeeping*, September 1962, 154.

12. Guttmacher, "How Safe?" 127.

13. Gregory Pincus, "Tell Me, Doctor," *Ladies' Home Journal*, June 1963, 50.

14. William L. Laurence, "Report on New Oral Contraceptive," *New York Times*, 19 February 1963, A6; "Enovid Exonerated," *Newsweek*, 29 June 1964, 81.

15. David Boroff, "Sex: The Quiet Revolution," *Esquire*, July 1961, 96.

16. Boroff, "Sex: The Quiet Revolution," 96, 98.

17. Ellen Willis, "The Birth-Control Pill," *Mademoiselle*, January 1961, 54, 112.

18. Willis, "Birth-Control Pill," 113; Gloria Steinem, "The Moral Disarmament of Betty Coed," *Esquire*, September 1962, 97, 153–157.

19. Steinem, "Moral Disarmament," 156–157.

20. Steinem, "Moral Disarmament," 157.

21. Andrew Hacker, "The Pill and Morality," *New York Times Magazine*, 21 November 1965, 138–139; "Contraception: Freedom from Fear," *Time*, 7 April 1967, 80.

22. "Birth Control: The Pill and the Church," *Newsweek*, 6 July 1964, 51.

23. "Birth Control: The Pill and the Church," 51, 55.

24. "Birth Control: The Pill and the Church," 52.

25. "Birth Control: The Pill and the Church," 54.

26. "Birth Control: The Pill and the Church," 52.

27. Morton Mintz, "The Golden Pill: We Can't Yet Be Sure It's Safe," *The New Republic*, 2 March 1968, 18–20. The direct quotation appeared on page 20.

28. Steven M. Spencer, "The Birth Control Revolution," *Saturday Evening Post*, 15 January 1966, 22.

29. "The Pill: How It Is Affecting U.S. Morals, Family Life," *U.S. News & World Report*, 11 July 1966, 62–65. The direct quotations appeared on pages 62–63 ("With birth control now . . .") and 63 ("There is less talk . . ." and "Marital infidelity is . . .").

30. For the quotation, see Watkins, *On the Pill*, 49. For other positive assessments of the media's role in reporting on the pill, see McLaughlin, *The Pill, John Rock, and the Church*, especially 137–139, 154–155, 165–166, 172–173.

31. James R. Petersen, *The Century of Sex*: Playboy's *History of the Sexual Revolution, 1900–1999* (New York: Grove, 1999), 261. On six million American women using the birth control pill, see also Mintz, "The Golden Pill," 18.

32. Brody, "Pill: Revolution in Birth Control," A34; Petersen, *Century of Sex*, 276.

33. On the pill being embraced because of positive feelings toward scientific developments, see Mintz, "Golden Pill," 20.

34. "The Remarkable Pill," *Newsweek*, 30 January 1961, 71; "Contraception: Freedom from Fear," *Time*, 7 April 1967, 80; Boroff, "Sex: The Quiet Revolution," 96, 98–99.

35. Willis, "Birth-Control Pill," 54–55; Steinem, "Moral Disarmament," 97, 153–155; Brody, "Pill: Revolution in Birth Control," A1, A34. On women finding success in the news business by focusing on stories that they were uniquely qualified to cover, see Kay Mills, *A Place in the News: From the Women's Pages to the Front Pages* (New York: Dodd, Mead, 1988), especially 236–252.

36. On the news values that journalists use to determine the importance of a story, see, for example, Brian S. Brooks, George Kennedy, Daryl R. Moen, and Don Ranly (The Missouri Group), *News Reporting and Writing*, 7th edition (New York: Bedford/St. Martin's, 2002), 5–6.

Chapter Two

1. "Growing Wonder," *Playboy*, October 1963, 119.

2. Although the definition of pornography has varied over time, it generally is understood to refer to material that is designed to sexually arouse the intended viewer.

3. On Hugh Hefner being the catalyst for the Sexual Revolution, see Kevin Burns, director, "Hugh Hefner: American Playboy," Arts & Entertainment Biography (video), Van Ness Films, Inc., New York, 1996.

4. Louis Chunovic, *One Foot on the Floor: The Curious Evolution of Sex on Television from* I Love Lucy *to* South Park (New York: TV Books, 2000), 46.

5. On men's magazines before *Playboy*, see Tom Hickman, *The Sexual Century* (London: Carlton, 1999), 116; Frederick S. Lane III, *Obscene Profits: The Entrepreneurs of Pornography in the Cyber Age* (New York: Routledge, 2000), xvi; James R. Petersen, *The Century of Sex*: Playboy's *History of the Sexual Revolution, 1900–1999* (New York: Grove, 1999), 228.

6. Soft-core porn is generally understood to be limited to nudity, while hard-core porn involves vaginal, oral, or anal penetration. "Sweetheart of the Month," *Playboy*, undated issue that appeared in November 1953, 19. For background on the early history of *Playboy*, see Hickman, *Sexual Century*, 116–119; Calvin Tomkins, "Mr. Playboy of the Western World," *Saturday Evening Post*, 23 April 1966, 100.

7. The Frank Sinatra interview was in February 1963, the Beatles in February 1965, Fidel Castro in January 1967, the Rev. Martin Luther King Jr. in January 1965, and Malcolm X in May 1963.

8. On *Playboy* articles being pornographic but not "smutty or dirty," see Dennis Brissett and Robert P. Snow, "Vicarious Behavior: Leisure and the Transformation of 'Playboy' Magazine," *Journal of Popular Culture*, vol. 3, no. 3 (1969): 432.

9. "Playboy Puts Glint in the Admen's Eyes," *Business Week*, 28 June 1969, 143. The advertising agency was J. Walter Thompson.

10. Oriana Fallaci, "Hugh Hefner: I Am in the Center of the World," *Look*, 10 January 1967, 56; "The Pursuit of Hedonism," *Time*, 3 March 1967, 77; "'It'—Up to Date," *Time*, 4 June 1965, 58.

11. Bill Davidson, "Czar of the Bunny Empire," *Saturday Evening Post*, 28 April 1962, 34; Petersen, *Century of Sex*, 231. The comedian was named Mort Sahl.

12. On the Playmate photo being innovative, see Hickman, *Sexual Century*, 119.

13. *Playboy*, "Viva Victoria," September 1963, 117; "Unmelancholy Dane," January 1967, 133; "Winters' Welcome," December 1956, 42; "Bunny from Britain," May 1966, 110; "Schoolmate Playmate," January 1958, 35; "Growing Up Glamorous," December 1964, 46.

14. *Playboy*, "Queen of Clubs," October 1962, 96; "Winters' Welcome," December 1956, 42; "Miss June Takes a Jaunt Through Central Park," June 1956, 35; "Spice from the Orient," April 1967, 103; "Homing Pigeon," March 1969, 109.

15. *Playboy*, "Growing Wonder," October 1963, 123; "Manhattan Mannequin," March 1963, 89; "Screen Gem," September 1967, 133; "Winters' Welcome," December 1956, 42; "Miss June Takes a Jaunt Through Central Park," June 1956, 35.

16. Tomkins, "Mr. Playboy," 96; "Can You Bare It?" *Forbes*, 1 March 1971, 18; "Urbunnity," *Newsweek*, 6 January 1964, 48.

17. On the extent of the Playboy empire, see Lane, *Obscene Profits*, especially 26–27; Tomkins, "Mr. Playboy," 96–101; "Can You Bare It?" *Forbes*, 1 March 1971, 17–21.

18. *Playboy*, "The Old Pro," January 1969, 51; "Vanishing Virgins," February 1969, 47; "Use It or Lose It," February 1969, 47.

19. *Playboy*, Harriet F. Pilpel, "Contraception and Freedom," January 1969, 51; "Gutter Crawling," April 1969, 69; "Laissez Faire," April 1969, 69.

20. *Playboy*, September 1963, 152; April 1969, 220; March 1963, 65.

21. On *Playboy* being the first magazine to send nude images through the mail, see Hickman, *Sexual Century*, 119. "The Nudist Jayne Mansfield," *Playboy*, June 1963, 124; "Two Definitions of Obscenity," *Time*, 21 June 1963, 44.

22. Diana Lurie, "In Hefnerland, Women Are Status Symbols," *Life*, 29 October 1965, 70; "Urbunnity," *Newsweek*, 6 January 1964, 49; Fallaci, "Hugh Hefner," 57.

23. *Playboy*, Stephen Yafa, "The Campus Mood," September 1969, 197; Richard Warren Lewis, "The Swingers," April 1969, 226; "Sexual Evolution," April 1969, 68.

24. *Playboy*, "Another Other Woman," April 1969, 68; "Adultery and Neurosis," January 1969, 50.

25. "The Playboy Advisor," *Playboy*, October 1963, 47.

26. Lewis, "Swingers," 150, 216.

27. Lewis, "Swingers," 150.

28. Lewis, "Swingers," 216, 219, 220.

29. "The Pursuit of Hedonism," *Time*, 3 March 1967, 78; "The Boss of Taste City," *Time*, 24 March 1961, 55; Tomkins, "Mr. Playboy," 99; "Hugh Hefner's Jet Black Bunny," *Look*, 2 June 1970, 63; "Bunny Hunting," *Newsweek*, 2 March 1970, 71; "Can You Bare It?" *Forbes*, 1 March 1971, 17; "Playboy Puts Glint in the Admen's Eyes," *Business Week*, 28 June 1969, 143.

30. Tomkins, "Mr. Playboy," 100; Lurie, "In Hefnerland," 70.

31. *Playboy* began allowing pubic hair to be visible with its January 1971 centerfold. "Bunny Hunting," *Newsweek*, 2 March 1970, 71–72; "Penthouse v. Playboy," *Time*, 7 November 1969, 88.

32. Petersen, *Century of Sex*, 228; John Brady, "Nude Journalism," *Journal of Popular Culture*, vol. 9, no. 1 (1975): 153; Burns, "Hugh Hefner: American Playboy."

33. Hugh Hefner, "Foreword," in Petersen, *Century of Sex*, ix.

Chapter Three

1. On the Ursula Andress entrance being the most memorable in film history, see James Chapman, *Licence to Thrill: A Cultural History of the James Bond Films* (New York: Columbia University Press, 2000), 84; Steven Jay Rubin, *The Complete James Bond Movie Encyclopedia* (Chicago: Contemporary Books, 1995), 11. On the scene being the sexiest in movie history, see "Ursula Andress Voted Sexiest Screen Moment," *EXP Magazine*, 19 December 2003–29 January 2004, 34.

2. *Playboy*, "She Is Ursula Andress," June 1965, 130–141; "James Bond's Girls," November 1965, 132–141, 144, 205–206; "Ursula," July 1966, 102–109; "Playboy Interview: Ian Fleming," December 1964, 97–98, 100, 102, 104, 106; "Playboy Interview: Sean Connery," November 1965, 75–76, 78, 80–84. Bond looked at *Playboy* in *On Her Majesty's Secret Service*.

3. Richard Schickel, "007 and a Grimy Cousin," *Life*, 7 January 1966, 8. After the 1960s, Sean Connery returned to the role of James Bond in *Diamonds Are Forever* in 1971 and again in *Never Say Never Again* in 1976. The other three actors who have filled the role are Roger Moore, Timothy Dalton, and Pierce Brosnan.

4. "Agent 007 Takes On a Solid-Gold Cad," *Life*, 6 November 1964, 116.

Notes

5. Chapman, *Licence to Thrill,* 69–70.

6. Chapman, *Licence to Thrill,* 13–14, 72; "007 Sights $2-Bil," *Variety,* 13 May 1987, 57; Nicholas Anez, "James Bond," *Films in Review,* 18/9–10, September/October 1992, 316; "Bondomania," *Time,* 11 June 1965, 59; Lietta Tornabuoni, "A Popular Phenomenon," in Oreste Del Buono and Umberto Edo, eds., *The Bond Affair* (London: R. A. Downie, 1966), 19.

7. "Bondomania," *Time,* 11 June 1965, 59; Chapman, *Licence to Thrill,* 114. The female star on the cover of *Life* was Shirley Eaton from *Goldfinger.*

8. Chapman, *Licence to Thrill,* 6. The condemnation was published in the Vatican newspaper *Osservatore Romano.*

9. Among the beauty queens appearing in the films were Daniela Bianchi in *From Russia With Love,* Miss Rome and runner-up to Miss Universe, and Claudine Auger in *Thunderball,* Miss France.

10. Nudity in motion pictures was restricted by the provisions of the Motion Picture Production Code that was established in 1930 and remained in effect until the ratings system was adopted in 1968.

11. Sylvia Trench was played by Eunice Gayson.

12. "Unredeemed Bond," *Newsweek,* 26 June 1967, 73.

13. For the Harry Saltzman quote, see Alan Barnes and Marcus Hearn, *Kiss Kiss Bang! Bang!: The Unofficial Bond Film Companion* (Woodstock, NY: Overlook, 1998), 9.

14. On George Lazenby being chosen because of his appearance, see Jeremy Black, *The Politics of James Bond: From Fleming's Novels to the Big Screen* (Westport, CT: Praeger, 2001), 124.

15. James Bond's two sex partners from the clinic were named Ruby, played by Angela Scoular, and Nancy, played by Catherina von Schell.

16. Pussy Galore was played by Honor Blackman.

17. Tom Hickman, *The Sexual Century* (London: Carlton, 1999), 145.

18. The woman in the bra and panties was named Jill Masterson and was played by Shirley Eaton.

19. The physical therapist was named Patricia Fearing and was played by Molly Peters.

20. Contessa Teresa de Vincenzo was played by Diana Rigg.

21. Fiona Volpe was played by Italian actress Luciana Paluzzi.

22. Helga Brandt was played by German actress Karin Dor.

23. Miss Taro was played by Zena Marshall, Bonita by Latina actress Nadja Regin. On red- and dark-haired women being stereotyped as villains, see Black, *Politics of James Bond,* 111.

24. On the voyeuristic technique's prominence in the Bond films, see Chapman, *Licence to Thrill,* 84; Laura Mulvey, "Visual Pleasure and Narrative Cinema," *Screen,* 16/3, Autumn 1975, 6–18; Bill Osgerby, *Playboys in Paradise: Masculinity, Youth and Leisure-Style in Modern America* (New York: Oxford University Press, 2001), 161.

25. Bond's repeated sex partner in *From Russia With Love* was named Tatiana Romanova and was played by Italian actress Daniela Bianchi.

26. The two gypsy women were named Vida and Zora and were played by actresses Aliza Gur and Martine Beswick; the belly dancer was named Leila, but the actress who filled the role was not identified in the film credits or in the numerous books that have been written about the Bond films. On the fight between the two gypsy women being irrelevant to the plot, see Barnes and Hearn, *Kiss Kiss Bang! Bang!,* 25; Chapman, *Licence to Thrill,* 87.

27. Among the actresses whose voices were dubbed, in addition to Andress, were Claudine Auger in *Thunderball,* Daniela Bianchi in *From Russia With Love,* Shirley Eaton in *Goldfinger,* Eunice Gayson in *Dr. No* and *From Russia With Love,* and Tania Mallet in *Goldfinger.*

28. On femme fatales, see "Hairy Marshmallow," *Time,* 31 May 1963, 80; "Agent 007," *Life,* 6 November 1964, 116. On James Bond's bride being killed, see A. H. Weiler, "Screen: James Bond," *New York Times,* 19 December 1969, 68.

29. "Yes to 'No,'" *The New Yorker,* 1 June 1963, 65–66; "Once More Unto the Breach," *Time,* 10 April 1964, 103–104; "Agent 007," *Life,* 6 November 1964, 116.

30. Weiler, "Screen: James Bond," 68.

31. On the "swinging bachelor," see James R. Petersen, *The Century of Sex: Playboy's History of the Sexual Revolution, 1900–1999* (New York: Grove, 1999), 266–267. On the quote by the producer, see Barnes and Hearn, *Kiss Kiss Bang! Bang!,* 4 (the quote was from Harry Saltzman, who along with Albert R. Broccoli co-produced the first nine James Bond films). On the "Bond is the perfect hero" quote, see Chapman, *Licence to Thrill,* 117. Books about the James Bond films include Kingsley Amis, *The James Bond Dossier* (London: Jonathan Cape, 1965; Pan, 1966); Barnes and Hearn, *Kiss Kiss Bang! Bang!;* Tony Bennett and Janet Woollacott, *Bond and Beyond: The Political Career of a Popular Hero* (London: Macmillan, 1987); Tony Bennett et al., *The Making of 'The Spy That Loved Me'* (Milton Keynes, UK: Open University Press, 1977); Raymond Benson, *The James Bond Bedside Companion* (London:

Boxtree, 1988); Black, *Politics of James Bond*; John Brosnan, *James Bond in the Cinema* (London: Tantivy, 1981); Chapman, *Licence to Thrill*; Del Buono and Eco, *Bond Affair*; Brian Dunbar, *Goldfinger* (London: York, 2001); Peter Haining, *James Bond: A Celebration* (London: Planet Books, 1987); Sally Hibbin, *The Official James Bond 007 Movie Book* (London: Hamlyn, 1987); Andy Lane and Paul Simpson, *The Bond Files: The Unofficial Guide to the World's Greatest Secret Agent* (London: Virgin, 1998); Sheldon Lane, ed., *For Bond Lovers* (London: Panther, 1965); Jay McInerney, Nick Foulkes, Neil Norman, Nick Sullivan, and Colin Woodhead, *Dressed To Kill: James Bond, the Suited Hero* (Paris: Flammarion, 1996); Garth Pearce, *The Making of GoldenEye* (London: Boxtree, 1995); Garth Pearce, *The Making of Tomorrow Never Dies* (London: Boxtree, 1997); Lee Pfeiffer and Lisa Philip, *The Incredible World of 007* (London: Boxtree, 1992); Lee Pfeiffer and Dave Worrall, *The Essential Bond: The Authorized Guide to the World of 007* (London: Boxtree, 1998); Andrew Rissik, *The James Bond Man: The Films of Sean Connery* (London: Elm Tree, 1983); Rubin, *James Bond Movie Encyclopedia*; Steven Jay Rubin, *The James Bond Films: A Behind the Scenes History* (London: Talisman, 1981); Patrick Rufo, *The James Bond Story* (Paris: WIN Productions, 1987); Graham Rye, *The James Bond Girls* (London: Boxtree, 1989); O. F. Snelling, *James Bond: A Report* (London: Panther, 1965); Adrian Turner, *Goldfinger: Bloomsbury Movie Guide No. 2* (London: Bloomsbury, 1998); Dave Worrall, *The Most Famous Car in the World: The Complete History of the James Bond Aston Martin DB5* (Christchurch, New Zealand: Solo, 1991).

Chapter Four

1. Paul Levine, *Miami Herald*, "Singer Exposed Self, 2 Spectators Testify," 18 August 1970, B1; "Jurors Hear Morrison Tape," 28 August 1970, C9.

2. Paul Levine, *Miami Herald*, "Judge Rejects Morrison Plea for Acquittal," 3 September 1970, D6; "Officer: Morrison Fans Feared," 26 August 1970, B2.

3. Steve Sink, "Morrison Gets 6-Month Sentence," *Miami Herald*, 31 October 1970, A1.

4. James Riordan and Jerry Prochnicky, *Break on Through: The Life and Death of Jim Morrison* (New York: William Morrow, 1991), 165; Jerry Hopkins, *The Lizard King: The Essential Jim Morrison* (New York: Fireside/Simon & Schuster, 1992), 11.

5. On Morrison's early years, see Ben Fong-Torres, "James Douglas Morrison, Poet: Dead at 27," *Rolling Stone*, 5 August 1971, 1, 34–39; Hopkins, *Lizard King*, 32–58; Riordan and Prochnicky, *Break on Through*, 25–92. Other books that are either biographies of Jim Morrison or that contain substantial biographical information about him include John Densmore, *Riders on the Storm: My Life with Jim Morrison and The Doors* (New York: Delacorte, 1990); Andrew Doe and John Tobler, *The Doors in Their Own Words* (New York: Perigee/Putnam, 1991); Jerry Hopkins and Daniel Sugerman, *No One Here Gets Out Alive* (New York: Warner, 1980); Dylan Jones, *Jim Morrison: Dark Star* (New York: Viking Studio Books/Penguin, 1990); Frank Lisciandro, *Jim Morrison: An Hour for Magic* (New York: Delilah, 1982); Frank Lisciandro, *Morrison: A Feast of Friends* (New York: Warner, 1991); Herve Muller, *Jim Morrison au-dela des doors* (Paris: Albin Michel, 1973); Daniel Sugerman, *The Doors: The Illustrated History* (New York: Quill/William Morrow, 1983).

6. Hopkins, *Lizard King*, 43.

7. Fong-Torres, "Morrison," 37.

8. Hopkins, *Lizard King*, 63, 66.

9. Hopkins, *Lizard King*, 75.

10. Howard Smith, "Scenes," *Village Voice*, 14 December 1967, 14.

11. Jerry Hopkins, "The Doors on Stage," *Rolling Stone*, 10 February 1968, 15; Paul Williams, "Rothchild Speaks," *Crawdaddy!* July/August 1967, 17; Gene Youngblood, "Doors Reaching for Outer Limits," *Los Angeles Free Press*, 1 December 1967, 6; "Swimming to the Moon," *Time*, 24 November 1967, 106; "This Way to the Egress," *Newsweek*, 6 November 1967, 101.

12. Jones, *Jim Morrison: Dark Star*, 68.

13. Riordan and Prochnicky, *Break on Through*, 15–16.

14. Riordan and Prochnicky, *Break on Through*, 55.

15. Richard Goldstein, "Shaman as Superstar," *New York*, 5 August 1968, 42; Hopkins, *Lizard King*, 75.

16. Pamela Des Barres, *I'm with the Band: Confessions of a Groupie* (New York: Beech Tree/William Morrow, 1987), 64–65.

17. Fong-Torres, "Morrison," 37.

18. Fred Powledge, "Wicked Go The Doors," *Life*, 12 April 1968, 88, 91–92; Riordan and Prochnicky, *Break on Through*, 144.

19. Hopkins, *Lizard King*, 86.

Notes

20. Goldstein, "Shaman as Superstar," 44; Smith, "Scenes," 14; Annie Fisher, "Riffs: Jiiimmieeeee!" *Village Voice*, 30 January 1969, 36; Shamrock O'Toole (pseudonym for Patricia Kennealy), "The Doors in New York," *Jazz & Pop*, April 1970, 50.

21. "New Haven Police Close 'The Doors,'" *New York Times*, 11 December 1967, 58; "Door Slammed for Obscene Reason," *Rolling Stone*, 20 January 1968, 4; Powledge, "Wicked Go The Doors," 87–94.

22. Riordan and Prochnicky, *Break on Through*, 207–208.

23. Among the books that discuss Courson and Morrison's relationship are Hopkins, *Lizard King*; Hopkins and Sugerman, *No One Here Gets Out Alive*; Riordan and Prochnicky, *Break on Through*.

24. Jones, *Dark Star*, 161–162.

25. Hopkins, *Lizard King*, 95, 108.

26. Hopkins, *Lizard King*, 95–97.

27. Riordan and Prochnicky, *Break on Through*, 127, 150.

28. Riordan and Prochnicky, *Break on Through*, 243.

29. Riordan and Prochnicky, *Break on Through*, 176, 181.

30. Riordan and Prochnicky, *Break on Through*, 297–298.

31. Riordan and Prochnicky, *Break on Through*, 298.

32. Riordan and Prochnicky, *Break on Through*, 298.

33. Riordan and Prochnicky, *Break on Through*, 299.

34. Riordan and Prochnicky, *Break on Through*, 300.

35. Larry Mahoney, "Rock Singer Charged," *Miami Herald*, 6 March 1969, B1.

36. Riordan and Prochnicky, *Break on Through*, 306–307, 418.

37. Hopkins and Sugerman, *No One Here Gets Out Alive*, 238; Riordan and Prochnicky, *Break on Through*, 306–307, 310, 541.

38. Jones, *Dark Star*, 10.

39. Riordan and Prochnicky, *Break on Through*, 334.

40. Hopkins, *Lizard King*, 159–160.

41. Hopkins, *Lizard King*, 172, 367–374.

Chapter Five

1. "Meet the Bunkers" aired 12 January 1971.

2. Steven D. Stark, *Glued to the Set: The 60 Television Shows and Events That Made Us Who We Are Today* (New York: Free Press, 1997), 163; Richard P. Adler, ed., *All in the Family: A Critical Appraisal* (New York: Praeger, 1979), xv.

3. John Leonard, "Bigotry as a Dirty Joke," *Life*, 19 March 1971, 10; "Family Fun," *Newsweek*, 15 March 1971, 64; Carroll Terry, "The New Trend in TV Comedies," *Good Housekeeping*, September 1972, 81.

4. Adler, *All in the Family*, xv.

5. Janet Staiger, *Blockbuster TV: Must-See Sitcoms in the Network Era* (New York: New York University Press, 2000), 98.

6. Staiger, *Blockbuster TV*, 98.

7. "TV: Speaking About the Unspeakable," *Newsweek*, 29 November 1971, 53. Archie was played by Carroll O'Connor, Edith by Jean Stapleton, Gloria by Sally Struthers, and Mike by Rob Reiner.

8. "Playboy Interview: Carroll O'Connor," *Playboy*, January 1973, 62.

9. Myron Roberts and Lincoln Haynes, "TV: Archie's Hang-ups," *The Nation*, 15 November 1971, 509; Arnold Hano, "Can Archie Bunker Give Bigotry a Bad Name?" *New York Times Magazine*, 12 March 1972, 32.

10. "Michael's Problem" aired 20 November 1971.

11. Christopher Porterfield, "Toppling Old Taboos," *Time*, 25 September 1972, 51.

12. Porterfield, "Toppling Old Taboos," 50; Roberts and Haynes, "TV: Archie's Hang-ups," 509. On *All in the Family* being the first program in entertainment television to broadcast an episode about homosexuality ("Judging Books by Covers"), see Stephen Tropiano, *The Prime Time Closet: A History of Gays and Lesbians on TV* (New York: Applause Theatre and Cinema Books, 2002), 186. "Judging Books by Covers" aired 9 February 1971; "The Threat" aired 30 September 1972.

13. On infidelity, see "Archie's Brief Encounter," which aired 22 September 1976; on rape, "Gloria, the Victim" and "Edith's 50th Birthday," 17 March 1973 and 16 October 1977; on menstruation, "The Battle of the Month," 24 March 1973; on menopause, "Edith's Problem," 8 January 1972; on vasectomies, "Gloria's False Alarm," 18

December 1976; on wife-swapping, "The Bunkers and the Swingers," 28 October 1972; on lesbianism, "Cousin Liz," 9 October 1977; on sexually aggressive wives, "Mike and Gloria Mix It Up," 5 January 1974.

14. Staiger, *Blockbuster TV,* 95; Donna McCrohan, *Prime Time, Our Time: America's Life and Times Through the Prism of Television* (Rocklin, CA: Prima, 1992), 224; Adler, *All in the Family,* xliv. The books are Adler, *All in the Family;* Spencer Marsh, *God, Man, and Archie Bunker* (New York: Harper & Row, 1975); Spencer Marsh, *Edith the Good* (New York: Harper & Row, 1977); Donna McCrohan, *Archie & Edith, Mike & Gloria: The Tumultuous History of All in the Family* (New York: Workman, 1987). The other works include Steven Capsuto, *Alternate Channels: The Uncensored Story of Gay and Lesbian Images on Radio and Television* (New York: Ballantine, 2000), 71–73; Louis Chunovic, *One Foot on the Floor: The Curious Evolution of Sex on Television from* I Love Lucy *to* South Park (New York: TV Books, 2000), especially 12–13, 61–65; David Marc and Robert J. Thompson, *Prime Time, Prime Movers: From* I Love Lucy *to* L.A. Law (Boston: Little, Brown, 1992), especially 49–60; McCrohan, *Prime Time,* 208–224; Staiger, *Blockbuster TV,* 81–113; Stanley Stark, "Toward an Anthropology of Dogmatism: Traditionalism, Modernism, Existentialism, and the Counterculture: 'All in the Family,'" *Psychological Reports,* vol. 29 (1971): 819–830; Stark, *Glued to the Set,* 162–167; Howard F. Stein, "'All in the Family' as a Mirror of Contemporary American Culture," *Family Process,* vol. 13, no. 3 (1974): 279–315.

15. "Gloria, the Victim" aired 17 March 1973; McCrohan, *Prime Time,* 218.

16. Hano, "Can Archie Bunker Give Bigotry a Bad Name?" 127.

Chapter Six

1. "Dear Cosmopolitan," *Cosmopolitan,* July 1972, 201.

2. "Cosmo's Playmate of the Year!—Why?" *Cosmopolitan,* April 1972, 185.

3. Amy Kennedy, "Burt Reynolds, the New Sex Star," *Vogue,* July 1972, 86–87, 111, 113; Claire Safran, "The Burt Reynolds Nobody Knows," *Redbook,* January 1974, 72–73, 110–112; "Playmate of the Month," *Newsweek,* 10 April 1972, 57–58; Roger Ebert, "What Kind of Playmate Is Burt?" *New York Times,* 26 March 1972, B13.

4. For the quote, see Melissa Hantman, "Helen Gurley Brown," *Salon,* 26 September 2000. On the circulation growth, see Paula Kamen, *Her Way: Young Women Remake the Sexual Revolution* (New York: New York University Press, 2000), 225.

5. On biographical details about Helen Gurley Brown, see Shana Alexander, "Singular Girl's Success," *Life,* 1 March 1963, 60, 65–67; Nora Ephron, "Helen Gurley Brown Only Wants to Help," *Esquire,* February 1970, 117–118; Stephanie Harrington, "Two Faces of the Same Eve," *New York Times Magazine,* 11 August 1974, 11, 36; *Helen Gurley Brown: The Original Cosmo Girl,* A&E Television Networks (Video) (New York, 1996); Roxanne Roberts, "The Oldest Living Cosmo Girl," *Washington Post,* 31 January 1996, D1; Randall Rothenberg, "The Cosmo Girl at 25," *New York Times,* 21 April 1990, 31–32; Alex Witchel, "Go Ahead, Say It," *New York Times,* 1 April 1993, C1, C6.

6. Harrington, "Two Faces," 11; Roberts, "The Oldest Living Cosmo Girl," D1.

7. Harrington, "Two Faces," 11; Ephron, "Helen Gurley Brown Only Wants to Help," 75.

8. Helen Gurley Brown, *Sex and the Single Girl* (New York: Bernard Geis, 1962), 7.

9. Since its founding in 1886, *Cosmopolitan* had been a general-circulation magazine, emphasizing fiction during some periods of its history and at other times focusing on public affairs.

10. Florence King, "Brief Encounters," *Cosmopolitan,* September 1975, 191.

11. Richard Atcheson, "The Wayward Co-ed and the Willing Prof," *Cosmopolitan,* February 1972, 139.

12. King, "Brief Encounters," 191–192.

13. King, "Brief Encounters," 192.

14. Mona Williams, "The Cheaters," *Cosmopolitan,* February 1972, 127; Irma Kurtz, "Creative Infidelity," *Cosmopolitan,* July 1973, 146.

15. Kurtz, "Creative Infidelity," 146.

16. Witchel, "Go Ahead, Say It," C6.

17. Barbara Howell, "The Sexually Selfish Lover," *Cosmopolitan,* January 1974, 32, 37.

18. Tom Burke, "Here's Barbi . . . Hugh Hefner's Playmate," *Cosmopolitan,* September 1973, 70; David Reuben, "The Sexually Deprived Wife," *Cosmopolitan,* January 1972, 79; Constance Bogen, "The Sexually Obsessed Woman," *Cosmopolitan,* March 1972, 86.

19. *Cosmopolitan,* April 1972, 169.

20. Jeannie Sakol, "Why Girls Can't Have Orgasms . . . and What to Do About It," *Cosmopolitan,* May 1974, 209, 263.

21. David Reuben, "Masturbation and Other Pleasures," *Cosmopolitan,* March 1974, 140–141.

22. Sakol, "Why Girls Can't Have Orgasms," 209.

23. Harrington, "Two Faces," 10, 76.

24. Ephron, "Helen Gurley Brown Only Wants to Help," 75, 117.

25. "Big Sister," *Time*, 9 February 1968, 60; "Down with 'Pippypoo,'" *Newsweek*, 18 July 1966, 60; M. J. Sobran Jr., "Diets and Diaphragms," *National Review*, 2 April 1976, 335.

26. Brian McNair, *Striptease Culture: Sex, Media and the Democratization of Desire* (New York: Routledge, 2002), 23; Kamen, *Her Way*, 225.

Chapter Seven

1. For the quotation, see www.phildonahue.philtalks.com. William Brashler, "Blessed Are the Women of America," *Esquire*, 30 January 1979, 42; Phil Donahue & Co., "Donahue's Love Affair with His Audience," *Chicago Tribune*, 13 April 1980, L4; "From Dayton to the World," *Broadcasting*, 2 November 1992 (advertising supplement with unnumbered pages inserted in the magazine); Abe Peck and Laura Green, "The Cool Art of Creating a Hot Dialogue," *Chicago Sun-Times*, 9 April 1980, 37; Roger Simon, "There's No Phil Donahue Without the Audience," *TV Guide*, 27 May 1978, 27.

2. On the size of the *Donahue* audience, see Larry Green, "The Donahue Touch Seduces America," *Los Angeles Times*, 18 February 1980, E1; Abe Peck and Laura Green, "Come Share with Me," *Chicago Sun-Times*, 7 April 1980, 39; Joel Swerdlow, "Donahue's Dilemma," *Washington Post*, 27 January 1980, G1, G4.

3. Harry F. Waters, "The Talk of Television," *Newsweek*, 29 October 1979, 77.

4. Simon, "No Phil Donahue Without," 25–26. Although *All in the Family* did not deal with the abortion issue, a CBS spin-off of the program titled *Maude* devoted two episodes to the topic in November 1972. In the segments, the title character in the sitcom became pregnant at the age of forty-seven and then aborted the fetus. The two segments created a great deal of controversy, including anti-abortion advocates conducting public demonstrations and several CBS stations refusing to air the segments.

5. On Donahue's early life, see Abe Peck and Laura Green, "Phil Donahue's Roots," *Chicago Sun-Times*, 6 April 1980, E1–E3, E14; Swerdlow, "Donahue's Dilemma," G1, G4.

6. On Donahue's early career, see "From Dayton to the World"; Peck and Green, "Phil Donahue's Roots," E1.

7. On Phil Donahue being the most popular talk show host on television by mid-1978, see Brashler, "Blessed Are the Women," 41.

8. Jeanne Albronda Heaton and Nona Leigh Wilson, *Tuning in Trouble: Talk TV's Destructive Impact on Mental Health* (San Francisco: Jossey-Bass, 1995), 17; Swerdlow, "Donahue's Dilemma," G4; Waters, "Talk of Television," 77.

9. For the quotation, see www.phildonahue.philtalks.com. Diane K. Shah, "Heeere's . . . Phil Donahue!" *Newsweek*, 13 March 1978, 85; Simon, "No Phil Donahue Without," 26; Waters, "Talk of Television," 77.

10. Brashler, "Blessed Are the Women," 47; Swerdlow, "Donahue's Dilemma," G4; Starkey Flythe Jr., "Phil Donahue," *Saturday Evening Post*, December 1976, 71; Lee Margulies, "Talk Show for, by the Audience," *Los Angeles Times*, 30 August 1976, D12; Ann Marie Lipinski, "The Women Behind Donahue," *Chicago Tribune*, 22 April 1979, L1. Burt Reynolds's relationship was with singer and television personality Dinah Shore.

11. Abe Peck and Laura Green, "The Interviewer Puts His Views on the Record," *Chicago Sun-Times*, 8 April 1980, 57.

12. Joseph Sobran, "Television: Acute Philophobia," *National Review*, 25 July 1980, 914. On Phil Donahue being a pioneer on showcasing gays, see Larry Gross, *Up from Invisibility: Lesbians, Gay Men, and the Media in America* (New York: Columbia University Press, 2001), 185–187.

13. For the quotation, see www.phildonahue.philtalks.com. Brashler, "Blessed Are the Women," 42; Phil Donahue, "Putting the Blame on Fame," *Saturday Evening Post*, May/June 1980, 16; Peck and Green, "The Cool Art," 37.

14. Brashler, "Blessed Are the Women," 42; Donahue, "Putting the Blame on Fame," 16; Flythe, "Phil Donahue," 71; Peck and Green, "The Interviewer Puts His Views," 57; Simon, "No Phil Donahue Without," 28.

15. Swerdlow, "Donahue's Dilemma," G4.

16. Swerdlow, "Donahue's Dilemma," G4. On Donahue programs about incest, see also Howard Kurtz, "Father of the Slide," *The New Republic*, 12 February 1996, 12.

17. Gary Deeb, "WGN 'Saves' Bozo's Fans from Donahue Abortion Show," *Chicago Tribune*, 15 May 1975, C11; Green, "Donahue Touch Seduces," E9; Swerdlow, "Donahue's Dilemma," G4; Waters, "Talk of Television," 77.

Notes

18. Elaine Markoutsas, "The Phil Donahue I Know," *Good Housekeeping*, March 1980, 205; Peck and Green, "The Interviewer Puts His Views," 57; Peck and Green, "Phil Donahue's Roots," E14; Swerdlow, "Donahue's Dilemma," G1.

19. For the quotation, see www.phildonahue.philtalks.com. William Gildea, "A Bachelor Father's Drugstore Romance," *Washington Post*, 2 February 1978, C14.

20. Markoutsas, "Donahue I Know," 205.

21. Brashler, "Blessed Are the Women," 41; Phil Donahue & Co., "Donahue's Love Affair," L4; Flythe, "Phil Donahue," 71; Heaton and Wilson, *Tuning in Trouble*, 16; Peck and Green, "The Cool Art," 37; Shah, "Heeere's," 85; Waters, "Talk of Television," 77.

22. Giovanna Breu, "To TV's Phil Donahue, the Hand That Rocks the Cradle—and the Boat—Can Change America," *People Weekly*, 27 August 1979, 91.

23. Peck and Green, "The Interviewer Puts His Views," 57.

24. Brashler, "Blessed Are the Women," 48; Anne Gaylor, *Abortion Is a Blessing* (New York: Psychological Dimensions, 1975).

25. Mary Ann O'Roark, "Phil Donahue," *McCall's*, August 1978, 90.

26. On the *Donahue* program about abortion, see Brashler, "Blessed Are the Women," 48; Deeb, "WGN 'Saves' Bozo's Fans," C11; Donahue, "Putting the Blame on Fame," 16; Green, "Donahue Touch Seduces," E9; Margulies, "Talk Show for," D12; O'Roark, "Phil Donahue," 90; Sobran, "Television: Acute Philophobia," 914; Waters, "Talk of Television," 77.

27. Deeb, "WGN 'Saves' Bozo's Fans," C11.

28. Deeb, "WGN 'Saves' Bozo's Fans," C11.

29. Deeb, "WGN 'Saves' Bozo's Fans," C11.

30. On Donahue's appearances on the *Today* show, which continued for eighteen months, see Markoutsas, "Donahue I Know," 127.

31. Donahue, "Putting the Blame on Fame," cover, 12–14, 16; Phil Donahue and Company, *Donahue, My Own Story* (New York: Simon & Schuster, 1978); O'Roark, "Phil Donahue," 86, 90, 93, 188; Mary Ann O'Roark, "Marlo Thomas," *McCall's*, August 1978, 86, 89–90; Simon, "No Phil Donahue Without," cover, 25–30; Waters, "Talk of Television," cover, 76–79, 81. Donahue and Thomas married in 1980.

32. Breu, "To TV's Phil Donahue," 91; Green, "Donahue Touch Seduces," E9; Markoutsas, "Donahue I Know," 205; Simon, "No Phil Donahue Without," 25.

33. Brashler, "Blessed Are the Women," 41; Gildea, "A Bachelor Father's," C1.

Chapter Eight

1. Gerald Clarke, "Sanitizing the Small Screen," *Time*, 29 June 1981, 83; Harry F. Waters, "The New Right's TV Hit List," *Newsweek*, 15 June 1981, 101–103; Jill Williams, "The Drive to Clean Up Television," *Saturday Evening Post*, 7 November 1981, 74–77. The National Federation for Decency was later renamed the American Family Association.

2. Clarke, "Sanitizing the Small Screen," 83; William A. Henry III, "Another Kind of Ratings War," *Time*, 6 July 1981, 17–18, 20; Susan Schiefelbein, "Guardians of the Airwaves," *Saturday Review*, 16 September 1978, 26–28; Waters, "New Right's TV Hit List," 101–103.

3. Somers left the program in November 1980 because of a salary dispute. Other blond actresses then filled the role.

4. Chris Mann, *Come and Knock on Our Door: A Hers and Hers and His Guide to Three's Company* (New York: St. Martin's, 1998), xiii, xv.

5. Mann, *Come and Knock*, 1. The first recurring gay character on a television series was Peter Panama, a designer who appeared in the cast of the ABC comedy *The Corner Bar*, during the 1972 season. Another character, Jodie Dallas, played by Billy Crystal, appeared in the cast of *Soap*, an ABC sitcom that aired from 1977 to 1981.

6. John J. O'Connor, "TV: A Sex Comedy by Innuendo," *New York Times*, 31 March 1977, C25; Gerald Weales, "Television," *The Nation*, 2 September 1978, 189–190; James Brown, "ABC Opens 3 Seasons in One," *Los Angeles Times*, 15 March 1977, D12.

7. "A Man About the House" aired 15 March 1977.

8. "Jack and the Giant Killer" aired 14 April 1977; "Chrissy's Date" aired 13 October 1977.

9. "It's Only Money" aired 21 April 1977.

10. "A Man About the House" aired 15 March 1977; "And Mother Makes Four" aired 24 March 1977. Helen was played by Audra Lindley, and Stanley was played by Normal Fell.

11. "Roper's Car" aired 1 November 1977.

12. "No Children, No Pets" aired 7 April 1977.

13. "A Man About the House" aired 15 March 1977; "And Mother Makes Four" aired 24 March 1977; "No Children, No Pets" aired 7 April 1977.

14. "Alone Together" aired 25 October 1977; "Janet's Promotion" aired 27 September 1977; "Jack's Navy Pal" aired 7 February 1978; "Good Old Reliable Janet" aired 19 September 1978.

15. "Roper's Car" aired 1 November 1977.

16. Mann, *Come and Knock*, 132. The producer was Bernie West.

17. Mann, *Come and Knock*, 3. ABC's programming chief was Fred Silverman.

18. "And Mother Makes Four" aired 24 March 1977.

19. Mann, *Come and Knock*, 68, xv.

20. "Chrissy's Date" aired 13 October 1977.

21. Gary Powers, "Three's Company," *Saturday Evening Post*, September 1978, 62–63; Carolyn See, "The Short Jerky Girl," *TV Guide*, 4 August 1979, cover, 22–23, 25–26; Lois Armstrong, "Couples," *People Weekly*, 22 May 1978, 72–73, 75, 77; Edwin Miller, "The Fun's No Fake," *Seventeen*, February 1980, 140–141, 150, 152; Phyllis Battelle, "John Ritter," *Good Housekeeping*, March 1980, 68, 71–72, 74–75.

22. Merrill Rogers Skrocki, "Is Three Company?" *McCall's*, August 1979, cover, 51.

23. Mann, *Come and Knock*, 51.

24. "A Man About the House" aired 15 March 1977.

25. "And Mother Makes Four" aired 24 March 1977; "Cyrano de Tripper" aired 8 November 1977; "Jack and the Giant Killer" aired 14 April 1977.

26. Mann, *Come and Knock*, 52.

27. Steven Capsuto, *Alternate Channels: The Uncensored Story of Gay and Lesbian Images on Radio and Television* (New York: Ballantine, 2000), 144; Stephen Tropiano, *The Prime Time Closet: A History of Gays and Lesbians on TV* (New York: Applause Theatre and Cinema Books, 2002), 225. "Roper's Car" aired 1 November 1977; "Jack Looks for a Job" aired 20 September 1977.

28. "And Mother Makes Four" aired 24 March 1977; "Jack and the Giant Killer" aired 14 April 1977.

29. Mann, *Come and Knock*, 17.

30. Harry F. Waters, "Sex and TV," *Newsweek*, 20 February 1978, cover, 54–55, 57–61.

31. Gerard Jones, *Honey, I'm Home!: Sitcoms, Selling the American Dream* (New York: Grove Weidenfeld, 1992), 236; Louis Chunovic, *One Foot on the Floor: The Curious Evolution of Sex on Television from* I Love Lucy *to* South Park (New York: TV Books, 2000), 79; Mann, *Come and Knock*, 44.

Chapter Nine

1. Stanley Kauffmann, "Stanley Kauffmann on Films," *The New Republic*, 23 August 1980, 25.

2. Richard Corliss, "Killer!" *Time*, 16 November 1987, 74.

3. Carrie Rickey, "Sex and the Silver Screen," *Mademoiselle*, June 1982, 125.

4. On infidelity as a prominent theme in 1980s movies, see Corliss, "Killer!" 72, 74; Jack Kristin, "The Many Faces of Eve," *American Film*, April 1989, 38–41, 62; Tom O'Brien, "Keeping Things Taut," *Commonweal*, 9 October 1987, 565; Lawrence O'Toole, "Fatal Attraction," *Maclean's*, 21 September 1987, 58; Rickey, "Sex and the Silver Screen," 188; Richard Schickel, "The War Between the Mates," *Time*, 28 September 1987, 69.

5. Stanley Kauffmann, "Stanley Kauffmann on Films," *The New Republic*, 23 August 1980, 25. *Dressed to Kill*, which was directed by Brian De Palma, was released in 1980 by MGM Studios.

6. Corliss, "Killer!" 75. *Fatal Attraction*, which was directed by Adrian Lyne, was released in 1987 by Paramount Pictures.

7. *No Way Out*, which was directed by Roger Donaldson, was released in 1987 by Orion Pictures.

8. On 1980s movies communicating that infidelity by women leads to death, see David Ansen, "Nightmare on Madison Avenue," *Newsweek*, 28 September 1987, 76; Fred Bruning, "Sex and the Psychopath Factor," *Maclean's*, 23 November 1987, 7; Lisa Henricksson, "Back to the Boudoir," *Rolling Stone*, 17–31 December 1987, 147–148; Stanley Kauffmann, "Stanley Kauffmann on Films," *The New Republic*, 19 October 1987, 27; Kristin, "The Many Faces of Eve," 39, 62; Richard Schickel, "Hot Films," *Time*, 17 August 1987, 62.

9. On 1980s movies using women's bodies as objects, see Pauline Kael, "The Current Cinema," *The New Yorker*, 30 December 1985, 68; Stanley Kauffmann, "Stanley Kauffmann on Films," *The New Republic*, 23 August 1980, 25; Kristin, "The Many Faces of Eve," 39; Rickey, "Sex and the Silver Screen," 188; Colin L. Westerbeck, Jr., "Fashion Statement," *Commonweal*, 29 August 1980, 467.

Notes

10. Kristin, "The Many Faces of Eve," 40.

11. Stanley Kauffmann, "Stanley Kauffmann on Films," *The New Republic*, 23 August 1980, 25.

12. On 1980s movies promoting male dominance, see David Ansen, "We Shall Overcome," *Newsweek*, 30 December 1985, 59; Vincent Canby, "Film: 'No Way Out,'" *New York Times*, 14 August 1987, C3; "Expensive Turnoff," *Working Woman*, March 1986, 164.

13. "Expensive Turnoff," 164; Michael Musto, "9½ Reeks," *Saturday Review*, May/June 1986, 78. *9½ Weeks*, which was directed by Adrian Lyne, was released in 1986 by MGM Studios.

14. Lawrence O'Toole, "More Than Just a Gigolo," *Maclean's*, 4 February 1980, 49. *American Gigolo*, which was directed by Paul Schrader, was released in 1980 by Paramount Pictures.

15. Henry Edwards, "Sex-Rated," *Vogue*, April 1989, 237. On 1980s movies highlighting kinky sex, see also Joy Gould Boyum, "Movies," *Glamour*, May 1986, 235; David Denby, "England Spins," *New York*, 3 March 1986, 129.

16. Musto, "9[fr 1/2] Reeks," 78.

17. Corliss, "Killer!" 75.

18. *Risky Business*, which was directed by Paul Brickman, was released in 1983 by Warner Brothers Studios.

19. Jack Kroll, "Blood, Broads and Bucks," *Newsweek*, 15 March 1982, 78. On 1980s movies connecting sex and violence, see also Edward Donnerstein and Daniel Linz, "Sexual Violence in the Media: A Warning," *Psychology Today*, January 1984, 14–15; Pat Dowell, "Sex Makes a Comeback," *Psychology Today*, September 1988, 65; Ron Rosenbaum, "Should Sex Rate an 'X'?" *Mademoiselle*, June 1987, 46; James W. Wall, "Editorials: Fighting the Media's Eroticizing of Violence," *Christian Century*, 3 October 1984, 891.

20. O'Toole, "Fatal Attraction," 58; Bruning, "Sex and the Psychopath Factor," 7.

21. Corliss, "Killer!" 76.

22. Lawrence O'Toole, "Just When It Was Safe to Return to the Shower . . . ," *Maclean's*, 28 July 1980, 54.

23. On 1980s movies glamorizing prostitution, see David Ansen, "Love for Sale," *Newsweek*, 15 August 1983, 64; Lawrence O'Toole, "Adolescent Fantasies," *Maclean's*, 15 August 1983, 46; Pauline Kael, "The Current Cinema," *New Yorker*, 5 September 1983, 109; Richard Schickel, "Pinkeye," *Time*, 11 February 1980, 95.

24. Robert Hatch, "Films," *The Nation*, 16–23 August 1980, 165.

25. Kael, "The Current Cinema," 5 September 1983, 109; Ansen, "Love for Sale," 64.

26. Robert Hatch, "Films," *The Nation*, 23 February 1980, 219; Stanley Kauffmann, "Stanley Kauffmann on Films," *The New Republic*, 1 March 1980, 25. On *American Gigolo* redefining male escorts, see Schickel, "Pinkeye," 95; Mitch Tuchman, "Gigolos," *Film Comment*, March/April 1980, 49–52.

27. For the quote, see Charla Krupp, "Does Safe Sex Sell?" *Glamour*, July 1988, 156; the producer was Don Simpson. On 1980s movies not sending messages about safe sex, see David Ansen, "An August Heat Wave," *Newsweek*, 24 August 1987, 60; Henriksson, "Back to the Boudoir," 148; Krupp, "Does Safe Sex Sell?" 156; Schickel, "Hot Films," 62.

Chapter Ten

1. To view a print version of the ad, see http://www.davidtoc.com/ck/ckad.cfm?Ad_ID=228.

2. "The Bum's Rush in Advertising," *Time*, 1 December 1980, 95.

3. On the ad beginning a movement toward more sexual content in ads, see Jennet Conant, "Sexy Does It," *Newsweek*, 15 September 1986, 62; John A. Conway, "The Rag Trade Shuffle," *Forbes*, 2 January 1984, 16; Stuart Elliott, "Has Madison Avenue Gone Too Far?" *New York Times*, 16 December 1991, C6; Kim Foltz, "A Kinky New Calvinism," *Newsweek*, 11 March 1985, 65; Marcia Pally, "Brief Encounters," *Film Comment*, July/August 1984, 16; Pamela Sherrid, "Ragman," *Forbes*, 15 February 1982, 33.

4. "Sultry Jeans Ads Banned by WABC, WCBS-TV," *New York Times*, 20 November 1980, D1; "WNBC Also Bans Sultry Jeans Ads," *New York Times*, 21 November 1980, D5; Kathryn Buxton, "Personalities," *Washington Post*, 11 February 1982, D2.

5. Jeffrey A. Trachtenberg, "'It's Become Part of Our Culture,'" *Forbes*, 5 May 1986, 134.

6. Andrew Sullivan, "Flogging Underwear," *The New Republic*, 18 January 1988, 20.

7. "Sultry Jeans Ads Banned," D1, D7; "WNBC Also Bans Sultry Jeans Ads," D5; "I Wish You Hadn't Asked That, Daddy," *Fortune*, 17 November 1980, 112; Shirley Clurman, "Calvin Klein," *People*, 18 January 1982, 94. On the ad being described as "sexy," see Sherrid, "Ragman," 33; Conway, "Rag Trade Shuffle," 16; on the ad being described as "scandalous," see Conant, "Sexy Does It," 62; Foltz, "Kinky New Calvinism," 65.

8. Buxton, "Personalities," D2.

Notes

9. On Calvin Klein's contributions to American fashion, see Michael Gross, "The Latest Calvin," *New York,* 8 August 1988, 20–29; Melissa Sones, "Superstar Success Fitting Calvin Klein to a Tee," *Los Angeles Times,* 13 December 1987, VI16–VI19. For the quotation, see "Sultry Jeans Ads Banned," D7.

10. "Bum's Rush," 95.

11. "Sex Roles Modified in Changing of Ads," *New York Times,* 13 May 1985, D1; Ellen Goodman, "The 'Successful Woman as Sex Object' Syndrome," *Washington Post,* 12 October 1982, A13.

12. "Bum's Rush," 95.

13. Some sources spell the Underwear Man model's name Tom Hinthaus.

14. On the significance of Underwear Man, see Janice Castro, "Calvin Meets the Marlboro Man," *Time,* 21 October 1985, 69; Gross, "Latest Calvin," 27; Tom Shales, "Those Incredible Hunks," *Washington Post,* 27 November 1983, G9.

15. To view the ad, see http://www.davidtoc.com/ck/ckad.cfm?Ad_ID=178.

16. Shales, "Those Incredible Hunks," G1, G9.

17. Shales, "Those Incredible Hunks," G1, G9.

18. "Jim Palmer Pitches 'Style' for Jockey," *New York Times,* 29 August 1982, C23. On Palmer's modeling, see also Shales, "Those Incredible Hunks," G9; Trachtenberg, "'It's Become Part of Our Culture,'" 134.

19. On the ads being targeted at gay men, see "Jim Palmer Pitches 'Style' for Jockey," C23; Pally, "Brief Encounters," 17.

20. Shales, "Those Incredible Hunks," G9; Sullivan, "Flogging Underwear," 20; Castro, "Calvin Meets the Marlboro Man," 69.

21. Elliott, "Has Madison Avenue Gone Too Far?" C6; Sones, "Superstar Success," VI16. To view the ads of the couples, see http://www.davidtoc.com/ck/ckad.cfm?Ad_ID=154. To view the ad of the three nude couples, see http://www.davidtoc.com/ck/ckad.cfm?Ad_ID=151.

22. Foltz, "Kinky New Calvinism," 65; Michael Gross, "New Fashion Ads," *New York Times,* 19 April 1986, 52.

23. Sullivan, "Flogging Underwear," 22. The professor's name was Jacob Jacoby.

24. Conant, "Sexy Does It," 62.

25. Foltz, "Kinky New Calvinism," 65.

26. Gross, "New Fashion Ads," 52; Sones, "Superstar Success," VI16.

27. Gross, "New Fashion Ads," 52.

28. Conant, "Sexy Does It," 62; Sones, "Superstar Success," VI16.

29. Lee Margulies, "Networks to Keep Ban on Contraceptive Ads," *Los Angeles Times,* 27 November 1986, F1.

Chapter Eleven

1. One study of prime-time television looked at every program that aired during a one-week period in 1989 and did not find a single mention of AIDS; see Louis Chunovic, *One Foot on the Floor: The Curious Evolution of Sex on Television from* I Love Lucy *to* South Park (New York: TV Books, 2000), 126.

2. Jim Miller, "Rock's New Women," *Newsweek,* 4 March 1985, 48; Michael Goldberg, "Madonna Seduces Seattle," *Rolling Stone,* 23 May 1985, 20; David Edelstein, "Seek and Ye Shall Founder," *Village Voice,* 2 April 1985, 56.

3. J. Randy Taraborrelli, *Madonna: An Intimate Biography* (New York: Berkeley Books, 2001), 8. On Madonna's commitment to communicating substantive messages, see also Mikal Gilmore, "Madonna Mystique," *Rolling Stone,* 10 September 1987, cover, 36–38, 87–88; Cathleen McGuigan, "The New True Blue Madonna," *Newsweek,* 14 July 1986, 71; Joel D. Schwartz, "Virgin Territory," *The New Republic,* 26 August 1985, 30–31; Davitt Sigerson, "Madonna," *Rolling Stone,* 17–31 July 1986, 121–122; Bill Zehme, "Madonna Candid Talk," *Rolling Stone,* 23 March 1989, cover, 51–53, 56–58, 180, 182.

4. On Madonna's biography, see Georges-Claude Guilbert, *Madonna as Postmodern Myth* (Jefferson, NC: McFarland, 2002), especially 27–28; "Madonna Goes All the Way," *Rolling Stone,* 22 November 1984, 14–16, 18, 20, 81; "Madonna: She's One Lucky Star!" *Teen,* January 1985, 39; Miller, "Rock's New Women," 48–55; John Skow, "Madonna: Why She's Hot," *Time,* 27 May 1985, cover, 76–77; Taraborrelli, *Madonna.*

5. "Madonna: She's One Lucky Star!" 39. The photos appeared in the two magazines in September 1985; see "Like a Pinup," *Time,* 22 July 1985, 61.

6. Taraborrelli, *Madonna,* 38; Guilbert, *Madonna as Postmodern Myth,* 168; Matthew Rettenmund, *Encyclopedia Madonnica* (New York: St. Martin's, 1995), 1.

7. Carl Arrington, "Madonna," *People Weekly,* 11 March 1985, 113; Rettenmund, *Encyclopedia Madonnica,* 140.

Notes

8. Taraborrelli, *Madonna*, 95. On Madonna's appearance on the awards show, see also Miller, "Rock's New Women," 51–52.

9. On messages in "Like a Virgin," see Schwartz, "Virgin Territory," 31.

10. Rettenmund, *Encyclopedia Madonnica*, 34.

11. Taraborrelli, *Madonna*, 20, 22.

12. Rettenmund, *Encyclopedia Madonnica*, 42; Donald Wildmon, "Madonna," *USA Today*, 10 March 1989, A10.

13. Skow, "Madonna: Why She's Hot," cover, 74–77; Arrington, "Madonna," 113; "Madonna Goes All the Way," *Rolling Stone*, 22 November 1984, 16, 81.

14. Taraborrelli, *Madonna*, 131; David Perel, "Madonna's Former Roommate Has AIDS," *National Enquirer*, 21 October 1986, 14.

15. Perel, "Madonna's Former Roommate," 14.

16. Perel, "Madonna's Former Roommate," 14. On Madonna's relationship with Sean Penn, see Gilmore, "Madonna Mystique," 88; Fred Schruers, "Can't Stop the Girl," *Rolling Stone*, 5 June 1986, 28, 30–32, 59–60; Carol Wallace, "Desperately Seeking Matrimony," *People Weekly*, 8 July 1985, 24; Amy Wilentz, "This Time the Gown Was for Real," *Time*, 26 August 1985, 67; Roger Wolmuth, "Madonna Lands Her Lucky Star," *People Weekly*, 23–24, 26–27; Zehme, "Madonna Candid Talk," cover, 56–57.

17. Taraborrelli, *Madonna*, 131.

18. Vince Aletti, "Madonna," *Rolling Stone*, 27 August 1987, 17.

19. Kate Saunders, "Sister Superior," *The Sunday Times of London*, 15 July 1990, G1; Aletti, "Madonna," 17. For the full lyrics, see www.musicsonglyrics.com/M/Madonna.

20. Rettenmund, *Encyclopedia Madonnica*, 5.

21. On messages in "Papa Don't Preach," see McGuigan, "New True Blue Madonna," 71; Sigerson, "Madonna," 121–122. For the lyrics, see www.musicsonglyrics.com/M/Madonna.

22. McGuigan, "New True Blue Madonna," 71; Georgia Dullea, "Madonna's New Beat Is a Hit, But Song's Message Rankles," *New York Times*, 18 September 1986, B1. The Planned Parenthood spokesman was Alfred Moran.

23. Georgia Dullea, "Madonna's New Beat Is a Hit, But Song's Message Rankles," *New York Times*, 18 September 1986, B9; Rettenmund, *Encyclopedia Madonnica*, 133. The critic was Joyce Millman.

24. Gilmore, "Madonna Mystique," 87.

25. Guilbert, *Madonna as Postmodern Myth*, 168–169.

26. Mark Miller, "Madonna: From Boy Toy to Breathless," *Newsweek*, 25 June 1990, 46; Richard Lacayo, "Madonna," *People Weekly*, Fall 1989 special issue, 50; Brian McNair, *Striptease Culture: Sex, Media and the Democratization of Desire* (New York: Routledge, 2002), 67.

27. For the lyrics, see www.musicsonglyrics.com/M/Madonna.

28. Schwartz, "Virgin Territory," 31; Helen Gurley Brown, "Madonna," *Rolling Stone*, 19 December 1985, 85.

29. On messages in "Open Your Heart," see Aletti, "Madonna," 17; Gilmore, "Madonna Mystique," 87.

30. For the full lyrics, see www.musicsonglyrics.com/M/Madonna.

31. Madonna filed the petition for divorce on 25 January 1989, and the divorce became final on 14 September 1989. Saunders, "Sister Superior," G1. For the full lyrics, see www.musicsonglyrics.com/M/Madonna.

32. On messages in "Express Yourself," see Miller, "Madonna," 46.

33. Rettenmund, *Encyclopedia Madonnica*, 61; Gilmore, "Madonna Mystique," 87.

34. Jay Cocks, "Madonna Draws a Line," *Time*, 17 December 1990, 74–75; Zehme, "Madonna Candid Talk," cover, 51; Saunders, "Sister Superior," G1; Steve Dougherty, "Madonna Exposes, MTV Opposes," *People Weekly*, 17 December 1990, 54.

35. Miller, "Madonna," 46; Saunders, "Sister Superior," G1.

36. Fred Schruers, "Lucy Stars," *Rolling Stone*, 9 May 1985, 27–29; William A. Henry III, "Madonna Comes to Broadway," *Time*, 16 May 1988, 98–99; James McBride, "Hollywood Sizzle," *People Weekly*, 13 May 1985, 42; Tom Hickman, *The Sexual Century* (London: Carlton, 1999), 224.

37. Miller, "Rock's New Women," 48; Bill Barol, "Women in a Video Cage," *Newsweek*, 4 March 1985, 54.

Chapter Twelve

1. *Vanity Fair*, September 1992, 262–263.

2. Larry Gross, *Up from Invisibility: Lesbians, Gay Men, and the Media in America* (New York: Columbia University Press, 2001), 238.

3. On the explosion of gay content in the media during the 1990s, see Steven Capsuto, *Alternate Channels: The Uncensored Story of Gay and Lesbian Images on Radio and Television* (New York: Ballantine, 2000), especially 247–248,

Notes

306; "Gay Rights Groups Laud NBC for Showing 'Law' Lesbian Kiss," *Hollywood Reporter*, 11 February 1991, 38; Gross, *Up from Invisibility*, especially 143–183; Suzanna Danuta Walters, *All the Rage: The Story of Gay Visibility in America* (Chicago: University of Chicago Press, 2001); Stephen Tropiano, *The Prime Time Closet: A History of Gays and Lesbians on TV* (New York: Applause Theatre & Cinema, 2002), especially 56, 89, 168.

4. On the relative abundance of gay men compared to lesbians, see Capsuto, *Alternate Channels*, 340–351; Larry Gross, "Out of the Mainstream: Sexual Minorities and the Mass Media," in Michelle A. Wolf and Alfred P. Kielwasser, *Gay People, Sex, and the Media* (New York: Harrington Park, 1991), 21; Larry Gross and James D. Woods, eds., *The Columbia Reader on Lesbians and Gay Men in Media, Society, and Politics* (New York: Columbia University Press, 1999), 7; Erik Meers, "Hunky Business," *The Advocate*, April 1, 2003, 39; Walters, *All the Rage*, 161. A variety of factors have been identified as contributing to the media's tendency to pay more attention to gay men than to lesbians. One of those factors is sexism; just as American mores required that *Playboy* had to come before *Cosmopolitan* and Jim Morrison had to blaze a sexual trail in music before Madonna did, gay men had to move onto the nation's cultural radar screen before gay women did (see Walters, *All the Rage*, 161). A second factor is that many people find it much more acceptable to see women having physical contact than to see men having physical contact—much less having sex—and so male-male relationships are a much more compelling media topic (see Meers, "Hunky Business," 39). A third factor is that gay men gained a presence on television and in films, while lesbians did not, because there are more gay men in positions of power in Hollywood than there are lesbians; conventional wisdom is that a "Gay Mafia" came to exist and saw to it that gay men gained a presence in media products, with some of the men being open about their sexuality but others remaining closeted (see Gross, *Up from Invisibility*, 5). A fourth factor may be economics; the media perceive gay men as a more attractive target audience for advertisements than they perceive lesbians because, first, men generally make higher salaries than women do and, second, most gay men don't have children so they tend to have larger expendable incomes—and therefore more money to spend on the products being advertised—than lesbians do.

5. For discussion of and reproductions of gay-themed ads, see the Commercial Closet Web site at http://www.commercialcloset.org. Specifically on the Benetton ad, see http://www.commercialcloset.org/cgi-bin/iowa/portrayals.html?record=422, and on the Abercrombie & Fitch ads, see http://www.commercialcloset.org/cgi-bin/iowa/portrayals.html?record=413 and http://www.commercialcloset.org/cgi-bin/iowa/portrayals.html?record=350. On depictions of gay men in mainstream advertising in the 1990s, see Meers, "Hunky Business," 38–39; Michael Wilke, "Selling Sex," *Genre*, March 2003, 64–67.

6. *Philadelphia* was directed by Jonathan Demme, released by TriStar Pictures, and rated PG–13; *The Birdcage* was directed by Mike Nichols, released by MGM Studios, and rated R; *My Best Friend's Wedding* was directed by P. J. Hogan, released by TriStar Pictures, and rated PG–13.

7. "The Puppy Episode" aired 30 April 1997. "Yep, I'm Gay!" *Time*, 14 April 1997, cover; Bruce Handy, "Roll Over, Ward Cleaver," *Time*, 14 April 1997, 78–85; Patricia Brennan, "NBC's Buddy Sitcom Doesn't Play It Straight," *Washington Post*, 14 February 1999, Y6; Jess Cagle, "As Gay as It Gets?" *Entertainment Weekly*, 8 May 1998, 26–32; Walters, *All the Rage*, 86–94. On *Ellen* and the events surrounding it, see also Capsuto, *Alternate Channels*, 378–403; Tropiano, *Prime Time Closet*, especially 245–249.

8. Brennan, "NBC's Buddy Sitcom," Y6. *Will & Grace* premiered in September 1998.

9. The "don't ask, don't tell" segment aired on *60 Minutes* on 12 December 1999.

10. "Advise and Resent" aired 29 February 2000. Will is played by Eric McCormack; Jack is played by Sean Hayes. Steve Lopez, "To Be Young and Gay in Wyoming," *Time*, 26 October 1998, 38, 40.

11. Rita Kempley, "The Feel-Bad Hits of the Summer," *Washington Post*, 3 August 1997, G1; Robin Givhan, "House of Dreams," *Washington Post*, 16 July 1997, D1; Robin Givhan, "Versace: The Guru of Glamour," *Washington Post*, 20 July 1997, F3.

12. For the quote, see Capsuto, *Alternate Channels*, 406–407. On the two different types of gay men on one program, see Tropiano, *Prime Time Closet*, 250–251. On the focus group members, see A. J. Jacobs, "When Gay Men Happen to Straight Women," *Entertainment Weekly*, 23 October 1998, 23.

13. Hal Hinson, "'The Birdcage,'" *Washington Post*, 8 March 1996, B1. The son was played by Dan Futterman.

14. Hillary Johnson and Nancy Rommelmann, *The Real Real World* (New York: MTV Books, 1995), 91.

15. For the quote, see Johnson and Rommelmann, *Real Real World*, 104. Capsuto, *Alternate Channels*, 336; Joseph Hanania, "Resurgence of Gay Roles on Television," *Los Angeles Times*, 3 November 1994, F12; Johnson and Rommelmann, *Real Real World*, especially 90–91, 104–105; Tropiano, *Prime Time Closet*, 182.

16. On gay characters being either villains or victims, see Gross, *Up from Invisibility*, 143; Walters, *All the Rage*, 139.

17. Brian McNair, *Striptease Culture: Sex, Media and the Democratization of Desire* (New York: Routledge, 2002), 139.

18. "Girls Interrupted" aired 2 May 2000; "Acting Out" aired 22 February 2000.

Notes

19. John Robinson, "Frank Discusses Being Gay," *Boston Globe*, 30 May 1987, A1; Ellen Goodman, "The Barracks and the Closet," *Washington Post*, 10 July 1993, A19; "Statement by Barney Frank," *Congressional Record*, 13 October 1998, H10815.

20. On the pink condom ad, see http://www.commercialcloset.org/cgi-bin/iowa/portrayals.html?record=239. On the "H.I.V. POSITIVE" ads, see http://www.commercialcloset.org/cgi-bin/iowa/portrayals.html?record=560, http://www.commercialcloset.org/cgi-bin/iowa/portrayals.html?record=562, and http://www.commercialcloset.org/cgi-bin/iowa/portrayals.html?record=561. On the "Pieta" ad, see http://www.commercialcloset.org/cgi-bin/iowa/portrayals.html?record=559.

21. Hal Hinson, "Our Hate–Love Relationship," *Washington Post*, 26 December 1993, G8.

22. On the AIDS-related conversations that took place during the series, see Capsuto, *Alternate Channels*, 336; Gross, *Up from Invisibility*, 172; Hanania, "Resurgence of Gay Roles on Television," F12; "HIV, and Positive," *People Weekly*, 28 November 1994, 185; Johnson and Rommelmann, Real *Real World*, especially 112–113, 158; David Kronke, "MTV Tells Us About Sex, and Somehow It Gets Trite," *Baltimore Sun*, 2 November 1994, D3; Eric Morgenthaler, "The Last Chapter of 'Pedro's Story' Is Drawing to a Close," *Wall Street Journal*, 21 October 1994, A1; "Pedro Zamora," *Life*, January 1995, 110; "Pedro Zamora/1972–1994," *St. Petersburg Times*, 12 November 1994, A1; Richard Roeper, "Zamora Showed AIDS Exists in 'Real World,'" *Chicago Sun-Times*, 16 November 1994, 11; Tropiano, *Prime Time Closet*, 182; Shaila M. Yates, "Gay Actor Impressed Youth," *Cleveland Plain Dealer*, 28 November 1994, E2.

23. Johnson and Rommelmann, Real *Real World*, 91, 113.

24. Hanania, "Resurgence of Gay Roles on Television," F12; Morgenthaler, "The Last Chapter of 'Pedro's Story'," A1; Roeper, "Zamora Showed AIDS Exists in 'Real World,'" 11; "HIV, and Positive," 185; "Pedro Zamora," 110.

25. Johnson and Rommelmann, Real *Real World*, 112.

26. The *Will & Grace* episode titled "Girl Trouble" aired 26 October 2000.

27. Gross, *Up from Invisibility*, 42.

28. Gross, *Up from Invisibility*, 164–165; "AIDS Fuels His Fury," *New York Post*, 17 July 1997, 1; Joel Achenbach, "The Killer Virus Motive," *Washington Post*, 19 July 1997, F1.

29. David Ansen, "Gay Films Are a Drag," *Newsweek*, 18 March 1996, 71. See also Brian Lowry, "Number of Gay TV Characters Plummets," *Los Angeles Times*, 16 September 2002, F10.

Chapter Thirteen

1. "Martin Returns" aired 8 September 1994.

2. On *Martin* being the first sitcom to feature sexually suggestive plotlines between two African Americans, see Harry F. Waters, "Amusing Ourselves to Def," *Newsweek*, 15 February 1993, 47.

3. For the quotes, see Kristal Brent Zook, *Color by Fox: The Fox Network and the Revolution in Black Television* (New York: Oxford University Press, 1999), 105. On Fox's motivation not being "racial altruism" but a desire to increase profits, see Robin R. Means Coleman, *African-American Viewers and the Black Situation Comedy: Situating Racial Humor* (New York: Garland, 1998), 118. Among the shows that fit into Fox's African-American programming strategy were *In Living Color* (1990–1994), *Living Single* (1993–1997), *Martin* (1992–1997), *New York Undercover* (1994–1998), *Roc* (1991–1994), *The Sinbad Show* (1993–1994), and *South Central* (1994). Martin aired at 8 p.m., *Living Single* at 8:30 p.m.

4. Christopher John Farley, "Hip-Hop Nation," *Time*, 8 February 1999, 56. Rap music is a form of rhymed storytelling accompanied by highly rhythmic, electronically based music; it began in the mid-1970s in the South Bronx section of New York City as part of hip-hop, an African-American and Afro-Caribbean youth culture that includes graffiti, breakdancing, and rap music. On *Jungle Fever* and *The Best Man* being major box-office successes, see Roger Ebert, "Jungle Fever," *Chicago Sun-Times*, 7 June 1991; Desson Howe, "Jungle Fever," *Washington Post*, 7 June 1991; Janet Maslin, "'The Best Man,'" *New York Times*, 22 October 1999; Wesley Morris, "Nicely Performed Romantic Comedy," *San Francisco Examiner*, 22 October 1999.

5. After *Martin* aired for six seasons on Fox, reruns were broadcast on other networks, including USA. Gina was played by Tisha Campbell. On sexual content in *Martin*, see Coleman, *African-American Viewers*, 123, 164; Beretta E. Smith-Shomade, *Shaded Lives: African-American Women and Television* (New Brunswick, NJ: Rutgers University Press, 2002), 41–43, 46–47.

6. "Judging by the Cover" aired 29 August 1993; "Another Saturday Night" aired 30 March 1995; "Stormy Weather" aired 2 February 1995. Regine was played by Kim Fields Freeman, the married man was played by Cylk Cozart, and Maxine was played by Erika Alexander. After *Living Single* aired for five seasons on Fox, reruns were

Notes

broadcast on other networks, including USA. On sexual content in *Living Single*, see Coleman, *African-American Viewers*, 125; Smith-Shomade, *Shaded Lives*, 41–43, 46, 180.

7. *Jungle Fever*, which was directed by Spike Lee, was released in 1991 by Universal Studios and was rated R; *The Best Man*, which was directed by Malcolm D. Lee, was released in 1999 by Universal Studios and was rated R. The woman in *The Best Man* who suggests the one-night stand is played by Nia Long, and the man who accepts the offer is played by Taye Diggs.

8. Ice Cube was born O'Shea Jackson and was raised in South Central Los Angeles by his two parents who worked at the University of California, Los Angeles.

9. http://lyrics.astraweb.com/displayp.cgi?ice_cube..amerikkkas_most_wanted.

10. Greg Kot, "Rock Turns Mean and Ugly," *Chicago Tribune*, 18 November 1990, XIII5. On scholarship that discusses booty rap as an articulation of the socioeconomic problems encountered by inner-city youth, see Houston A. Baker Jr., *Black Studies, Rap and the Academy* (Chicago: University of Chicago Press, 1993); Venise Berry, "Redeeming the Rap Music Experience," in Jonathan S. Epstein, ed., *Adolescents and Their Music* (New York: Garland, 1994), 165–187; Robin D. G. Kelley, "Kickin' Reality, Kickin' Ballistics: Gangsta Rap and Postindustrial Los Angeles," in William Eric Perkins, ed., *Droppin' Science* (Philadelphia: Temple University Press, 1996), 117–158; Cheryl L. Keyes, "At the Crossroads: Rap Music and Its African Nexus," *Ethnomusicology*, vol. 40, no. 2 (Spring–Summer 1996), 223–249; Nathan McCall, *What's Going On? Personal Essays* (New York: Random, 1997).

11. "Got to Be There" aired 5 September 1993; "Whoop! There It Ain't" aired 12 December 1993. Cole was played by Carl Anthony Payne II, and Tommy was played by Thomas Mikal Ford.

12. "Silver Bells" aired 15 December 1997; "Worlds Without Love" aired 2 November 1998; "Making Spirits Bright" aired 14 December 1998. Renee was played by Lisa Nicole Carson, Ally was played by Calista Flockhart, and the married man was played by Richard T. Jones. After *Ally McBeal* aired for five seasons on Fox (1997 through 2002), reruns were broadcast on other networks, including FX.

13. The football player was played by Morris Chestnut, and the friend was played by Terrence Howard.

14. 2 Live Crew was based in Miami. The group was led by Luke Skyywalker (born Luther Campbell), and its other members were Fresh Kid Ice (born Chris Wong Won), Mr. Mixx (born David Hobbs), and Brother Marquis (born Mark Ross).

15. http://lyrics.astraweb.com/displayp.cgi?2_live_crews_greatest_hits.

16. On African-American women being highly sexualized on the Fox network programs that targeted black viewers, see Smith-Shomade, *Shaded Lives*, 47.

17. "Buried Pleasures" aired 1 November 1999.

18. Greg Braxton, "'Living Single' Is Living Large on Fox," *Los Angeles Times*, 9 December 1993, A1. "Fatal Distraction" aired 9 January 1994; "Love Is a Many Splintered Thing" aired 17 April 1994. The source was played by Adam Lazarre-White, and the writer was played by Richard Whiten. Queen Latifah was born Dana Owens.

19. http://lyrics.astraweb.com/displayp.cgi?geto_boys..grip_it_on_that_other_level. The Geto Boys was based in Houston. Members of the group included Bushwick Bill (born Richard Shaw), Scarface (born Brad Jordan), and Willie "D" Dennis.

20. The Spike Lee character's wife was played by Veronica Webb, and the Wesley Snipes character's wife was played by Lonette McKee.

21. The Wesley Snipes character's father was played by Ossie Davis and his mother by Ruby Dee; the white woman was played by Annabella Sciorra.

22. http://lyrics.astraweb.com/displayp.cgi?ice_cube..death_certificate.

23. "Editorial," *Billboard*, 23 November 1991, 8.

24. James R. Petersen, *The Century of Sex: Playboy's History of the Sexual Revolution, 1900–1999* (New York: Grove, 1999), 458; "Appeals Court Rules 'Nasty' Not Obscene," *Washington Post*, 8 May 1992, B4; Laura Parker, "Federal Judge Finds LP Obscene," *Washington Post*, 7 June 1990, A1. The judge who made the original ruling was Jose A. Gonzalez Jr.

25. http://lyrics.astraweb.com/displayp.cgi?2_live_crews_greatest_hits.

26. Kot, "Rock Turns Mean and Ugly," XIII4.

27. http://lyrics.astraweb.com/displayp.cgi?geto_boys.. grip_it_on_that_other_level.

28. During the decade, the rate of HIV infection among African Americans increased at a rate nearly six times that among whites. See Tony Pugh, "AIDS Epidemic Surges; Gays, Blacks Hit Hardest," *Miami Herald*, 1 June 2001.

29. According to the 2000 Census, 43 percent of African-American families were headed by single mothers, compared to 13 percent of white families (see Andrew Herrmann, "Black Single Moms Show Poorly in Income Survey," *Chicago Sun-Times*, 26 April 2003). The figure of twenty-four was derived by adding together five characters from *Martin* (Gina, Pam, Big Shirley, Sheneneh, and Mama Payne), four from *Living Single* (Khadijah, Max, Regine, and Synclaire), two from *Ally McBeal* (Renee and Corretta, an African-American attorney who joined the

cast in 2001), nine from *Jungle Fever* (Drew, Vera, Vivian, Orin, the Wesley Snipes character's mother, and Drew's three female friends), and four from *The Best Man* (Jordan, Robin, Mia, and Shelby).

30. Kot, "Rock Turns Mean and Ugly," XIII4; Brent Staples, "Editorial Notebook," *New York Times*, 27 August 1993, A28; George Will, "America's Slide into the Sewer," *Newsweek*, 30 July 1990, 64.

31. Kot, "Rock Turns Mean and Ugly," XIII4.

32. Tricia Rose, *Black Noise: Rap Music and Black Culture in Contemporary America* (Hanover, NH: University Press of New England/Wesleyan University Press, 1994), 1, 2.

33. Kot, "Rock Turns Mean and Ugly," XIII5; Sara Terry, "Hip-Hop Leaps into World Youth Culture," *Christian Science Monitor*, 5 May 1999, 10. On the rebellious nature of rock 'n' roll and other youth-oriented music, see Robert Pattison, *The Triumph of Vulgarity: Rock Music in the Mirror of Romanticism* (New York: Oxford University Press, 1987), especially 3–12, 207–212; Rhoda Rabkin, "Children, Entertainment, and Marketing," *Consumers' Research*, June 2002, 14–18, 29.

34. For the quote, see James T. Jones IV, "Rap Sales Stand Up to Backlash," *USA Today*, 3 February 1994, D1. On the impact of rap music, see Mary E. Ballard and Steven Coates, "The Immediate Effects of Homicidal, Suicidal, and Nonviolent Heavy Metal and Rap Songs on the Mood of College Students," *Youth and Society*, vol. 27, no. 2 (December 1995): 148–168; Amy Binder, "Constructing Racial Rhetoric: Media Depictions of Harm in Heavy Metal and Rap Music," *American Sociological Review*, vol. 58, no. 6 (December 1993): 753–767; Jonathon S. Epstein, David J. Pratto, and James K. Skipper, "Teenagers, Behavioral Problems, and Preferences for Heavy Metal and Rap Music: A Case Study of a Southern Middle School," *Deviant Behavior*, vol. 11, no. 4 (1990): 381–394; Kevin J. Took and David S. Weiss, "The Relationship Between Heavy Metal and Rap Music and Adolescent Turmoil: Real or Artifact," *Adolescence*, vol. 29, no. 115 (Fall 1994): 613–621; Stephen R. Wester, Cynthia L. Crown, Gerald L. Quatman, and Martin Heesacker, "The Influence of Sexually Violent Rap Music on Attitudes of Men with Little Prior Exposure," *Psychology of Women Quarterly*, vol. 21, no. 4 (December 1997): 497–508.

Chapter Fourteen

1. Lawrence K. Grossman, "Spot News: The Press and the Dress," *Columbia Journalism Review*, November/December 1998, 34.

2. Marvin Kalb, *One Scandalous Story: Clinton, Lewinsky, and Thirteen Days that Tarnished American Journalism* (New York: Free Press/Simon & Schuster, 2001), 205; *World News Tonight*, 23 January 1998.

3. The first American newspaper was *Publick Occurrences, Both Forreign and Domestick*, founded in Boston on September 25, 1690.

4. Kalb, *One Scandalous Story*, 6–7.

5. "My 12-Year Affair with Bill Clinton," *Star*, 23 January 1992, 1; James R. Petersen, *The Century of Sex: Playboy's History of the Sexual Revolution, 1900–1999* (New York: Grove, 1999), 471.

6. *Nightline*, 23 January 1992; Howard Kurtz, "Reports on Clinton Pose Quandary for Journalists," *Washington Post*, 30 January 1992, A14.

7. The *60 Minutes* segment aired 26 January 1992.

8. On the use of the term Zippergate to denote the sex scandal involving Bill Clinton, see Tom Hickman, *The Century of Sex* (London: Carlton, 1999), 22.

9. *World News Tonight*, 11 February 1994.

10. Kalb, *One Scandalous Story*, 30, 32–33. On Paula Jones being characterized as "trailer trash," see Matthew Dallek, "When the Best Defense *Isn't* a Good Offense," *Salon*, 20 June 1997.

11. Evan Thomas with Michael Isikoff, "Clinton v. Paula Jones," *Newsweek*, 13 January 1997, 34. For the full article, see also cover, 26–32. Paula Jones filed her sexual harassment lawsuit against President Clinton in May 1994, and the U.S. Supreme Court handed down its ruling in May 1997.

12. Howard Kurtz, "Paula Jones Speaks to National Media About Clinton Suit," *Washington Post*, 17 June 1994, A11; Michael Kelly, "An Emerging Strategy," *Washington Post*, 27 January 1998, A17.

13. Kalb, *One Scandalous Story*, 69–73. The reporter was Michael Isikoff.

14. Kalb, *One Scandalous Story*, 80. The lawyer who e-mailed the material to Matt Drudge was George Conway.

15. Matt Drudge, "NEWSWEEK KILLS STORY ON WHITE HOUSE INTERN," *Drudge Report*, 18 January 1998.

16. Susan Schmidt, Peter Baker, and Toni Locy, "Clinton Accused of Urging Aide to Lie," *Washington Post*, 21 January 1998, A1.

17. Schmidt, Baker, and Locy, "Clinton Accused," A1.

18. *Today*, 22 January 1998.

Notes

19. John F. Harris and Dan Balz, "Clinton More Forcefully Denies Having Had Affair or Urging Lies," *Washington Post*, 27 January 1998, A1.

20. Kalb, *One Scandalous Story*, 59.

21. Kalb, *One Scandalous Story*, 204–205.

22. Kalb, *One Scandalous Story*, 205.

23. John M. Broder, "The President Under Fire: The Overview; Ex-Intern Offered to Tell of Clinton Affair in Exchange for Immunity," *New York Times*, 24 January 1998, A1; Jeff Leen, "Lewinsky: Two Coasts, Two Lives, Many Images," *Washington Post*, 24 January 1998, A1; "Immunity Deal for Ex-Intern Rejected," *Miami Herald*, 24 January 1998, A1; "Lewinsky Rejected Immunity Last Week but Now Seeks Deal," *Seattle Times*, 24 January 1998, A1.

24. Amy Goldstein and William Claiborne, "Aide's Interest in President Was Known to Friends," *Washington Post*, 29 January 1998, A1; Howard Kurtz, "Lewinsky's Past: A Matter of Credibility or Curiosity?" *Washington Post*, 30 January 1998, D1; Kim Murphy, "Ex-Intern Allegedly Boasted of Sex," *Los Angeles Times*, 28 January 1998, A15; Kim Murphy, "Teacher: Lewinsky Boasted about Affair," *Seattle Times*, 28 January 1998, A1; Jules Witcover, "The Scandal: Where We Went Wrong," *Columbia Journalism Review*, March/April 1998, 19. Monica Lewinsky began working at the White House as an unpaid intern in early July 1995, was hired for a job dealing with correspondence at the White House office of legislative affairs in late November 1995, and was transferred to a public affairs job at the Pentagon in April 1996.

25. Richard A. Serrano, "Clinton Under Fire: Phone Sex by Clinton Alleged," *Los Angeles Times*, 24 January 1998, A1; Matt Drudge, "SHE HAD SEX WITH CIGAR," *Drudge Report*, 22 August 1998; David Jackson, "Witness Said Ready to Testify," *Dallas Morning News*, 26 January 1998, A1; Howard Kurtz, "Dallas Paper's Story Traveled Far Before Being Shot Down," *Washington Post*, 28 January 1998, D1.

26. *Nightline*, 21 January 1998; *Today*, 22 January 1998; Marc Fisher, "The Buzz: Washington Sinks Its Teeth into the Clinton Story," *Washington Post*, 23 January 1998, D1; David Willman, "Clinton Under Fire: Starr Builds Case Against Ex-Intern," *Los Angeles Times*, 24 January 1998, A1.

27. Howard Kurtz, "In Lewinsky Saga, a Cast of Dozens," *Washington Post*, 2 March 1998, C1; Frank Rich, "Journal: The Body Count," *New York Times*, 11 February 1998, A29; Robert Scheer, "Media Fall for a Sorry Tale of Leaks and Lies," *Los Angeles Times*, 3 February 1998, A7; Geraldo Rivera, *Rivera Live!*, 8 July 1998.

28. Michael Kazin, "Good Bill?" *Mother Jones*, September/October 1998, 54.

29. Howard Kurtz, "With a Heavy Topic, Nation's Newspapers Weigh In," *Washington Post*, 13 September 1998, A31. Among the newspapers that reprinted the entire report were the *Baltimore Sun*, *Boston Globe*, *Chicago Tribune*, *Los Angeles Times*, *New York Post*, *Philadelphia Inquirer*, *Washington Post*, and *Washington Times*.

30. Kurtz, "With a Heavy Topic," A31.

31. "Special Report: Part II," *Washington Post*, 12 September 1998, A29.

32. "Special Report: Part III," *Washington Post*, 12 September 1998, A31.

33. "Special Report: Part III," A31.

34. "Special Report: Part XII," *Washington Post*, 12 September 1998, A45.

35. Richard Benedetto, "Clinton Must Do Something Bold to Achieve Greatness in History," Gannett News Service, 13 November 1999.

36. Howard Kurtz, "At First Blush, TV Reporters Stumble Over Sordid Details," *Washington Post*, 12 September 1998, E1. The CNN correspondent reading the passage was Candy Crowley; the CBS correspondent interrupted by Rather was Sharyl Attkisson.

37. Nature of President Clinton's Relationship with Monica Lewinsky, B. Evidence Establishing Nature of Relationship, 1: Physical Evidence, section headed I, 57.

38. Peter Baker, "Clinton, Jones Reach Settlement," *Washington Post*, 14 November 1998, A1. The judge hearing the case dismissed Jones's lawsuit on 1 April 1998, saying that her complaint, if true, would not constitute a violation of the law. Two weeks later, Jones announced that she would appeal the dismissal.

39. Eric Pianin, "Clinton Impeached," *Washington Post*, 20 December 1998, A1.

40. Peter Baker and Helen Dewar, "Prosecutors Start to Present Clinton Case Today," *Washington Post*, 14 January 1999, A1. President Andrew Johnson was impeached in 1868 on charges of violating the Tenure of Office Act, which prohibited the president from dismissing any official who had been appointed with Senate consent without first obtaining Senate approval. The impeachment process against the Democratic president was, in reality, motivated by his Republican opponents. Johnson was acquitted by a single vote, but his party then chose not to nominate him for reelection and the Republican candidate, Ulysses S. Grant, was voted into office.

41. Peter Baker and Helen Dewar, "Clinton Acquitted," *Washington Post*, 13 February 1999, A1.

42. Laura Sessions Stepp, "Buddy Sex Replaces Serious Relationships for Some Young People," *Minneapolis Star Tribune*, 16 March 2003; "No-Strings 'Buddysex' a Fact of Life for Many Teens," *Providence Journal*, 23 February

Notes

2003. On oral sex becoming widespread among teenagers, see also Laura Sessions Stepp, "Parents Are Alarmed by an Unsettling New Fad in Middle Schools: Oral Sex," *Washington Post,* 8 July 1999, A1; Barbara Vobejda, "Scandal's Legacy: A Blush of Open Sex Talk," *Washington Post,* 12 February 1999, A1.

43. Kevin Merida, "Hill Doesn't Rise to Flynt's Bait," *Washington Post,* 7 October 1998, D1; Jeffrey Toobin, *A Vast Conspiracy: The Real Story of the Sex Scandal That Nearly Brought Down a President* (New York: Random House, 1999), 364; Eric Pianin, "Clinton Impeached; Livingston Quits as Designated House Speaker," *Washington Post,* 20 December 1998, A1; Guy Gugliotta, "The Right Guard," *Washington Post,* 12 May 1998, D1; Howard Kurtz, "A Chill in the Marble Halls," *Washington Post,* 11 September 1998, D1; Howard Kurtz, "Report of Hyde Affair Stirs Anger," *Washington Post,* 17 September 1998, A15; Petersen, *Century of Sex,* 485.

44. Howard Kurtz, "The Slow Start of Something Big," *Washington Post,* 30 July 2001, C1; Maureen Dowd, "Liberties; The Girl Who Vanished," *New York Times,* 20 June 2001, A23; Jonathan V. Last, "Dangerous Liaisons," *Los Angeles Times,* 12 August 2001, M1.

45. Joe Conason and Gene Lyons, *The Hunting of the President: The Ten-Year Campaign to Destroy Bill and Hillary Clinton* (New York: St. Martin's: 2000), 370–371.

Chapter Fifteen

1. Peter Travers, "American Pie," *Rolling Stone,* 8–22 July 1999, 163.

2. Patrick Goldstein, "Back to School, Dude," *Los Angeles Times,* 15 April 1998, A1.

3. Jeff Giles, "Fear and Lusting," *Newsweek,* 12 July 1999, 62; Travers, "American Pie," 163. An R rating means that any viewer under the age of seventeen must be accompanied by a parent or adult guardian; an NC–17 rating means that no viewer seventeen years of age or younger can be admitted.

4. Jane D. Brown, Jeanne R. Steele, and Kim Walsh-Childers, *Sexual Teens, Sexual Media: Investigating Media's Influence on Adolescent Sexuality* (Mahwah, NJ: Lawrence Erlbaum, 2002), 5; D. Haffner, "Facing Facts: Sexual Health for American Adolescents," *Journal of Adolescent Health,* issue 22 (1998): 453–459.

5. *American Pie,* which was directed by Paul Weitz, was released in 1999 by Universal Studios. Kevin was played by Thomas Ian Nicholas, and Vicky was played by Tara Reid.

6. Richard Corliss, "To Live and Buy in L.A.," *Time,* 31 July 1995, 65. *Clueless,* directed by Amy Heckerling, was released in 1995 by Paramount Pictures; the film was rated PG–13. The boy who meets Cher's standards is named Josh and was played by Paul Rudd.

7. *Dawson's Creek* aired from 1998 to 2003, and the episode titled "High Risk Behavior" aired 13 January 1999. Andie was played by Meredith Monroe, and Pacey was played by Joshua Jackson.

8. On the new perception of oral sex, see Laura Sessions Stepp, "The Buddy System: Sex in High School and College, What's Love Got to Do With it?" *Washington Post,* 19 January 2003, F1, F4.

9. Erik Hedegaard, "There's Something about Virgins," *Rolling Stone,* 19 August 1999, 96.

10. The best friend was played by Stacey Dash, and the boyfriend was played by Donald Faison.

11. David Ansen, "In a Class by Herself," *Newsweek,* 26 April 1999, 67. *Election,* which was directed by Alexander Payne, was released in 1999 by Paramount Pictures; the film was rated R. The quarterback was played by Chris Klein.

12. Steve Stifler was played by Seann William Scott. The quotation was by Jim, who was played by Jason Biggs.

13. Frazier Moore, "How 'Friends' Talk Amongst Themselves," *Los Angeles Times,* 26 March 1995, 9. *Friends* aired on NBC from 1994 to 2004. Monica was played by Courteney Cox Arquette, Joey was played by Matt LeBlanc, Ross was played by David Schwimmer, and Rachel was played by Jennifer Aniston. "The One with the Blackout" aired 3 November 1994.

14. Paul was played by Eddie Kaye Thomas, and the character known as Stifler's mom—her first name is never mentioned—was played by Jennifer Coolidge.

15. The episode in which Pacey and the teacher begin their affair, titled "Kiss," aired 3 February 1998. The teacher was played by Leann Hunley.

16. "Baby" aired 24 February 1998, and "The One Where Ross and Rachel . . . You Know" aired 8 February 1996.

17. "The All-Nighter" aired 18 November 1998, and "Hurricane" aired 17 February 1998. Jen was played by Michelle Williams, Dawson by James Van Der Beek, and Chris by Jason Behr.

18. "The One Where Chandler Can't Remember Which Sister" aired 9 January 1997.

19. Travers, "American Pie," 163. Jim's date was played by Alyson Hannigan.

20. "High Risk Behavior" aired 13 January 1999, "Hurricane" aired 17 February 1998, and "The All-Nighter" aired 18 November 1998.

Notes

21. "The One with the Kips" aired 29 October 1998, and "The One Where Rachel Tells Ross" aired 11 October 2001.

22. Elinor Burkett, "Now Targeted for '92: MTV Condom Ads," *Miami Herald*, 22 November 1991; Stevenson Swanson, "Taboo on TV Condom Ads Largely Unfounded, Study Says," *Chicago Tribune*, 20 June 2001.

23. On STDs among teenagers, see Richard M. Perloff, *Persuading People to Have Safer Sex* (Mahwah, NJ: Lawrence Erlbaum, 2001), 26; on adults in cross-generational affairs suffering but teenagers not, see David Denby, "School Spirit," *The New Yorker*, 26 April–3 May 1999, 192.

24. Tom Carson, "Girlie Shows," *Esquire*, January 1999, 36; Rick Marin, "My So-Called Soap," *Newsweek*, 19 January 1998, 68; Bruce Fretts, "Remote Patrol," *Entertainment Weekly*, 3 April 1998, 78; Brian Lowry, "Teens Flow to 'Creek,'" *Los Angeles Times*, 3 March 1998, 1; "Jailed Ex-Teacher Likely Impregnated by Teen," *Los Angeles Times*, 15 March 1998, 8.

25. Craig Tomashoff, "The Joy of Six," *People*, 17 April 1995, 80.

26. Marc Silver, "Sex and Violence on TV," *U.S. News & World Report*, 11 September 1995, 65.

27. Giles, "Fear and Lusting," 63. "Hurricane" aired 17 February 1998.

28. "RAND Study Finds Entertainment TV Can Help Teach Responsible Sex Messages," RAND Corporation news release, 3 November 2003. The RAND Corporation is a nonprofit research organization, and the teenagers were questioned as part of a larger study of television and adolescent sexuality. The psychologist was Rebecca Collins.

Chapter Sixteen

1. "What Goes Around Comes Around" aired 8 October 2000. The woman, Samantha, was played by Kim Cattrall; the boy, Sam, was played by Jacob Pitts.

2. The premier episode aired 3 December 2000. The man, Brian, was played by Gale Harold; the boy, Justin, was played by Randy Harrison.

3. *Sex and the City* debuted in June 1998 and continued for six seasons, ending in February 2004. *Queer as Folk* debuted in December 2000 and was still on the air in 2004. Reruns of both programs continued to be broadcast, and the various seasons are also available on VHS and DVD for both rental and purchase.

4. Steve Vineberg, "The Courage to Aim Both High and Low," *New York Times*, 22 July 2001, B28; Tom Shales, "Showtime's Shockingly Bold 'Queer as Folk,'" *Washington Post*, 2 December 2000, C1.

5. On full-frontal female nudity on *Sex and the City*, see "Attack of the Five Foot Ten Woman," which aired 18 June 2000; "One," which aired 14 September 2003. On full-frontal female nudity on *Queer as Folk*, see episode 9 in the first season, which aired 11 February 2001; episode 10 in the first season, which aired 18 February 2001. On full-frontal male nudity on *Queer as Folk*, see episode 11 in the first season, which aired 25 February 2001; episode 6 in the second season, which aired 10 February 2002; episode 9 in the second season, which aired 10 March 2002; episode 12 in the second season, which aired 7 April 2002; episode 9 in the third season, which aired 11 May 2003; episode 10 in the third season, which aired 18 May 2003. The episode built around the word "cunt" was titled "The Power of Female Sex" and aired 5 July 1998.

6. New episodes of both shows aired on Sundays and were rebroadcast later in the week. On *Sex and the City* and *Queer as Folk* having more leeway in their content because they aired on pay-cable channels, see Tom Shales, "'Queer as Folk,'" *Washington Post*, 5 January 2002, C1; Bernard Weinraub, "Cable TV Shatters Another Taboo," *New York Times*, 20 November 2000, E1. On the number of subscribers to HBO and Showtime in 2000, see Weinraub, "Cable TV Shatters Another Taboo," E1. On the rate of increase in subscribers, see Bill Carter, "On Television: Serious Tone Adds to Success of 'Sex and the City,'" *New York Times*, 13 August 2001, C1.

7. Howard Rosenberg, "'Sex,' Act III; HBO's Lusty 'Sex and the City,'" *Los Angeles Times*, 9 June 2000, A1; Yahlin Chang and Veronica Chambers, "Sex and the Single Girl," *Newsweek*, 2 August 1999, 60. *Sex and the City* grew out of the experiences of Candace Bushnell, who wrote a column titled "Sex and the City" for the *New York Observer* newspaper as well as a novel titled *Sex and the City*. Miranda was played by Cynthia Nixon, and Charlotte was played by Kristin Davis.

8. Michael is played by Hal Sparks, Emmett by Peter Paige, and Ted by Scott Lowell.

9. "Politically Erect" aired 11 June 2000.

10. "The Awful Truth" aired 13 June 1999.

11. "Valley of the Twenty-Something Guys" aired 28 June 1998.

12. The premier episode aired 3 December 2000.

13. The premier episode aired 3 December 2000.

14. Episode 3 of the third season aired 16 March 2003.

15. Episode 5 of the first season aired 7 January 2001.

16. The college student was in "What Goes Around Comes Around" that aired 8 October 2000. The dildo model was in "Escape from New York" that aired 10 September 2000. The wrestling coach was in "My Motherboard, My Self" that aired 15 July 2001. Samantha fears she has already slept with every attractive man in Manhattan in "The Chicken Dance" that aired 18 July 1999. Samantha began the lesbian relationship in "Defining Moments" that aired 10 June 2001. For the quotation, see Chang and Chambers, "Sex and the Single Girl," 60.

17. The premier episode aired 3 December 2000.

18. Carter, "On Television," C1. On *Sex and the City* covering serious sexual issues, see also Julie Salamon, "The Relevance of 'Sex' in a City That's Changed," *New York Times*, 21 July 2002, B1. The headline on the cover highlighted Michael Rowe, "The Queer Report," *The Advocate*, 15 April 2003, 40–42, 45–48. On *Queer as Folk* covering serious sexual issues, see also Joyce Millman, "The Gayest Story Ever Told," *Salon*, 29 November 2000.

19. Abortion was a topic on "Coulda, Woulda, Shoulda" that aired 5 August 2001. Menopause was a topic on "The Big Time" that aired 30 July 2000. Infertility was a topic on "Coulda, Woulda, Shoulda" that aired 5 August 2001. Breast cancer was a topic on "Catch-38" that aired 18 January 2004 and "Out of the Frying Pan" that aired 25 January 2004, among others. The biological clock was a topic of "Evolution" that aired 15 August 1999.

20. Carrie began her affair in "Easy Come, Easy Go" that aired 6 August 2000. Big was played by Chris Noth, and Aidan was played by John Corbett. Vineberg, "Courage to Aim," B28.

21. The episode about the struggle between Carrie's head and heart was titled "Easy Come, Easy Go" and aired 6 August 2000. The episode in which Carrie tells Big she will not sleep with him a second time was titled "All or Nothing" and aired 13 August 2000. The episode in which Carrie says she hates herself was titled "Running with Scissors" and aired 20 August 2000. The episode with Carrie talking to herself was titled "All or Nothing" and aired 13 August 2000. The episode with Charlotte snapping at Carrie was titled "Running with Scissors" and aired 20 August 2000.

22. "Don't Ask, Don't Tell" aired 27 August 2000. Big's wife, Natasha, was played by Bridget Moynahan.

23. The episode with Michael's quotation was number 7 in the first season, which aired 28 January 2001. The episode about Emmett and the couple was number 3 in the second season, which aired 20 January 2002.

24. The episode about being addicted to pornography was number 5 in the second season, which aired 3 February 2002. Episodes about drugs being required for sex included episode 3 in the first season, which aired 10 December 2000; episode 10 in the third season, which aired 18 May 2003; episode 11 in the third season, which aired 25 May 2003; episode 12 in the third season, which aired 8 June 2003; and episode 13 in the third season, which aired 15 June 2003. The episode about Brian and Justin negotiating the parameters of their open relationship was number 6 in the second season, which aired 10 February 2002.

25. "Sex and Another City" aired 17 September 2000.

26. "Running with Scissors" aired 20 August 2000.

27. The episode about Charlotte getting crabs was titled "Twenty-Something Girls Vs. Thirty-Something Women" and aired 26 September 1999. The episode about Miranda discovering the STD was titled "Are We Sluts?" and aired 16 July 2000.

28. The episode about Miranda struggling with her pregnancy was titled "Coulda, Woulda, Shoulda" and aired 5 August 2001. The episode about Miranda struggling with her responsibilities as a single mother and a partner in a law firm was titled "Hop, Skip, and a Week" and aired 27 July 2003.

29. Weinraub, "Cable TV Shatters Another Taboo," E1; Shales, "Showtime's Shockingly Bold 'Queer as Folk,'" C1; James Poniewozik, "It's Here, It's Queer, Get Used to It," *Time*, 27 November 2000, 79. The premier episode aired 3 December 2000.

30. The episode about the gay–straight alliance was number 16 in the first season, which aired 8 April 2001. The episode about Justin and Daphne having sex was number 19 in the first season, which aired 29 April 2001. Daphne is played by Makyla Smith. The episode about Justin wanting to bareback was number 7 in the second season, which aired 17 February 2002.

31. The episode about Michael's trip was number 7 in the first season, which aired 28 January 2001. Michael's boyfriend, David, was played by Chris Potter. The episode about Ted attending the party was number 3 in the second season, which aired 20 January 2002. The episode about Emmett being "the safe-sex poster boy" was number 11 in the first season, which aired 25 February 2001.

32. Episodes about men suffering from STDs included one about Michael having gonorrhea, number 8 in the first season, which aired 4 February 2001; Michael having crabs, number 9 in the first season, which aired 11 February 2001; Brian having crabs, number 10 in the third season, which aired 11 May 2003; a young man on the street having anal warts, number 12 in the second season, which aired 7 April 2002. The episode about Michael's mother collapsing was number 8 in the first season, which aired 4 February 2001. Vic was played by Jack Weatherall, and Michael's mother is played by Sharon Gless. Episodes about Ben and Michael struggling with the

Notes

HIV issue included number 6 in the second season, which aired 10 February 2002; number 7 in the second season, which aired 17 February 2002; and number 9 in the second season, which aired 10 March 2002. Ben is played by Robert Gant.

33. Vineberg, "Courage to Aim," B28 (for "vulgar"); Hal Boedeker, "Sex and the TV: Fox, HBO Take Us to Sleazy New Lows," *Orlando Sentinel*, 11 November 2001, E3 (for "salacious"); Weinraub, "Cable TV Shatters Another Taboo," E1 (for "sensation for sensation's sake"); Howard Rosenberg, "Sex and the Steel City," *Los Angeles Times*, 2 December 2000, F1 (for "an assembly line of orgasms"). On *Sex and the City* as educational television, see Sarah Hepola, "Television: Her Favorite Class: 'Sex' Education," *New York Times*, 22 June 2003; Walter Kirn, "The Way We Live Now: Sex-Ed Night School," *NYTimes.com*, 16 November 2003; Stephanie Lehmann, "Educational Television," *Salon*, 19 July 2002; Rodger Streitmatter, "'Sex and the City': Educational TV at Its Best," *Gay Today*, 2 September 2003; "TV Teaches Teenagers about Sex," Associated Press, 20 December 2002. On *Queer as Folk* as educational television, see Lynn Elber, "Solid Crossover Appeal Bolsters 'Queer as Folk,'" *Los Angeles Times*, 4 January 2000, F38; Caryn James, "In a Gay World, Without the Usual Guides," *New York Times*, 3 December 2000, B27; Rodger Streitmatter, "'Queer as Folk': Gay Public Health Pioneer," *Gay Today*, 3 December 2001.

34. On accolades for the adultery plotline, see Carter, "On Television," C1; Hepola, "Television: Her Favorite Class"; Vineberg, "Courage to Aim," B28; "Is Sex and the City Ruining Your Sex Life?" *Mademoiselle*, July 2001, 66. One of the episodes showing the consequences of Carrie's adulterous affair ("Running with Scissors," which originally aired on 20 August 2000) was nominated for the 2001 Shine (Sexual Health IN Entertainment) Award, in the comedy episode category, from the Media Project, a nonprofit organization concerned with media portrayals of adolescent sexuality. On accolades for the plotline portraying Miranda's difficulties, see Carter, "On Television," C1; Hepola, "Television: Her Favorite Class." The episode in which Miranda decided not to have an abortion ("Coulda, Woulda, Shoulda," which originally aired on 5 August 2001) received the 2002 Shine Award, in the comedy episode category, from the Media Project. On accolades for the safe-sex messages, see James, "In a Gay World," B27; Poniewozik, "It's Here, It's Queer," 79; Streitmatter, "'Queer as Folk': Gay Public Health Pioneer." The premiere in which Justin and Brian used a condom (the episode originally aired on 3 December 2000) was nominated for the 2001 Shine Award, in the scene stealer category, from the Media Project.

35. "Hot Child in the City" aired 24 September 2000. The girl, named Jenny, was played by Kat Dennings.

36. The episode, number 7 in the second season, aired 17 February 2002. The episode won the 2002 Shine Award, in the drama episode category, from the Media Project.

37. Michael said he would protect himself in episode 7 of the second season, which aired 17 February 2002. Ben told Michael about the realities of his illness in episode 9 of the second season, which aired 10 March 2002.

38. Ben and Michael made love for the first time in episode 9 of the second season, which aired 10 March 2002.

Chapter Seventeen

1. For the quotes, see David Amsden, "Generation XXX," *New York*, 20 October 2003, 32. On the $2 billion figure, see Frederick S. Lane III, *Obscene Profits: The Entrepreneurs of Pornography in the Cyber Age* (New York: Routledge, 2000), xv.

2. Thomas E. Weber, "As Other Internet Ventures Fail, Sex Sites Are Raking in Millions," *Wall Street Journal*, 20 May 1997, A1.

3. Weber, "As Other Internet Ventures Fail," A1; Amsden, "Generation XXX," 32.

4. Eric Schlosser, "The Business of Pornography," *U.S. News & World Report*, 10 February 1997, 42; Vic Sussman, "Sex on the Net," *USA Today*, 20 August 1997, A1; Anthony Flint, "Skin Trade Spreading Across U.S.," *Boston Globe*, 1 December 1996, A1. On the revenues for the porn industry totaling $10 billion, see also Tom Hickman, *The Century of Sex* (London: Carlton, 1999), 224; "Porn in the U.S.A." segment on *60 Minutes*, CBS, 23 November 2003.

5. Lane, *Obscene Profits*, xiv, xix; Linton Weeks, "Pornography Goes from XXX to Zzz," *Washington Post*, 24 February 2003, C1.

6. Weeks, "Pornography Goes from XXX to Zzz," C1; on mainstream magazines quoting porn stars, see, for example, Stacey Grenrock Woods, "You've Got Questions, She's Got Answers," *Esquire*, June 2003, 72, and "Does Size Really Matter?" *FHM*, November 2003, 155; on adult films being viewed in hotel rooms, see "Porn in the U.S.A." segment on *60 Minutes*, CBS, 23 November 2003; *Family Business* premiered in 2003 and began its second season in January 2004.

7. Weeks, "Pornography Goes from XXX to Zzz," C1.

8. The author conducted the search on 4 October 2003.

9. Ray Glass, "In Favor of Technology; Vivid's *Party Favors* Shines," Spectator.net, accessed 4 October 2003 at www.spectator.net/1170/pages/1170_party_favors.html. *Party Favors* was created by Vivid Video in 1998 and was later featured on www.adultvideoxxx. The film stars Christian Steel as the husband, Tia Bella as the wife, Ian Daniels and Cheyenne Silver as one couple, Vince Voyeur and Dee as the other couple, and Corinne Williams as the single woman.

10. See, for example, www.pussyquota.com.

11. Thomas E. Weber, "'The X-Files: For Those Who Scoff at Internet Commerce, Here's a Hot Market," *Wall Street Journal*, 20 May 1997, A1.

12. *Head Over Heels* was created by Vivid Video in 1998 and was later featured on www.amazingtails.com. The film stars Joel Lawrence and Janine Harper.

13. The author conducted the search on 4 January 2004.

14. Lane, *Obscene Profits*, 128–129.

15. The author conducted the search on 3 January 2004.

16. The author conducted the search on 4 January 2004.

17. Amsden, "Generation XXX," 32.

18. Matt Marion, "Bedroom Confidential," *Men's Health*, May 2002, 125.

19. Lane, *Obscene Profits*, xxii.

20. Lisa de Moraes, "CBS Gave 90 Million an Eyeful," *Washington Post*, 3 February 2004, C1.

21. Jonathan Krim, "House Acts to Boost Penalty for Indecency," *Washington Post*, 12 March 2004, E1.

22. Leslie Walker, "Janet Jackson Replays Super Among Searches," *Washington Post*, 8 February 2004, F7.

23. Anchor Carol Costello used the phrase on "CNN Live at Daybreak" on 10 February 2004.

24. Lisa de Moraes, "Flags Keep Dropping on Super-Bowl Stunt," *Washington Post*, 5 February 2004, C1.

25. de Moraes, "CBS Gave 90 Million an Eyeful," C1; "Vulgar TV: Gosh, How (Yawn) Shocking," *USA Today*, 5 February 2004.

26. David Segal, "The Grammys' Hip-Hop Parade," *Washington Post*, 9 February 2004, C1. Justin Timberlake won awards for best pop vocal album for *Justified* and best male pop vocal performance for "Cry Me a River."

Chapter Eighteen

1. "The Reality of Reality TV," Bravo, 8 September 2003.

2. Melissa Wujick, "Dating Shows," *Lumberjack Online*, 10 October 2002. On reality TV shows being pornography, see also Monica Collins, "E! Explores True Lies of MTV Megahit 'Real World,'" *Boston Herald*, 24 August 2003, 55. By no means are all reality television programs pornographic; shows such as ABC's *The Bachelor* and *The Bachelorette* have placed their emphasis on romance rather than seeking to arouse lustful feelings in their viewers. Also, sexual content on porn sites and reality TV shows differ dramatically in their level of explicitness; much of the sexual content on the Internet can rightly be labeled hard-core pornography, as it is characterized by full nudity, erect penises, and vaginal penetration, while even the most explicit sexual content on reality television is soft-core pornography that is limited to partial nudity and genitalia that, when shown at all, is either blurred or otherwise obscured.

3. Liza Mundy, "Question Reality," *Washington Post*, 20 July 2003, W10; Tom Shales, "'Real World' in Paris," *San Diego Union-Tribune*, 3 June 2003, E6.

4. Hank Stuever, "Getting Down and Dirty in the Hot Tub," *Washington Post*, 31 January 2003, C1.

5. Paul Farhi, "TV's New Reality," *Washington Post*, 17 February 2003, A1.

6. Bravo's *Queer Eye for the Straight Guy* marathon began at 1 p.m. and continued until midnight on 1 January 2004.

7. Patricia Leigh Brown, "Hey There, Couch Potatoes: Hot Enough for You?" *New York Times*, 27 July 2003, D1. *Blind Date* premiered in September 1999 and was still airing daily in 2004.

8. *Blind Date* has been the subject of a lengthy study in a scholarly journal; see Justin DeRose, Elfriede Fursich, and Ekaterina V. Haskins, "Pop (Up) Goes *Blind Date*: Supertextual Constraints on 'Reality' Television," *Journal of Communication Inquiry*, vol. 27, no. 2 (April 2003): 171–189. *Blind Date* has been the subject of numerous articles in the popular press; see, for example, Alexandra Jacobs, "What Dethroned Seinfeld at 11? TV's Love Sensation, Blind Date," *New York Observer*, 13 November 2000, 3; Joe Newman, "*Blind Date*, Blind Luck," poppolitics.com, 2 August 2001; Karla Peterson, "'Blind Date' Thought Bubbles: 'I Smell Painful Fun,'" *San Diego Union-Tribune*, 26 October 2000, 3; Gail Pennington, "Dating Shows Match TV with Viewers Who Are Longing for Love," Centredaily.com, 2 July 2002; Louise Roug and Brian Lowry, "Dating Fame Games," *Los Angeles Times*, 18 August 2002, F10; Justin T. P. Ryan, "Reality Dating," freecongress.org, 29 July 2002; Wujick, "Dating Shows."

9. The episode aired 13 October 2001.

10. Episode 3 of season 11 aired several times during 2001.

11. Episodes 6, 7, and 11 of season 12 aired several times during 2002. Playboy DVD titled "Girls of Reality TV," released 5 August 2003; Sarah Preston, "Reality Chick," www.playboy.com/arts-entertainment/features/re-alitytv/.

12. Lawrie Mifflin, "TV Stretches Limits of Taste to Little Outcry," *New York Times*, 6 April 1998, A1; Tom Shales, "TV So Bad That Shame Isn't in Its Vocabulary," *Los Angeles Times*, 17 June 1996, F2; Tom Shales, "Wince More, With Feeling," *Washington Post*, 16 June 1996, G1. After half a dozen years of airing fairly routine talk-show fare, *The Jerry Springer Show* was about to be canceled when it was revamped in 1997 to showcase sexual content.

13. "Bizarre Betrayals" aired 13 March 2003.

14. "Feisty Females" aired 11 March 2003.

15. "Angry Women Face Off" aired 12 March 2003.

16. Nicholas Fonseca, "They're Here! They're Queer! And They Don't Like Your End Tables," *Entertainment Weekly*, 8 August 2003, cover, 24–28. On the runaway success of *Queer Eye*, see also Michael Giltz, "Queer Eye Confidential," *The Advocate*, 2 September 2003, 40–44; Tom Shales, "Reality TV: Nobodies' Home," *Washington Post*, 28 December 2003, N1, N4; Bruce C. Steele, "The Gay Rights Makeover," *The Advocate*, 2 September 2003, 42–43. *Queer Eye for the Straight Guy* premiered on 15 July 2003. Bravo and NBC are both owned by General Electric.

17. Carina Chocano, "Sharper Image," *Entertainment Weekly*, 8 August 2003, 62.

18. The Bravo Web site (www.bravotv.com) assigns numbers to the various episodes of *Queer Eye for the Straight Guy*, all of which have aired several times. The quotations are from episodes 115 and 108.

19. "The Reality of Reality TV," Bravo, 8 September 2003.

20. "The Reality of Reality TV," Bravo, 8 September 2003.

21. "Evan Marriott's 16th Minute," *Men's Journal*, August 2003, 74–77, 96–97. Marriott ultimately rejected Kozer and chose the other finalist, identified on the program only as Zora.

22. The two women were Paris Hilton, a hotel-chain heiress who is expected to inherit $30 million, and Nicole Richie, daughter of singer Lionel Richie. The sexual content of the series included images of the two young women wearing string bikinis as they washed a tractor and scenes in which the two girls were passionately kissed by two underage boys. *The Simple Life* originally aired in December 2003 and January 2004.

23. Michael Giltz, "Queer Eye Confidential," *The Advocate*, 2 September 2003, 44.

24. Lisa de Moraes, "On Fox, Reality Bites 'Boston Public,'" *Washington Post*, 14 April 2003, C7.

25. Tom Shales, "We're Mad as Hell," *Washington Post*, 19 March 1995, G1.

"Sexual Literacy"

1. "TV: Speaking About the Unspeakable," *Newsweek*, 29 November 1971, 53. For other early 1970s references to the potential of popular media being sex educators, see Robert Lewis Shayon, "TV–Radio," *Saturday Review*, 27 March 1971, 20; Chilton Williamson Jr., "Television," *National Review*, 11 April 1975, 401–402.

2. Marc Silver, "Sex and Violence on TV," *U.S. News & World Report*, 11 September 1995, 65; "Dawson Shines," *TV Guide* (on-line), 28–30 October 2000; Hilary E. MacGregor, "Media Project Teaches Safe Screen Sex," *Los Angeles Times*, 25 October 1999 (on-line edition). On the media as sex educators, see also Dale Kunkel, Kirstie M. Cope, and Erica Biely, "Sexual Messages on Television: Comparing Findings from Three Studies," *Journal of Sex Research*, vol. 36, no. 3 (August 1999): 230–236; Lawrie Mifflin, "TV Stretches Limits of Taste, to Little Outcry," *New York Times*, 6 April 1998, A1, B4.

3. For the quotes, see Jane D. Brown and Sarah N. Keller, "Can the Media Be Healthy Sex Educators?" *Family Planning Perspectives*, vol. 32, no. 5 (September/October 2000): 255–256. On the media as sex educators, see also Lynn Elber, "Solid Crossover Appeal Bolsters 'Queer as Folk,'" *Los Angeles Times*, 4 January 2000, F38; Sarah Hepola, "Television: Her Favorite Class: 'Sex' Education," *New York Times*, 22 June 2003; Caryn James, "In a Gay World, Without the Usual Guides," *New York Times*, 3 December 2000, B27; Sarah N. Keller and Jane D. Brown, "Media Interventions to Promote Responsible Sexual Behavior," *Journal of Sex Research*, vol. 39, no. 1 (February 2002): 67–72; Walter Kirn, "The Way We Live Now: Sex-Ed Night School," NYTimes.com, 16 November 2003; Stephanie Lehmann, "Educational Television," *Salon*, 19 July 2002; Rhoda Rabkin, "Children, Entertainment, and Marketing," *Consumers' Research*, June 2002, 14–18, 29; Rodger Streitmatter, "'Queer as Folk': Gay Public Health Pioneer," *Gay Today*, 3 December 2001; Rodger Streitmatter, "'Sex and the City': Educational TV at Its Best," *Gay Today*, 2 September 2003; "TV Teaches Teenagers about Sex," Associated Press, 20 December 2002. On young people turning to the media for information about sexual topics such as birth control, contraception, and pregnancy prevention, see Michael J. Sutton, Jane D. Brown, Karen M. Wilson, and Jonathan D. Klein, "Shaking the Tree of

Knowledge for Forbidden Fruit: Where Adolescents Learn about Sexuality and Contraception," in Jane D. Brown, Jeanne R. Steele, and Kim Walsh-Childers, eds., *Sexual Teens, Sexual Media: Investigating Media's Influence on Adolescent Sexuality* (Mahwah, NJ: Lawrence Erlbaum, 2002), 31; of the 7,000 young people who participated in the Commonwealth Fund Survey of the Health of Adolescents, 52.0 percent said they learn about the topics from magazines and 50.9 percent said they learn about the topics from television, which is only slightly fewer than the 52.5 percent who said they learn about the topics from their parents (girls in the survey relied on magazines for information on the sexual topics *more often* than they relied on their parents—63.9 percent turned to magazines, 56.3 percent turned to parents).

4. Brown and Keller, "Can the Media Be Healthy Sex Educators?" 256.

5. Ellen Benson, "Sword Swallowing," *Maxim*, September 2003, 66, 68, 70.

6. *Chicago*, directed by Rob Marshall, was released in 2002 by Miramax.

7. For the lyrics, see www.reallyrics.com/Lyrics/C000200040003.asp.

Index

Index